Taiwan in Transformation

1895-2005

The Challenge of a
New Democracy to an Old Civilization

Taiwan in Transformation

1895-2005

Chun-chieh Huang

Transaction Publishers
New Brunswick (U.S.A.) and London (U.K.)

Second paperback printing 2009
Copyright © 2006 by Transaction Publishers, New Brunswick, New Jersey.

All rights reserved under International and Pan-American Copyright Conventions. No part of this book may be reproduced or transmitted in any form or by any means, electronic or mechanical, including photocopy, recording, or any information storage and retrieval system, without prior permission in writing from the publisher. All inquiries should be addressed to Transaction Publishers, Rutgers—The State University, 35 Berrue Circle, Piscatatway, New Jersey 08854-8042. www.transactionpub.com

This book is printed on acid-free paper that meets the American National Standard for Permanence of Paper for Printed Library Materials.

Library of Congress Catalog Number: 2005054915
ISBN: 978-0-7658-0311-5 (cloth); 978-1-4128-0727-2 (paper)
Printed in the United States of America

Library of Congress Cataloging-in-Publication Data

Huang, Chun-chieh.
   Taiwan in transformation: 1895-2005 : the challenge of a new democracy to an old civilization / Chun-chieh Huang.
     p. cm.
  Includes index.
  ISBN 0-7658-0311-9 (alk. paper)
   1. Taiwan—Social conditions—1895-1945. 2. Taiwan—Social conditions—1945- 3. Taiwan—Civilization. 1. Title.

HN748.2.H83 2005
951.24'905—dc22
                                        2005054915

Contents

Preface ix

Acknowledgments xiii

Prologue xv

Part One: Retrospect 1

  1. The Taiwanese Nostalgia for Cultural China (1895–1950) 3

    1:1 The Rise and Formation of Cultural Nostalgia, 1895–1945 3

    1:2 The Fall and Dissipation of the Nostalgia, 1945–1950 14

    1:3 Implications and Lessons 24

  2. Postwar Taiwan in Historical Perspective 29

    2:1 Introduction 29

    2:2 The Rise and Fall of Agrarian Culture in Postwar Taiwan 31

    2:3 The Prewar Background and Its Problems 39

    2:4 The JCRR and Its Role in History 46

    2:5 Conclusion 51

  3. Transformation of Farmers' Social Consciousness (1950–1970) 53

    3:1 Introduction 53

3:2 Farmers' Social Consciousness in the Early
　　　　Period of Retrocession 57

　　3:3 Farmers' Social Consciousness in the 1970s 78

　　3:4 Conclusion 85

4. Transformation of Confucianism (1950–1980) 89

　　4:1 The Characteristics 89

　　4:2 The Approaches 94

　　4:3 The Propagation 117

　　4:4 Conclusion 122

5. A Contemporary Confucianist's Postwar Taiwan
　　Experience: The Case of Hsu Fu-kuan (1902–1982) .. 127

　　5:1 Cultural Impacts on People 128

　　5:2 Personal Formation of Culture 139

　　5:3 The Distinctiveness of Chinese Culture 144

　　Appendix 146

Part Two: Prospect 151

　6. The Development of Taiwanese Consciousness:
　　Retrospect and Prospect 153

　　6:1 Introduction 153

　　6:2 Stages of Development of "Taiwanese
　　　　Consciousness" 153

　　6:3 Characteristics of Taiwanese Consciousness 182

    6:4 Conclusion.. 185

7. "Mutual Historical Understanding": The Basis for "Taiwan- Mainland Relations in the Twenty-First Century 189

    7:1 Introduction 189

    7:2 The Importance of Historical Understanding....... 190

    7:3 Taiwan's Historicity: The Centripetal-Centrifugal Spirit 196

    7:4 Mainland's Historicity: Zealous Nationalism 212

    7:5 Historical Understanding: The Hope of the Relationship.. 216

Epilogue 219
Works Cited 231
Index of Names 249

Preface

The last decade of the twentieth century witnessed rapid changes not only in global politics but also in Taiwan's quests for new identities. The notorious martial law was lifted in July 1987, and long-repressed calls for democratization began to be heard that caught worldwide attention. In sync with the economic transformation, the entire world of thought in Taiwan underwent significant changes. Both economic and ideological restructuring have been basic elements of transformation in postwar Taiwan. Meawhile, the rapid democratization, hailed as "the second Taiwan miracle" by some politicians, has opened a Pandora's box and stirred a whirlwind of discord. Self-assertiveness and egocentrism verging on narcissism are but a few of the many centripetal forces at work in democratic Taiwan today. Is the old Taiwanese work ethic just a relic of the past? Is the goodhearted native openness now collapsing into a narcissistic decadence? Is Taiwan going to become an Armageddon of ideological wars?

The present volume contains seven of my essays on the 'where from' and the 'where to' of the Taiwan transformation. This book thus deals with some key problems that arose from the whirlpool of history and can be grasped and solved only in the context of history, the formation of Taiwanese consciousness and cross-strait relations, in particular. In essence, I seek to show that historical insights extrapolated from an understanding of history are the *sine qua non* for grasping and solving the basic problems facing Taiwan at present, including the Taiwan-Mainland relationship in the twenty-first century.

As a more Westernized frontier of the Chinese communities in East Asia, Taiwan has the advantages of a mature industrial infrastructure and a budding political democracy, which together boost the economy. The root of Taiwan's problems, however, is that its people lack historical consciousness when facing historical questions. Few Taiwanese can view their problems within a historical context. This sort of shortcoming is not unique to Taiwanese; it is equally discernable in American and European experts on problems in China. In this book, I situate the transformation of Taiwan—especially the development of Taiwanese consciousness, which since the lifting of the martial law has induced a dynamic ethos in Taiwan—in the frame, the context of history.

Where East Asia's pressing problems are usually identified as economic and political, I maintain that only mutual historical understanding that can solve the dilemma for people living across the straits. In addition to being *homo politicus* as Aristotle argues, or *homo economicus* as modern man insists, we are also *homo historien*, both shaping and being shaped by history, just like spiders working the web of history that crisscrosses the globe. I argue in this book that the solutions to problems facing the Chinese living on either side of the Taiwan Strait are to be found only in history.

This book represents a Taiwanese historian's reflections on the transformation of postwar Taiwan. I was born and raised in Taiwan; I am also a professional historian. This twofold biographical edge makes me an insider with an objective outlook. I have an inner understanding of Taiwan because I was born, raised and educated there. I have an objective understanding of Taiwan because of the historical perspective I take.

Having reflected on the changing social psychology, noting the rising naricissism in particular, I found that a new Taiwanese self-centeredness has been revealed vividly and concretely in public and administrative responses to the outbreak of SARS in the spring of 2003. Some hospitals in Taipei were focal points of public selfishness and administrative incompetence. Initially, hospital administrators misdiagnosed the cases and went on to send the patients away in a panic. Later, public officials set up quarantines for suspected SARS cases. But, misinformed about the meaning of quarintine, affected citizens complained that it violated basic human rights before self-righteously breaking out of the quarantine areas. Some SARS patients left their hospital and went to other hospitals but did not confess to their exposure to the SARS virus, thus spreading the ailment to other hospitals. As the phantom of SARS was wandering in the island of Taiwan, all of these events attest vividly to the problem of egocentrism in Taiwan today, a major theme of the present study.

Of course, nobody's viewpoint, no matter how personal *and* objective, can enjoy universal assent, much less be assured of its validity, whatever that means in this context. Thus, ultimately, what I offer in this volume are the personal views of a private citizen, humbly and conscientiously thought through. In light of these admitted shortcomings, I earnestly request the indulgence of the reader.

Chun-chieh Huang
Taipei, 2005

Acknowledgments

Five chapters of this book are revisions of papers that have appeared as book chapters or in journals. I am grateful to the publishers, who permitted me to use these previously published materials:

Chapters 2 and 5: Chun-chieh Huang and Teng-fu Tsao, eds., *Postwar Taiwan Experience in Historical Perspectives* (College Park: University Press of Maryland, 1998), pp. 17–35, 192–209.

Chapter 3: Stevan Harrell and Chun-chieh Huang eds., *Cultural Change in Postwar Taiwan* (Boulder, Colo.: Westview Press, 1993), pp. 111–134.

Chapter 4: Chun-chieh Huang and Erik Zürcher eds., *Norms and State in China* (Leiden: E. J. Brill, 1993), pp. 141–167.

Epilogue: Chun-chieh Huang, "Industry, Culture, Politics: The Taiwan Transformation," In *Culture, Politics and Economic Growth: Experience in East Asia,* ed. Richard Hardey Brown. (Studies in Third World Societies, Vol. 44, Williamsburg, Va.: The College of William and Mary, 1994).

Prologue

This volume deals with the transformation of Taiwan, particularly during the latter half of the twentieth century, from a historical perspective. I would like to begin with two key words: *Taiwan* and *transformation*.

1.

First, in terms of its culture and society *"Taiwan"* must be regarded as a Chinese community *par excellence*. Hence, we can analyze her "transformation" first in the cultural arena. The majority of "Taiwanese" are descendents of immigrants from coastal regions of Fujian and Guangdong. Taiwanese initially regarded the Mainland as their cultural and spiritual homeland. Chapter 1 deals with the vicissitudes of Taiwanese nostalgia for cultural China from 1895, when Taiwan was ceded to Japan. The feelings of cultural nostalgia in Taiwan were aroused by Japanese oppression and dissipated by the abuses of her mother country, China. Ironically, the nostalgia was dissipated precisely at the moment when Taiwan's desire to be enfolded in the mother country was realized. This drastic change in Taiwanese sentiment was due largely to the corruption, discrimination and abuses of power of the Nationalist government in 1950s. In the first chapter, we consider this historical process. The rise of cultural nostalgia in Taiwan was due to Japanese political oppression. Taiwanese naturally sought strength in their homeland culture. Taiwanese intellectuals, however, did not carry out any in-depth study of the Chinese cultural heritage. They only felt a yearning to land a foot on the soil of Mainland China, which turned out to be something remote and obsolete from what they had imagined. At the same time, the immediate occasion for the dissipation of cultural nostalgia in Taiwan was Chinese political corruption. This rapid dissipation was possible because the Taiwanese nostalgia was just a vague yearning for the historical heritage of Chinese culture.

The transformation in the cultural arena occurred primarily through Confucianism. In Chapter 4, I identify three approaches to the study of Confucianism in postwar Taiwan: historical, philosophical ("history of ideas"), and sociological. Drawing on questionnaires and statistical data, the latter approach was concerned with the actual contemporary situation and the survival of Confucian values in modern society. The propagation of Confucian values in postwar Taiwan took place at two levels: official (through schools, government-sponsored publications and social movements), and popular (through moralistic pamphlets issued by folk religious sects). At the official levels, the propagation of Confucian norms was strongly politicized; it was combined with modern nationalist sentiments, and was posed partly in response to anti-Confucianist movements (especially during the Cultural Revolution) in Mainland China. Despite these limited official aims, it can be said that Confucian scholars in Taiwan have been able to think and write free from obvious official constraint.

Among the "Contemporary New-Confucians" in postwar Taiwan and Hong Kong, Hsü Fu-kuan (1902–1982) stands out as a prominent figure. Chapter 5 examines the role of Hsü Fu-kuan in the intellectual history of China and Taiwan. Pondering China's prospects for the future, Hsü Fu-kuan identified himself as: (1) of the people; (2) practical-minded; and (3) agrarian-based. He formulated this identity in light of his study of Chinese culture. "Of the people" meant that he believed in setting up the *people* as the main political body, and he felt that China's future lay in democratic government. By "practical-minded," he meant that he approached China's Confucian tradition *critically,* with a view to putting its principles into practice and was not interested in formulating a transcendental or formalistic philosophy; By "agrarian-based," Hsü referred to his vision of China's future politics as being established by the owner-cultivator class. Hsü regarded these three aspects of his identity as complementary and not mutually opposed. He believed that China's hope for future development lay in establishing the people as the main body of government. The development and practice of Confucian principles had to go hand-in-hand with democratic rule, and he felt this practical development could make up for flaws found in contemporary Western democracies. Hsü also stipulated that the "people" set up "as the main body of government" should not limited to the urban middle class but should include the rural masses, particularly the ranks of toiling farmers and workers. In any case, democratic government had to be built upon the practical Confucianism implemented by the rural owner-cultivator class.

Second, the historic *transformation* of postwar Taiwan can be observed in Taiwan's transition from an agrarian to an industrial society. Chapter 2 discusses the transformation of Taiwan's infrastructure. We indicate three key phenomena in Taiwan's postwar development: (1) the emergence of the owner-cultivator class; (2) the rise of the middle class; and (3) the expansion of middle-class intelligentsia. These three social phenomena all revolved around Taiwan's transition from an agrarian to an industrial society. The emergence of the owner-cultivator class came earliest, and gave rise to the middle class and the expansion of middle-class intelligentsia in the 1970s.

Postwar agricultural renewal and the resulting economic development began with a series of land reform policies: the first was the 37.5 percent rent reduction policy implemented in 1949; next came the policy of offering of public lands for sale initiated in 1952. Then, in 1953, the Land-to-the-Tiller policy was launched. This series of land reform measures had a far-reaching effect on Taiwan's rural society. It reformed the old system of land tenure, boosted the owner-cultivator class, transferred land investment to industry and commerce, and stimulated increased agricultural production, thus laying the foundation for industrial development.

Beginning in 1953, the new agricultural policy in Taiwan was based on the principle of using agriculture to nurture industry and, in turn, industry to develop agriculture. Under this guiding principle, the agricultural policy during the twenty years between 1953 and 1972 could be described as a "developmental squeeze" in the sense that measures were adopted to promote the expansion of agricultural production while creating a surplus of manpower and materials. This surplus was transferred to non-agricultural sectors. From 1895 to 1960, most capital flowed into non-agricultural sectors, paving the way for rapid industrial expansion in the late 1960s. The development shift from agriculture to industry in postwar Taiwan set into motion a number of social and cultural changes such as: rapid urbanization, population growth and shifts, increased social mobility, expansion of educational opportunities, and expanded women's rights and opportunities.

Some scholars hail these major postwar transformations as hallmarks of the "economic miracle." This "miracle" has resulted in—as has been demonstrated in Chapter 3—the loss of folk traditions by shifting farmers' collective social consciousness from its traditional moral economy orientation, which was imbued with interpersonal, social feeling, to a profit-oriented individualistic approach. This shift in values, as measured by attitudes toward landlords and toward the Farmers' Associations, resulted from the penetration of outside forces, first under Japanese colonial rule and later under Kuomintang (KMT) rule, into a basically self-sufficient farming community. On the one hand, this transformation was a natural part of Taiwan's overall shift from agriculture to industry. On the other hand, the transformation was not entirely positive. Something was lost with the passing of the peasant community, and individual farmers were cast adrift in the unknown waters of capitalist society, without a clear compass of cultural values.

To sum up, the so-called "miracle" in postwar Taiwan led to chain reactions associated with the shift in mode of production. Culture, attitudes and thoughts changed, and Taiwan leaped from a traditional hierarchical society into a twentieth-century individualist, egalitarian society.

2.

Part Two of this book examines culture, attitude and thought. The most remarkable facet of the awakening of the "self" in Taiwan has been the volatile eruption of Taiwanese consciousness. A cluster of ideas branching out in many directions, Taiwanese consciousness is the product of various interrelated quests for cultural and political identity. In Chapter 6, we examine developments and metamorphoses of Taiwanese consciousness in unfolding political context. Early Taiwan featured local Chiong (漳, Zhang) consciousness and Chuan (泉, Quan) consciousness. Under Japanese rule, Taiwanese consciousness became broadly ethnic, a stout Chinese self-awareness against the oppressive Japanese imperialist tribe, ramified by the protest consciousness of the ruled against the rulers. History repeated itself during the Kuomintang regime, especially during the 228 Incident in 1947, when Taiwanese consciousness took the form of virulent provincial self-awareness against the Mainlanders, who now were the rulers. After the repeal of the martial law in August 1987, the concept of a 'New Taiwanese Consciousness' emerged to unite all residents in Taiwan, regardless of provincial origin in protest of the oppressive Communist regime on the Mainland. Thus, we see a clear element of protest throughout the unfolding Taiwanese consciousness.

The rapid awakening of individualism in Taiwan has led to the problem of excessive individual self-assertiveness. The eruption of self-assertiveness in Taiwan that followed the lifting of Martial Law in 1987 can readily be observed in every area, be it agriculture, politics, industry-commerce or education. Now, as we face Taiwan's "growth problem" of selfhood, I wish to urge that we see a maturity problem in the Taiwanese refusal to acknowledge the "fellowship of beings" that constitute the center of the self. This can be stated as a problem of mutuality and of intersubjectivity which forms not only the major challenge that Taiwan has to face, but can be seen as a key to paving the way to a more constructive Taiwan-Mainland relationship in the twenty-first century. The last chapter analyzes the basic weaknesses in the two quick-fix proposals for cross-strait relations: quick unification with Mainland, and quick independence of Taiwan from Mainland. Only a solid understanding of the historical experience of both Taiwan and the Mainland can ground a successful solution to bringing about peaceful coexistence. The mutual thriving of Taiwan and Mainland will be the *sine qua non* for resolving the Taiwan-Mainland relationship in the twenty-first century. It is on this note of hope and confidence that I close this venture to entwine the future of Taiwan and Chinese communities.

Part 1

Retrospect

1

The Taiwanese Nostalgia for Cultural China

(1895–1950)

Our study of the transformation of Taiwan begins with a reflection on the vicissitudes of Taiwanese nostalgia for cultural China. This chapter explores: (1) the 'where from', (2) the 'what' and 'where to', and (3) the 'why' of Taiwanese nostalgia for the Chinese homeland-culture, as it unfolded from the Japanese occupation (1895–1945) until the 1950s. In general, Taiwanese nostalgia for Chinese culture as their 'home': (1) was first aroused by the oppression of the alien Japanese rule, (2) was a psychological yearning for homecoming and as such was brutally disappointed and dissipated individually, also when Taiwanese stepped onto the soil of Mainland China, and, collectively, when Taiwan was ruled by the Nationalist government. This is a sad chronicle of the spiritual journey of Taiwanese souls, which teaches us to steep ourselves in the age-old Chinese cultural *heritage*.

1:1 The Rise and Formation of Cultural Nostalgia, 1895–1945

The Chinese who immigrated to Taiwan from the coastal regions of Fujian and Guangdong regarded Mainland China as their "homeland". Later, their nostalgia for Chinese culture was aroused and strengthened by two factors: (1:1:a.) suffering under Japanese political oppression, and (1:1:b.) Taiwanese identifying with Chinese culture (but not with any political regime in China). Last, (1:1:c.), we consider the excitement Taiwanese felt at the moment of their homecoming back to their mother-country.

1:1:a. Rather than describe the Japanese colonial regime in detail, we will consider several Tawanese reactions to perceived colonial oppression. We draw upon the firsthand materials left to us by the intellectual Yeh Jung-chung 葉榮鐘 (1900–1956), the writer Wu Cho-liu 吳濁流 (1900–1976), the doctor *cum* writer Wu Hsin-jung 吳新榮 (1906–1967), and the intercoastal merchant Wu San-lien 吳三連 (1899–1988). Their writings rank among the most notable expressions of consciousness of collective identity in Taiwan.

Yeh Jung-chung was a fervent follower of the eminent landlord Lin Hsien-tang 林獻堂 (1881–1956). Yeh reminisced with feeling about his childhood impressions of Tangshan (唐山), that is, Mainland China. His elders had liked to say: "Tangshan shan chang-chang (唐山山長長),"[1] which contrasted with the impressions of Japanese prejudice he had suffered. Yeh wrote,[2]

> Our homeland feeling and our people's consciousness, I would say, were aroused by the Japanese prejudice and oppression. Their prejudice and oppression made it quite clear to the Taiwanese that the Japanese 'Principle of Unity, Assimilation and Equality' is a pure sham. Their bullying and oppression provoke in us a strong centripetal force toward our motherland, just as a child would cry out for its mother when bullied.
>
> The Japanese people try in every way to assimilate the Taiwanese people. Yet, they wouldn't necessarily be happy if they were to see us completely assimilated and completely Japanese. All they want to do is to make us Taiwanese forget our motherland and colonize us into the second-class citizens, "second" to what they call "motherland people."

---

[1] "Long long Mountains of the Tang Land (China)."
[2] Yeh Jung-chung, *Xiaowu dazhu ji* (Taichung: Zhongyang Shuju, 1977), p. 24.

1. The Taiwanese Nostalgia for Cultural China (1895–1950) 5

Clearly, their official policy is contradicted by their individual behavior. But, their bullying and oppressive behavior amount to giving a rich chemical fertilizer to the sprouts of our homeland feelings and to our people's consciousness, nurturing them until they grow large and unshakable. The problem is that people like me, born after the Japanese occupation, have only a vague idea of our motherland. We cannot handle or step into our motherland, it is just a virtual reality to us. Deep in our hearts, we always have a yearning to touch our actual motherland.

Yeh expressed this on behalf of his generation—yearning for the untouched soil, unseen rivers and unclimbed mountains of their motherland, where they no longer had relatives or acquaintances. All they possessed were just abstract ideas and vague impressions—gathered from the writings they happened to have[3]—about a history and culture they had not personally experienced. All they had was a reactive feeling, that "centripetal force," for their homeland, their *Volksgeist*.

Yeh recalled that whenever people protested, the Japanese always threatened them with "if you don't like being Japanese, you can just go back to China." In such an oppressive atmosphere, Taiwanese sentiments naturally grew fervent toward the homeland; the more oppression the Taiwanese people faced, the deeper their cultural nostalgia became. If the Japanese really had put into practice what they had preached about 'Equal Treatment' and 'Becoming One Body with All Peoples,' the Taiwanese cultural nostalgia for China might not have grown to such white heat. Although language, writing, conventions and customs are ties that bind an eth-

---

[3] In the colonial period, the Japanese understandably never encouraged any reading of "Chinese culture," much less any in-depth studies.

nic community together, political rule had the final say on whether Taiwanese people could accommodate themselves to Japanese rule.[4] In his writings, Wu Cho-liu also expressed cultural nostalgia for China aroused by Japanese oppression. What was Taiwanese "love of motherland?" Wu wrote:[5]

> Although the love of motherland, being invisible, is only an idea and impression, this love always subtly pulls at my heart like the force of gravity, as irresistible as the feeling of an orphan child cut off from his unseen unknown parents, but who keeps yearning to see them. It does not matter to him what sort of people they may be, he simply yearns to be back in their arms, to feel warm all over. This instinctive sort of attachment goes out to our motherland; it is a feeling that can be known only by those who have it. Perhaps only those who have suffered from the bullying and oppression of the alien tribe can understand this feeling.

This sentiment was echoed in the writings of Wu Hsin-jung, a medical doctor in Yen-shui (鹽水), Tainan, during the Japanese occupation. His diary contains an entry expressing his concerns about Mainland China during the Sino-Japanese War (1937–1945) when the Japanese were committing unspeakable atrocities. He also felt anguish over the dismemberment of China:[6]

> In Peking, Wang Kemin organized the Temporary Government of the ROC over the provinces of Hebei, Shanxi, Shandong and Henan. In Suiyüan, King De established the Self-Government Alliance of Mongolia over Inner Mongolia. Previously, Zheng Xiaoxu (鄭孝胥) had estab-

---

[4] Yeh Jung-chung, op. cit., pp. 212–213.
[5] Wu Cho-liu, *Wuhuaguo* (Taipei: Qianwei chubanshe, 1988), p. 40.
[6] Ibid., p. 68.

1. The Taiwanese Nostalgia for Cultural China (1895–1950)   7

lished Manchu imperial rule over the three provinces in Northeastern China. Ku Lun (庫倫) had organized the Republic of Outer Mongolia. O, how sad! Our nation has now been dismembered. But for a great leader, our country will soon be occupied by several foreign powers, and incessant turmoil will follow.

Again,[7]

A whistle sounded last night alerting us to the news that Wuhan (武漢) has fallen to the Japanese troops. The heart of China has been taken. Before this we lost the brain area of Nanjing (南京) and the two hands of Beijing and Guangzhou. All China has now are the two legs of Gansu (甘肅) and Shanxi (陝西) on the left and Yunnan (雲南) and Guizhou (貴州) on the right. How can we manage? Like Yuan barbarian Kublai and Qing barbarian Aisin Chüelo of old, Japan has now taken over the Central Plains. Can our Chiang Kai-shek be as heroic as Yue Fei (岳飛) of the Song or Zheng Cheng-gong (鄭成功) of the Ming?

In Taiwan, Wu worried about Mainland China just as Zheng Chenggong or Koxinga had done at the end of the Ming dynasty. On finishing Pearl S. Buck's classic novel *The Good Earth* on December 21, 1947, Wu empathized with suffering Chinese peasants and villagers, sighing that "only revolutionary methods peculiar to China can solve China's especially complex problems."[8]

Another intellectual, Yang Chao-chia 楊肇嘉 (1891–1976) from Ching-shui (清水), Taichung, described the conditions in

---

[7] Ibid., p. 73.
[8] Ibid., p. 32.

Taiwan under the Japanese occupation as follows:[9]

> Previously in Taiwan several newspapers were published. They were all banned in 1936 when Japan started planning to invade China. All bookstores and private schools teaching Chinese were also closed. But, our cultural spirit could not be suppressed. If you do not believe so, just look at how the Taiwanese are still using their own Chinese language and writing; many poetry clubs continue to operate, many bookstores and private schools are still run without being publicized, and in many places we have musical organizations for southern and northern Chinese music. Even geisha girls at the taverns continue to sing Chinese songs; they sell their entertainment but not themselves to be 'soiled and shamed' by Japanese men. The very few of them who do business with the Japanese are nicknamed 'barbarous chicken.' The very few of our ladies who are married to Japanese are nicknamed 'barbarous liquor bottle.' They are despised all over and have nowhere to stand.

Yang recalled that once, when he had gone abroad to Japan to study, a Tai-sho (大正) Exposition was being planned. With the help of a friend, he arranged to be a guide at the Association of Sino-Japan Relations for some high-ranking official visitors from China. He made friends with some of these dignitaries, who felt sympathetic to him in his position and encouraged him to visit Mainland China, saying, "The Chinese Motherland does need Taiwanese youth like you to assist in national reconstruction." This encouragement impressed Yang deeply and heightened his sense of national consciousness.[10]

---

[9] Yang Chao-chia, *Yang Chao-chia huiyilu* (1) (Taipei: Sanmin shujü, 1977), p. 4.
[10] Yang Chao-chia, op. cit., pp. 100–101.

1. The Taiwanese Nostalgia for Cultural China (1895–1950)

Chung I-jin 鍾逸人 (1921–) was imprisoned because of his resistance against the Japanese. Chung wrote of a fellow prisoner he met: "When I learned that he was also from Taiwan, I felt a deep camaraderie with him. As he was often led out to be 'corrected' by the high officer torturer, I felt an irrepressible hatred towards the Japanese."[11] Examples like these are too numerous to recount. They all serve to show how the compatriot-feeling and cultural nostalgia were aroused by the Japanese oppression.

1:1:b. Again, this nostalgia for China was strictly cultural and not political. Wu Cho-liu expressed this point well,[12]

> The Taiwanese love both their land and their motherland passionately. All can be found to have such love. But, this love of motherland is never love of the Qing dynasty, which is a Manchu regime, not a Han regime. The Sino-Japanese War (1894) was a war fought by the Manchus with the Japanese; it was the Manchus who were defeated, not the Chinese or Han. Although, temporarily, Taiwan is being occupied by Japan, it will certainly be recovered and the Han-Chinese people will definitely work to reconstruct and reestablish their nation. Even in our dreams, we firmly believe that Han-Chinese troops will arrive to liberate Taiwan. The idea of a beautiful, great mother country called 'China' or 'Han' lies at the bottom of our Taiwanese hearts.

Again,[13]

> At the time, battles of resistance against the Japanese

---

[11] Chung I-jen, *Xinsuan liushinian--Er-er-ba shijian rrchi budui: Zhang Chung I-jen huiyilu* (Taipei: Ziyou shidai chubanshe, 1986), p. 37.
[12] Wu, op. cit., p. 40.
[13] Wu, op. cit., pp. 38-40.

broke out spontaneously and without organization; they were uncoordinated. Nobody from the outside instigated them. Deep in their hearts, the Taiwanese affirm that their forefathers had spent years of unspeakable pain and effort establishing our villages in developing Taiwan. Every inch of our soil is soaked with their blood, sweat and tears. Not a few of them sacrificed their lives protecting the villages, fighting off pestilence, plague and intruders. Those dead heroes and heroines are now enshrined in our revered Gi-bin Bio (I-min Temple); their spirits are called Gi-Bin Ia (Father Patriots) and our Fathers' Friends. Year after year, no greater amount of money or time is spent than for our big festivals in honor of those brave and glorious spirits. The spirit of Gi-bin Bio has been flowing in our veins and we feel instinctively that protecting our villages against invasion is our sacred duty. This feeling expresses itself upon sighting enemies from without. Upon hearing the arrival of Japanese troops, our anti-Japanese sentiment welled up and the anti-Japanese ideology was born, turning into anti-Japanese . . . struggles . . . This fervent love of our land is echoed in our feeling of love for our homeland . . . This is not love for the Qing dynasty; in our hearts it is this land of 'Han,' this beautiful, great mother country.

They felt a deep and passionate nostalgia for the motherland, Han-China. People in Taiwan regarded their homeland culture as linked with their souls; they felt organically at one with it. Yang Chao-chia observed a Taiwanese student in Beijing express this sentiment,[14]

The student from Taiwan in Beijing claimed that Taiwan

---

[14] Yang, op. cit., p. 65.

1. The Taiwanese Nostalgia for Cultural China (1895–1950)   11

and China's destinies were bound together. To rely on the mother country to restore Taiwan, we must engage in the labor to reestablish our mother country. This is the way to save Taiwan. This view seems accurate. Therefore, besides some who studied the humanities, others learned how to fight. Taiwanese soldiers, such as Ssu Shao-wen and Wang Min-ning, left Beijing University to join in the common fight against Japan.

One year before the Japanese occupation started in 1894, Christian millionaire Li Chun-sheng 李春生 (1834–1924) also echoed this sentiment, "Honored to have been born in Zhuxia (諸夏, China), I have always liked the Middle Kingdom (China) . . . Born in China, just as were my parents, I keenly feel for my ancestors' graves (in China)."[15] Similarly, after citing his three life-hopes, i.e., to build his own home, to educate his children and to travel all over the world, Wu Hsin-jung added, "Finally, I hope my bones will be buried on the Mainland."[16] Wu wrote the following in his diary after the War, on June 29, 1950:[17]

I am deeply afraid that the destiny of Taiwan will include some serious repercussions on China. We will always claim that Taiwan belongs to the Taiwanese, but that it also belongs to the Chinese. For this claim, I am willing to sacrifice my life.

1:1:c. In this connection, the Taiwanese initially felt exuberance at the retrocesson of Taiwan to the mother country. They were ecstatic in two ways when they first made contact with China: individually, when they went to the Mainland on their own, and, collectively, when the Chinese rulers came over to receive Taiwan

---

[15] Li Chun-sheng, *Zhujin xinji* (Fuzhou: Meihua Shuju, 1984), Vol. 1, p. 71.
[16] Chang Liang-tse, op. cit., p. 91.
[17] Chang Liang-tse, *Wu Hsin-jung riji [Zhanhou]*, p. 51.

from the defeated Japanese.

Individual contact with Mainland China is exemplified by Yeh Jung-chung who, while strolling in the city of Andong (安東) in Manchuria, heard a handicapped person strumming a musical instrument and singing Beijingese tunes and melodies. Yeh commented,[18]

> This man completely absorbed me. Knowing nothing about Beijingese tunes, I had no way of telling how well he played. But, I felt a resonance in my heart. What it was I did not know, either. I just felt deeply touched and grateful, full of longing and craving, almost in tears. At that time, I did not have time to reflect on why I reacted in that way. But, in fact, this was not a problem of value judgment or of ideas or ideals. If I were compelled to put it into words, I'd perhaps call it a resonance of 'blood.'

Collective contact with Mainland China was no less moving and impressive an experience for the Taiwanese. The return of Taiwan to China on August 15, 1945 was a grand event for all Taiwanese, "Happy leaving brutal winds, bitter rain,/elated at seeing the flag of blue skies, white sun, (喜離淒風苦雨景, 快睹青天白日旗)" was a verse couplet seen hanging in Taipei. At the time, Wu San-lien was residing at Hefenghang in Tianjin (天津). After carefully listening to news of the Japanese surrender on the radio, he felt he was in paradise, and gushed[19]

> As a member of the resistance against Japan, I naturally had dreams of victory. My first dream was to go home in time to see with my own eyes the Japanese flag being

---

[18] Yeh, op. cit., pp. 26–27.
[19] Dictated by Wu San-lien, edited and written by Wu Feng-shan, *Wu San-lien huiyilu* (Taipei: Zilibao Xi, 1991), pp. 102–103.

1. The Taiwanese Nostalgia for Cultural China (1895–1950) 13

lowered for the last time from the Parliament Building in Taipei and our national flag of blue sky and white sun gradually hoisted. My second dream was to see those Japanese who had always bullied my Taiwanese brothers repent and apologize to us, especially those Japanese who grabbed Mr. Lim Hian-tong just because Mr. Lim insisted that China was his mother country at the party celebrating the start of Tai-tiong governance in 1936. My third dream was to unite all the Taiwanese in the rebuilding of Taiwan.

Chung I-jin who was in Taiwan on August 15 and actually did see the national flag of blue-sky-white-sun being hoisted for the first time, gave this moving account:[20]

At last, I saw what I had been longing for, something that had been long hidden deep in my heart the symbol of my mother country, the national flag of China. Standing in front of a watch-and-clock store, quietly staring at that flag alone for a long time, I finally could not contain the excitement any more. To an old man strolling out of the store, I asked in Peijing Mandarin, 'Is this flag yours? Can I buy it?'. . . He nodded that I could have it, saying in a heavy Fuzhou accent, 'Ten yen'. At once, I pulled out a 50 yen bill and gave it to him. He was about to give me 40 yen in change, but I shook my head to indicate, 'No need to.' As I turned around to leave, he bowed a deep bow of gratitude.

In early December 1945, Chung took part in training the Central Officers in the Three People's Principles Youth Corps (三民主義青年團), so eager was he to put his ideals into practice.

---

[20] Chung, op. cit., pp. 277–278.

1:2 The Fall and Dissipation of the Nostalgia, 1945–1950

This saga of national nostalgic consciousness remains incomplete, however, until we tell its tragic sequel. The same Mr. Chung served as a captain in the twenty-seventh Platoon fighting against government troops following the notorious 228 Incident in 1947. At just the moment when the dream of making contact with the motherland was fulfilled, the brutal actuality of China-caused Taiwanese nostalgia for Chinese homeland culture to dissipate rapidly. This love contained a searing tension between the ideal and the real, between cultural identity and political identity. To this tragic sequel we now turn, to be followed by an analysis of the contents and implications of this popular nostalgia in Section 3.

The nostalgic enthusiasm most Taiwanese felt for their motherland collapsed (1:2:a.) when they went to Mainland China individually, and (1:2:b.) soon after they, collectively, welcomed back representatives of their homeland who had arrived to recover Taiwan from the defeated Japanese.

1:2:a. Some Taiwanese went to Mainland China individually, and received a culture shock that wiped out their longing for homecoming to China. This culture shock consisted of two elements: the dire conditions in which ordinary people lived and the low level of public morality there. Consider two examples of the former and one of the latter:

Wu Cho-liu went to the Mainland, and gave this account:[21]

> When I first landed on the Mainland I could not understand a word of what they said. Although I was in my home country, I felt I was in a foreign land. . . . The train to Nanjing was horribly packed. People queued up

---

[21] Wu, op. cit., pp. 120–123.

forming a snake-line for a complex check-in. Since I was a Japanese citizen, I went to a different station to be checked in; my luggage was not even examined. The Shanghai station had been bombed recently and was a mere temporary shack. The railroad carriage was wide; the train was wider than those in Taiwan. Every passenger carried a lot of luggage, very few did not. All the train stations along the line were temporary shacks, showing signs of the bitter battles of previous days. The scenes we passed through were all marked by desolation; it was a completely different world from the prosperity of Shanghai. Shanghai was the center of exploitation by many nations, with horribly imposing high-rises and skyscrapers. The foreigners residing in that extraterritorial region were disgustingly and audaciously haughty beyond words.

A stay of three or four days made me feel a deep sorrow for the plight of being Chinese. Hordes of streaming animal-like beggars were wretched shadows of human beings just getting by, while the foreigners were perversely domineering and tyrannical beyond description.

Such scenes dealt a shocking blow to the vision of a beautiful mother China in the heart of Mr. Wu!

Mr. Yeh Jung-chung of Lukang (鹿港) wrote another account after visiting Manchuria:[22]

> The city of Andong was prosperous with shops lined up closely together like comb-teeth, just that. . . the storefronts and signs were like what were seen thirty years

---

[22] Yeh, *op. cit.*, pp. 26–27.

ago in Lukang, my hometown. I asked myself, 'Is this my mother-country?' I walked and walked, and could not find anything that soothed my inner longing of many years. . . . In the jostling streets, I saw many Japanese; Japanese and Russian stores were strewn here and there. "Is this my home-country?" I asked myself ... I could only shake my head without admitting, "yes." Frankly, I had no specific concrete image I could use as a standard by which to gauge what would count as my 'mother country.' Yet, as a matter of fact, I found myself protesting against the scenes I witnessed before my eyes. This realization completely broke me down.

The rhetorical question, "Is this my home country?" reveals the extent to which their dream of a beautiful mother China had been devastated. Thus, these Taiwanese felt acute culture shock when they visited Mainland China individually. Peng Ming-min (彭明敏, 1923–), of a eminent family in Kaohsiung, traveled with his parents to Shanghai, Nanjing and other places on the Mainland when he was five. He reminisced on that trip later[23]

> This trip gave my parents an opportunity to compare the conditions in Mainland China with those in Taiwan following decades of Japanese occupation. They were, of course, impressed by the vast territory and nostalgic for the land of their forefathers. Yet, as to social development, industrialization, education, public health and sanitation, they felt that the Mainland still had much room for improvement compared to Taiwan.

These Taiwanese not only felt culture shock when they went to Mainland China individually, they felt shocked at the people's

---

[23] Peng Ming-min, *Ziyou di ziwei* (Taipei: Qianwei chubanshe, 1988), pp. 28–29.

low public moral standards there. Wu Chin-chuan 吳金川 was a native of Tainan who worked for the Central Bank in Manchuria during the war and served as board director of the Changhua Bank in Taiwan after the war. He went to Nanchang (南昌) with Chiang Ching-kuo to serve in the New Life Movement and felt shocked at the sleazy falsehoods in China. He reminisced on the situation at the time:[24]

> When I was in Nanchang I stayed at the hotel for the airplane pilots, which was supposed to be the best in the area. Upon entering my room, I found that people had already opened and gone through my luggage. Soon afterward, a young person appeared with a name card claiming to hold a B.A. from Japan's Meiji University, cordially offering his services to guide and show me around. I knew in fact he meant "I will bring you to places you may go see; I won't bring you to places you may not go see." This situation remains the same today. I treated him to a lunch that noon, but then told him I needed rest and let him go. Afterwards, I went out alone everywhere, including places I was not supposed to go. I found that places I was not supposed to go were about 10 years behind in the standard of living. I realized then that the so-called 'New Life Movement' was quite superficial. While the main streets showed indications of what New Life required; places outside the city could not bear inspection.

What the Taiwanese saw when they went to Mainland China was the glaring inconsistency between the showy appearance and

---

[24] "Wu Chin-chuan Xiansheng fangwen jilu (Records of visits to Mr. Wu)," in *Goushu lishi (5) --Riju shidai Taiwanren fu dalu jingyan* (Taipei: Zhongyang yanjiuyüan jindaishi yanjiuso, 1994), p. 130.

the shabby reality that turned out to be the truth about the China they had dreamed about. Inevitably, their dream was crushed.

1:2:b. Collectively, the Taiwanese were equally disappointed when Chinese officials came over to "receive" Taiwan from the defeated Japanese. Their disappointment was occasioned by three factors: (2.2.1.) political corruption; (2.2.2.) ethnic prejudice; and (2.2.3.) lingering suspicions the Taiwanese were traitors to China (*Hanjian*, 漢奸).

Immediately following the arrival of Chinese government officials, the Taiwanese tasted rank political corruption; this fact is documented throughout the annals of the modern history of Taiwan. Wu San-lien's report is highly representative:[25]

> Our tender feelings toward the Mainlanders were almost entirely destroyed by their corrupt words and behavior when they came to "recover" Taiwan. This was the same in northern China as in Taiwan. Mainlanders wanted gold, silver, vehicles, houses, women; those "five prizes of successful candidates" (*wuzi deng ke*, 五子登科) in government administration.
>
> When I returned to Taiwan in 1946 for 2 or 3 days, my ears kept hearing complaints about those Mainland receivers; I could not help but feel deeply disappointed. Our Taiwan brethren had danced in the streets for joy at returning home to China; now they were doused from their necks down with the foul liquor of Chinese corruption! Returning to Tianjin, I told a countryman of mine that the situation in Taiwan now was no different than a petroleum repository, waiting for a single lit match to ig-

---

[25] Wu, op. cit., pp. 107–108.

1. The Taiwanese Nostalgia for Cultural China (1895–1950)   19

nite. As to be expected, the tragic 228 Incident erupted soon afterwards.

Chen Cheng-tien 陳正添 was born in Pu-tzu (朴子), Chiayi (嘉義) prefecture, studied armored vehicles at school and went to Henan (河南) province to join the Chinese army. He said,[26]

> Since 1949, when the central government withdrew from China to come over and administer Taiwan, the so-called money culture has been thriving everywhere—'take some as you receive,' 'money first, then thanks,' 'red envelope (filled with bribe money)' and the like. In recent years, guns, drugs and looting have become rampant. Public peace and security have deteriorated; a gambling atmosphere is everywhere; social law and order have deteriorated; public decency is nowhere to be seen. The situation has reached a very serious level, making all of us feel gravely worried.

Chung I-jen also talked about the comportment of those Chinese "receivers" at the time:

> The Mainlanders had *only* one prominent desire in mind: how to 'loot' Japanese properties, how to take over geishas of Peng-lai Koh (蓬萊閣) and Chiang Shan Lou (江山樓). They never acknowledged Premier (Sun Yat-sen, 孫中山), never asked what were the Three People's Principles. How sad! How pitiful!

Tragically, the dreams of the Taiwanese were washed away overnight by this influx of Chinese political corruption and im-

---

[26] "Chen Cheng-tien xiansheng fangwen jilu," in *Goushu lishi (wu)-- Riju. shidai Taiwanren fu dalu jingyan,* op. cit., p85.

morality.

The second cause for the dissipation of Taiwanese nostalgia was the Mainlanders' snobbishness. Those "goa-seng lang" (外省人, outsiders) lorded over the throne of the departing Japanese, and continued the Japanese-style oppression over the island. Wu Choh-liu had this to say about the early period of Taiwan retrocession:[27]

> Government and party alike never trusted any Taiwanese person, it was exactly like during the Japan period. Mainlanders who took over after the Japanese occupied all the top levels of government adminstration; Taiwanese just played insignificant roles. Those who understood the situation were the Taiwanese down here; those ignorant 'goa seng lang (outsiders)' were up there. How could any smooth operations be possible at all? Worse still, those 'goa seng lang' were more bureaucratic than the Japanese had been, and with a superiority complex to boot; things naturally got into a terrible mess. Corruption was as commonplace as our meals at home. Most of them thought only of selfish profiteering and were oblivious to public welfare or benefit. The business of takeover naturally grew into snags and brawls. They also issued an excessive amount of banknotes that resulted in inflation everyday. News from Tainan on December 24th reported that white rice was now over 100 yen per *dou* (Chinese peck). Thus, everywhere voices of criticism arose, and people came to call these 'outsiders' 'pigs'. Some '*poa soa*' (half Mainlanders, Taiwanese who had been on the Mainland) who came back from Chungking but were not employed by the government took this op-

---

[27] Wu Choh-liu, *Taiwan lianqiao* (Taipei: Qianwei chubanshe, 1989), p. 185.

portunity and voiced criticisms to vent their inner frustrations. It so happened that the government and the Party could not get along harmoniously; there was no agreement of opinion at all, they were always criticizing each other.

In fact, such corruption had been a staple for a long time in the Mainland itself, resulting in what Wu Choh-liu called the "orphan of Asia" complex. Hsu Hsien-yao 許顯耀 from Tainan took preparatory courses at the School of Engineering at Zhejiang University. He recalled that while studying there he met some Mainlanders who didn't even know where Taiwan was, just that it was a tiny island off the coast. They regarded the Taiwanese as beyond the pale of civilization, and gave Hsu the nickname Shengfan (生番, raw barbarian).[28] Mainlanders viewed Taiwanese who had lived under the Japanese occupation as "second-class citizens".[29] To feel the prejudice of two different ethnic groups like this was too much to bear.

Naturally, at the time, ethnic snobbery and corruption went hand-in-hand. Wu Choh-liu reported about his experiences on the Mainland:[30]

> Taiwanese were generally called 'potatoes' on the Mainland. They were regarded as Japanese spies and were not well regarded anywhere. . . Such an existence was a sorry one. This was mainly because during the pre-war period Japan had dispatched hoodlums from Taiwan to Xiamen, and trained them to run gambling

---

[28] "Hsu Hsien-yao xiansheng fangwen jilu (records of visits with Mr. Hsu)," *Goushu lishi (6) -- Riju shidai Taiwanren fu dalu jingyan* (Taipei: Zhongyang yanjiuyuan jindaishi yanjiuso, 1995), p. 90
[29] Ibid., p. 43
[30] Wu, op. cit., p. 125.

stops and 'opium dens' under the cover of their extraterritorial status. These practices resulted in generally foul feelings among Mainlanders toward the Taiwanese, as 'running dogs' of Japan. This was part of Japan's policy to drive a wedge between us. Nor would the Japanese trust the Taiwanese after the war, either; they just took advantage of them. Many Taiwanese had taken part in the war of resistance against Japan and sacrificied themselves for their motherland, and thus were under constant surveillance by the Japanese military police. My arrival on the Mainland made me realize how complex the position of Taiwanese people was.

Li Fu-hsu 李佛續 earned a degree in electrical engineering from the private Jinling University in Nanking during the Sino-Japanese War. During his student days he decided not to reveal he was Taiwanese in order to avoid senseless misunderstandings. He usually claimed to be from Minnan in Fujian province or a Hakka person from Guangdong. During the war he avoided bearing the brunt of anti-Japanese sentiment by claiming he was from Jinjiang in Fujian province, and even registered himself as such at the University.[31]

Huang Shun-chien 黃順興 of Hainan Island recalled that after the War military personnel from the Chinese government who came over to recover the island reviled Taiwanese as "*sangjia zhi quan* (喪家之犬, homeless dogs, outcasts)."[32] Their ethnic snobbery reached its zenith here.

The final occasion for the dissipation of nostalgia toward the Mainland was when Mainlanders unkindly and summarily branded

---

[31] "Li Fu-hsu xiansheng fangwen jilu," *Goushu lishi (6)—Riju shidai Taiwanren fu dalu jingyan*, op. cit., p. 56
[32] "Huang Shun-chien xiansheng fangwen jilu," *Goushu lishi* (6), p. 143.00

all Taiwanese people as "traitors to China (漢奸, *Hanjian*)" or "war criminals (戰犯, *zhanfan*)". Such name-calling was deeply offensive to the Taiwanese. Wu San-lien, who was engaged in commercial business on the Mainland at the time, wrote:[33]

> At the time when the Qing government ceded Taiwan, they did so without the consent of the Taiwanese, who thereafter, continually resisted Japanese occupation until they exhausted their weapons and finally had to accept the occupation. Under the Japanese high-pressure rule, the Taiwanese had to manage to survive, now that Taiwan belonged to Japan. It was not the fault of the Taiwanese that they had to become Japanese citizens, thus branding them as traitors to China leaves much room for discussion.

Lan Min 藍敏 (ninth generation granddaughter of celebrated Qing general Lan Ting-yuan, 藍鼎元) went further to bring this injustice to light:[34]

> I resented the epithet, "war criminal"; I claimed that Taiwan had no war criminals. Taiwan was ceded to Japan after the Sino-Japanese War because the government did not want this piece of land and did not want the people residing there. It was not because the people did not want their parents: the children grew up, their real parents and foster parents fought; their real parents won, then said that their children in Taiwan had helped the foster parents fight against them and wanted to imprison the children. All this makes no sense. I told this story to everyone I met in Nanking. At first no one wanted to pay

---

[33] Wu, op. cit., pp. 104–105.
[34] Tseng Chin-lan's record of Hsu Hsueh-chis visit, *Lan Min xiansheng fangwen jilu* (Taipei: Zhongyang yanjiuyuan jindaishi yanjiuso, 1995), p. 93.

attention. I went to the gates of Army General Commander Ho Ying-chin and stood there for a good many hours. Everyone was much afraid at the mention of 'war criminal,' and shunned us as if we were lepers. Later, as I persisted in telling the story, and by and by they ceased rushing about to apprehend people [as 'war criminals'].... After a long year and eight months [of such struggles], the epithet, "Taiwan war criminals" was finally dropped.

This injustice was the straw that broke the back of Taiwanese nostalgia. Lan Min was vindicated but her cultural nostalgia had vanished; her vindication was a declaration of independence from the cultural Mainland. In effect, the alien political wind of Japanese oppression had aroused Taiwanese cultural nostalgia for China but China's wind of political corruption dissipated all such nostalgia.

1:3 Implications and Lessons

1:3:a. Reflecting on Sections 1 and 2, we see a radical enigma. The rise and fall of Taiwanese cultural nostalgia for China is peculiar in two respects: first, this cultural nostalgia was aroused by alien oppression and then was dissipated by the abuse of Taiwan by the mother country. Second, the nostalgia was dissipated, not quelled, just at the moment when the opportunity to be enfolded in the mother country was at last realized.

This was dramatically portrayed in Mr. Chung's switch from enthusiastic participant in a government-sponsored youth training camp in nation-building to a captain in the twenty-seventh platoon of resistance forces against the government during the 228 Uprising.[35] Wu Cho-liu had described Taiwanese nostalgia for cultural

---

[35] Section 2 began with this dramatic story that was a sequel to the one that ended

China as something instinctive, like an orphan's yearning for its parents without considering "what they are really like."[36] This feeling was later snuffed out completely. Why? What happened? The standard answer is that the Chinese rulers mishandled Taiwan. Indeed, it was corrupt, prejudiced and abusive. But, such deep feelings of nostalgia could not be wiped away just by prejudicial politics or political oppression. Nor could anything be wrong with yearning for a motherland *culture*. What went wrong?

1:3:b. Superficially, politics aroused cultural nostalgia in Taiwan and politics dissipated it. We must consider what this fact means and try to learn from it. The occasion for the rise of cultural nostalgia in Taiwan was Japanese political oppression. It was appropriate for Taiwanese to seek strength in their homeland culture. However, the Taiwanese intellectuals did not study the Chinese cultural heritage in-depth, but merely yearned to be in touch with actualities in Mainland China which, at the time, were not particularly worthy objects of yearning. By the same token, the occasion for the dissipation of cultural nostalgia in Taiwan was Chinese political corruption. This dissipation was due to the fact that Taiwanese nostalgia was just a vague psychological yearning without deep passion for the actual treasures of Chinese culture.

The soul of English culture expressed in Shakespeare, Milton, Bentham, Coleridge and Carlyle is one thing; the pragmatic maneuvers of the British Empire that occasioned the American Revolution and the Great Resistance in India are quite another. Similarly, the ethical vigor of classical Confucianism is one thing, the obsequiousness and corruption of bureaucratic Confucianism is quite another. Yeh Jung-chung expressed this distinction well in refusing to identify corrupt governor Chen Yi 陳儀 (Kung-chia, 1883–1950)

Section 1.
[36] See Note 5 in Section 1 (p. 6) and the quotation from Mr. Wu.

with the 5000-year Chinese culture he yearned for:[37]

> We are so happy to have come out of Japanese shackles and return home to the bosom of our motherland. We can now welcome the rule of our home country. Yet, to say "welcome our home country" does not seem to be quite accurate to the present situation... Some say that Governor Chen Yi represents the ROC which, in turn, legitimately represents our mother country, so, therefore, welcoming Chen Yi amounts to the same thing as welcoming our motherland. Such a syllogism is valid; but this [our situation] is not a problem for syllogisms. What we yearn for is for our blood to flow back home, to the home of 5,000 years of history and culture. Mr. Chen Yi does not at all deserve to be the object of our profound yearning.

One shudders to think what would have happened if the baby of cultural heritage had been thrown out with the dirty bathwater of corrupt rule, if Shakespeare were to be cast down along with the British Empire, if classical Confucianism were to be overthrown together with the dynasties of traditional China.

We must learn an important lesson from the rise and fall of Taiwanese nostalgia for homeland Chinese culture. We only hope the Taiwanese learn from their bitter cultural-political history, and plunge into deep studies—as if their whole life and destiny depended on it—of the authentic *heritage* of the Chinese homeland culture. Confucius (551–479 B.C.), Mencius (371–289 B.C.?), Laozi and Zhuangzi (bt. 399-295 B.C.?), the Eight Great Writers of the Tang and Song dynasties, and many other Greats, are all waiting to teach us. They have all been tested repeatedly throughout

---

[37] Yeh, op. cit., pp. 212–213.

the ages and have not been found wanting or disappointing. They have not only survived these fiery tests, they have shined across the centuries offering enlightenment and vitality. We must learn from them to get through these trying times. Having nurtured ourselves on the real Chinese cultural heritage, we can then look squarely at all the socioeconomic problems and sociopolitical corruptions. We can then be spared the tragic rise and fall of our cultural nostalgia and avoid being buffeted by sociopolitical winds wherever they may come from.

"Those who refuse to learn from history will be condemned to repeat it," as Santayana solemnly warned us. We surely wish to spare ourselves another culture shock, another cultural crash, which would be much more dire than the economic and sociopolitical disasters we have been exposed to in the tumultuous history of Taiwan during the past century.

What is the lesson of our history? We should not throw out our dream together with corrupt actuality because there is nothing wrong with our dream and nostalgia. Rather, we should sublimate the nostalgia into an unshakable historic faith; for life without nostalgic dreams is not human. Our dream of returning to an ideal China must be transmuted to dreaming Confucius' dreams of restoring the ideal ancient China. Confucius proclaimed, "Zhou could survey the two preceding dynasties. How great a wealth of culture! And we follow upon Zhou." He also sighed, "How utterly have things gone to the bad with me! It is long now indeed since I dreamed that I saw the Duke of Zhou."[38] Arthur Waley — Confucius' British translator—commented,[39]

---

[38] *The Analects*, 3/14, 7/5. Quoted from *The Analects of Confucius*, translated and annotated by Arthur Waley (London: George Allen & Unwin and NY: Vintage Books 1938), pp. 97, 123.
[39] Ibid., p. 17.

> Were we to take them [ancient sages] in the order of their importance to him [Confucius], I think we should have to begin with the founders and expanders of the Zhou dynasty; for in his eyes the cultures of the two preceding dynasties found their climax and fulfillment in that of the early Zhou sovereigns. Above all, we should have to deal first with Tang, Duke of Zhou, who had not only a particular importance in the Lu State, but also a peculiar significance for Confucius himself.

Cultural nostalgia has been endorsed since before the time of Confucius in the Three Dynasties at the misty dawn of Chinese history. This dream has survived thousands of years of brutal political history in China. Our eternal nostalgia is shared by Dr. Martin Luther King (1929–1968) who proclaimed his moral "dream" of inalienable equality of human persons, especially those who are uprooted, displaced and oppressed. He dedicated his life to his dream of two hundred years. We should do no less for our nostalgia of several thousand years of history.

2
Postwar Taiwan in Historical Perspective
2:1 Introduction

The "Taiwan experience" has attracted the attention of scholars worldwide who examine it from a variety of theoretical standpoints, including classical economics, progressive dependency, world system theory and the relatively conservative historico-political and sociocultural theory.[1] Many international conferences on this theme have been organized in Taiwan and overseas, indicating just how important scholars take the Taiwan experience. Indeed, the various perspectives together allow us to arrive at a deeper understanding of the Taiwan experience.

In this chapter we examine the postwar Taiwan experience from yet another viewpoint: Taiwan's agriculture in historical perspective. To understand contemporary Taiwan we must understand our roots in our soil and the history of the agrarian experience here, especially since the end of World War II. This involves looking into the history of the Sino-American Joint Commission on Rural Reconstruction (JCRR; *zhongmei zhong guo nongcun fuxing lianhe weiyuanhui,* 中美中國農村復興聯合委員會), which existed between October 1, 1948 and March 16, 1979. The vantage of agrarian history offers us a particular insight into the postwar Taiwan experience and its broader significance.

Why is this the case? Three transformations in and from agrarian society were decisive in the formation of postwar Taiwan the emergence of: (1) a full owner-cultivator class; (2) a middle-

---

[1] For a review of recent discussions on "Taiwan Experience," cf. Edwin A. Winckler and Susan A. Winckler, et al., eds., *Contending Approaches to the Political Economy of Taiwan* (New York: M. E. Sharpe, Inc., 1988), pp. 3–19.

class; and (3) a middle-class intelligentsia.

The formation of the "full owner-cultivator" class led to the sudden disappearance of tenant farmers, mainly as a consequence of the Taiwan land reform policy. According to statistics, full owner-cultivators rose from 32.7 percent of the farming population in 1946 to 38 percent in 1952, to 59 percent in 1955, 64 percent in 1960, 80 percent in 1974, 82 percent in 1984 and reached an amazing 83.55 percent in 1992.[2] This phenomenon altered the traditional Chinese landscape wherein "the rich with farmlands by the thousands, the poor without space for a drill-bit." This new farmer ownership of land was followed by a new enthusiasm on the part of the farmers and then by benefits to the very industrialization that ushered in the modernization of Taiwan and the demise of agriculture.

The emergence of a middle-class coincided with the change to industrial society in postwar Taiwan. The percentage of farmers in the population steadily declined from 52.49 percent in 1952, to 49.8 percent in 1960 and to 20.5 percent in 1987. This corresponded to a decline in agricultural production; the ratio of agriculture in the Net Domestic Product (NDP) relative to industrial production dropped from 30 percent versus 18 percent in 1952, to 28.3 percent versus 28.9 percent in 1964, to 9.2 percent versus 44.7 percent in 1980, to 6.2 percent versus 47.1 percent in 1987 and to 5.9 percent versus 43.5 percent in 1989. These statistics indicate a shift in the economic balance in postwar Taiwan. This was the first time this sort of shift from agrarian to industrial society had occurred in Chinese history. This shift in economic balance also brought about socio-political changes[3] which, in turn, in-

---

[2] Rural Economic Division, JCRR, *Taiwan Agricultural Statistics, 1901–1965* (Taipei: JCRR, 1966), 9; *Taiwan Agricultural Year Book* (1993 edition), p. 310.

[3] See Walter Galenson ed., *Economic Growth and Structural Change in Taiwan: The Postwar Experience of the Republic of China* (Ithaca, N.Y. and London: Cornell Univer-

duced the emergence of the middle-class.

A middle-class intelligentsia emerged because the developing economy and society in Taiwan spawned an expansion of public education. An immediate impetus was the 'Nine Year Public Education Policy' (1968–1969). As a result, the illiteracy rate of people over six-years-old plummeted from 42 percent (1952) to 4.72 percent (1999). At the same time, the ratio of population with a middle-school education rose from 8.8 percent (1952) to 53.94 percent (1999).[4]

These facts are indicative of a crucial turning point in Taiwan history; they herald Taiwan's democratization. Roughly, they help us to demarcate the overall pattern of the Taiwan experience. Moreover, this series of related developments was initiated by changes in the nature of agrarian society in Taiwan, changes that continue to stimulate the development that catapulted Taiwan into the modern world. This is why we can make the claim that agrarian society is the root and the soil out of which the modern prosperity of Taiwan was born. Understanding the history of agriculture in Taiwan is a *sine qua non* for understanding the Taiwan experience.

2:2 The Rise and Fall of Agrarian Culture in Postwar Taiwan

The essential feature of the postwar Taiwan experience has been the rise and fall of traditional agrarian culture. This culture involves four interrelated characteristics: (1) it forms an agrarian economic system based on labor-intensive farming and a market trade economy; (2) an agrarian society dominated by blood relations; (3) farming has priority over purely commercial activities and (4) belief in the unity of Heaven (nature) and man (*tianren*

---

sity Press, 1979).
    [4] *Taiwan Statistical Data Book*, (2001), Table 2–4, p. 24.

heyi). This belief is a key theme in Confucianism which, along agrarianism, constituted the two pillars of Chinese culture for several thousand years.[5]

Agrarian culture and society in Taiwan underwent dramatic structural change and decline after World War II. The Land Reform Policy of the 1950s ushered in a series of institutional changes, accelerated by improvements in seeds and seedlings and soils and fertilizers, combined with technical innovations in irrigation, to modernize agriculture in Taiwan. The strengthening of agriculture in Taiwan stimulated the industrial development of the 1960s, which, in turn, led to a decline in agrarian economy and increased farmer alienation from the land and villages.

This sweeping change, with deep historic implications, grew out of the agrarian and economic policies formulated and implemented by the government.[6] The Great Divide in the history of postwar agrarian policy is 1972: we demarcate the pre-1972 period and the post-1972 period.

The pre-1972 period began in 1945, when Japan returned Taiwan to the Republic of China (ROC). This period was marked by a series of land reform policies, such as "The 375 Reduction of Land Taxes" (1949), "The Public Land Purchase Policy" (1952) and "The Land-to-the-Tiller Policy" (1953).

The post-1972 period began in September 1972, when the ROC government enacted "Important Implementation for the Speedy Reconstruction of Agriculture." The resulting meta-mor-

---

[5] See my "Zhongguo nongye chuantong ji qi jingzheng neihan: Wenti yu jieshi," in *Zhongguo wenming di jingshen* (I) (Taipei: Guangbo dianshi wenhua jijinghui, 1990), pp. 211–226.

[6] See Liao Cheng-hung, Huang Chun-chieh and Hsiao Hsin-huang. *Guangfuhou Taiwan nongye zhengci di yanbian: Lishi ji shehui di fenxi* (Taipei: Institute of Ethnology, Academia Sinica, 1986), Chapter 1.

phosis was stupendous; for the first time in Chinese history, Taiwan changed from an agrarian to an industrial-commercial society, initiating the so-called "economic miracle." This rapid transformation produced many social and cultural problems.

These agrarian policies reformed the old tenant system, helped owner-cultivators to become independent, spurred land investment for industrial and commercial use and indirectly promoted agricultural production. All of this laid a solid foundation for industrial development.[7]

From 1953 on, all agrarian policies were forged under the principle, "Agriculture cultivates industry; industry develops agriculture." This resulted in a mixed blessing for agriculture which suffered a severe "developmental squeeze."[8] First, the increase in agricultural production, accelerated by mechanization, led to a surplus of manpower and supplies that were transferred to no-agrarian, industrial sectors of society. Ironically, this resulted in impoverishment of the agricultural sector. The entire process, resulting in the rapid industrial development of the 1960s, began during the 1895-1960 period.[9]

During the twenty-year implementation of this agrarian policy, until 1972, agricultural development occurred in two stages. The first stage, (1953–1960), involving import substitution, occurred during the first two periods of plans for establishing an agrarian economy. The second stage, (1961-1972), involved exporting substitution, and was the third period of agricultural-economic

---

[7] Cf. Martin M.C. Yang, *Socio-Economic Result of Land Reform in Taiwan* (Honolulu: East-West Center Press, 1970).

[8] Cf. Teng-hui Lee, *Intersectoral Capital Flows in the Economic Development of Taiwan, 1895-1960* (Ithaca: Cornell University Press, 1972); Hsin-Huang Michael Hsiao, *Governmental Agricultural Strategies in Taiwan and South Korea, A Macrosociological Assessment* (Taipei: Institute of Ethnology, Academia Sinica, 1981), pp. 55–56.

[9] Teng-hui Lee, op.cit.

planning. Agricultural enterprises in both these stages were intended to cultivate industry. The first stage saw payment, with funds obtained by the export sales of agricultural products, of bills for imported industrial materials needed to nurture the burgeoning industry in Taiwan. The second stage burdened agriculture with the task of providing the export industry with sufficient food and labor resources.

An agricultural crisis arose with the completion of the third economic plan in 1965. The most serious problems were the impoverishment of agrarian labor power, investment and profits, as well as a reduction in the availability of agricultural land and the imbalance between agrarian and industrial development.[10]

Agrarian policies were then reversed from "oppressing" agricultural enterprises to "balancing" them with industry. "The Important Implementations for Speedy Construction of Agriculture Act" in 1972 (commonly called "Nine Great Plans") and "The Resumption of Organization and Implementation of Construction of the Great Corps of Eighty Thousand Farmers" in 1983[11] were official efforts to redress the imbalance of agricultural development. But, these political efforts were hampered by the effects of the free international market economy, Taiwan was threatened by an influx of competitive, foreign agricultural products. In addition, industrial waste was beginning to pollute the cultivated lands and no one had attempted to address these issues in public or political arenas. All sectors of the agrarian economy felt there was little choice but to take to the streets.[12] All this began with land reform, to which we shall now turn our attention.

---

[10] Chang Hsun-shun, "Jiashu nongcun jianshe zhongyao coshi duidong jingxing," *Taiwan nongye 9:2* (1973), pp.1–6.

[11] *Taiwan nongye jianshe dazhun zhi linshan zhi qi zhuzhi yaodian* (Nantuo: Department of Agriculture and Forestry, Taiwan Provincial Government, March, 1993).

[12] See above, note 5.

The Rise of Agrarian Culture

Land reform during the 1950s had a profound impact on development in postwar Taiwan. The greatest impact was, of course, in the changes in the distribution of land ownership. After land reform, the number of full owner-cultivators suddenly increased, as shown in statistics gathered by the JCRR. In 1946, the year the ROC took over Taiwan, 32.7 percent of people involved in agriculture were full owner-cultivators, while 28.19 percent were half owner-cultivators, and 39.11 percent were tenants. After land reform, by 1953, 54.86 percent were full owner-cultivators, 24.14 percent were half owner-cultivators, while the ratio of tenants had dropped to 21 percent. By 1960, the ratios were: 64.45 percent, 21.23 percent, and 14.32 percent, respectively.[13]

The second dramatic change took place in the farmers' own attitudes to agriculture. The immediate reaction of farmers to land reform during the 1950s and 1960s was one of pride and devotion to agrarian culture— they were dedicated to the land and held a positive outlook on farming as a lofty, meaningful way of life; farming seemed to be more than just a way to earning a living to them. Now that farmers owned the land they cultivated, they were confident and held a positive outlook. In 1952, the JCRR surveyed 875 farming families, and found that 85 percent of them believed that improvement of their lives would follow their ownership of land and 69 percent believed they would eventually own the land they were cultivating.[14] Thus, the early successes of land reform in the 1950s bolstered farmers' dedication to their land and led them to perceive farming as a lofty way of life.[15]

---

[13] Rural Economic Division, JCRR, *Taiwan Agricultural Staistics, 1905-1965* (Taipei: JCRR, 1966).
[14] Leo Po-erh (Rapper), *Taiwan muqian zhi nongcun wenti youqi jianglai zhi zhanwang* (Taipei: JCRR), p. 156.
[15] I conducted an investigation of the agricultural self-consciousness of Taiwan

The third impact of land reform was the change in farmer social consciousness that had resulted from reorganizing the farmers' associations. In 1950, the JCRR invited W. A. Anderson, Professor of Rural Sociology at Cornell University, to study and report on farm associations in Taiwan.

In August 1952, the ROC Executive Yuan issued "Temporary Plans for the Improvement of Farmers' Associations at All Levels," by which association members were to be divided into two groups: regular members and associate members. Association functions were greatly expanded to include sales, promotion of agribusiness, cattle insurance and trusts and banking.

As the farmers' associations became more versatile and effective, their significance grew in the eyes of the farmers. The farmers' associations were first established under Japanese colonial rule with the implementation of "Regulations for Farmers' Associations in Taiwan" (1907). After the retrocession of Taiwan to the ROC, the associations gained autonomy, even at local levels where the associations were owned by their farmer members.

Kuo Min-hsueh, a JCRR specialist and former student of Anderson, took part in the reorganization of the farmers' associations. He conducted a survey of member attitudes towards the associations, including the extent to which they identified with their associations. Kuo Min-hsueh found that farmer identification with farmers' associations rose consistently during 1950s. To the question, "Who do the farmers' associations belong to?" most members replied, "the farmers" or "the farmer members"; this answer had risen from 1.7 percent (1952), to 56 percent (1955), to 79.5 percent (1959).

---

farmers. See my essay in Liao Cheng-hung and Chun-chieh Huang, *Zhanhuo Taiwan Nongmin jiazhi quxiang di zhuanbian* (Taipei: Liejing chuban shiye yuxian kung-ssu, 1992), Chapter 4.

The same period witnessed a steady increase in farmers' association membership: from 20.7 percent (1952), to 85.6 percent (1955), and up to 94.2 percent (1959). So too, the number of farmers who took part in association meetings increased from 27.6 percent, to 57.2 percent, to 82 percent. Simultaneously, there was a rising cry for democratization of farmers' associations. The ratio of voices saying that the executive secretary should be nominated by popular election increased from 20.7 percent, to 66.5 percent, to 80.2 percent. Those who knew that the representatives of farmer members were elected, not simply nominated, increased from 32.8 percent, to 72.4 percent, to 82.7 percent.[16]

Positive attitudes to farmers' associations, thus, had resulted from land reform and reorganization of farmers' associations.

The Fall of Agrarian Culture

We now turn to the sad '60s sequel to the upbeat '50s story. The agrarian crisis of the 1960s alienated farmers from their land and caused them to become disenchanted with farming. The crisis involved two components: land and income.

Previously, land had been viewed as a precious family legacy on which the farmers' mission of working the soil and the life ideal of fulfilling the unity of heaven (nature) and man were based. By now, land had become a commodity to be purchased by speculators who could turn around and sell it for three or four times more than they paid for it. This was the product of an earlier crisis, the precipitous drops in agricultural prices due to the sudden influx of imported agricultural commodities. The farmers' incomes tumbled. The ratio of income from farming to total farmer income, i.e. including income from nonfarming activities, dropped from 66

---

[16] Kuo Min-hsueh, *Taiwan Nongye fazhan guiji* (Taipei: Taiwan Commercial Press, 1984), pp. 146-147. See especially Chapter 3 of this book.

percent (1966), to 45.2 percent (1971), to 28.8 percent (1981), until the ratio rose slightly to 31.7 percent (1984), to 36.7 percent (1985), reaching 38.1 percent (1987).

The above crises darkened the farmers' outlook. According to a 1984 survey of 450 farming families, 59.3 percent regarded farming as hopeless; the attitude was especially prevalent among residents living in areas devoted exclusively to farming: 48.6 percent were dissatisfied with farming as a way of life; 16.6 percent were *very* dissatisfied. Nonetheless, a majority of farmers (53 percent) were unwilling to abandon agriculture, 7 percent of them *extremely* unwilling. In areas with relatively few farmers, 76.2 percent were extremely unwilling. This attitude might have been due to lack of education among farmers or their lack of other skills or training for new jobs. More likely, this reaction was due to their attitudes towards their land; they grasped that land was a precious commodity on this small, densely populated island. In any case, they had grown disenchanted with the farm associations and took to the streets to demand relief from the impact of low-priced foreign imports.[17]

This drastic metamorphosis of farmer attitudes forms a keynote in the history of postwar Taiwan. It led to the formation of a pluralistic society, a turning away from the monolithic traditional society. This monolithic traditional society had bred political hegemony over the social, economic and cultural spheres of the community. Each sphere gained and welcomed its own autonomy with the dawn of a pluralistic society. This was because social pluralism makes it impossible for the mode of thinking of *one* sector of the society, one ideology, to dominate other sectors.[18]

---

[17] Liao and Huang, op. cit., Chapters 6 and 8.
[18] Chun-chieh Huang, "Industry, Culture, Politics: The Taiwan Transformation" in Richard Hardey Brown, ed., *Culture, Politics and Economic Growth: Experience in East*

Let us now look into the *origin* of this agrarian metamorphosis: the land reform. How well did it succeed?

2:3 The Prewar Background and Its Problems

Causes for Success of Land Reform

Three causes can be cited for the success of the historic land reform in the 1950s that marked the beginning of the postwar Taiwan experience: (1) the policymakers were separate from the landowners; (2) the policymakers from the Mainland were devoted to the task, while those from Taiwan raised no objection and (3) people at the time were eager to redress the unfair distribution of land ownership, a legacy from the Japanese era.

Authorities who had come from Mainland China in 1949 were homeless; they lacked family ties and were landless. This special situation in Taiwan at the time[19] rendered these policymakers immune from personal considerations in viewing the land reform. This separation of policymakers from landowners made the land reform implementation a relatively streamlined affair in Taiwan—unlike in other countries (e.g., the Philippines and some Central and South American countries) that, although sending experts to Taiwan to learn from Taiwan's success, failed in their own land reform attempts because they had failed to separate the policymakers from land owners themselves.

Second, the policymakers from the Mainland were fresh from their bitter experience with peasants in China and determined to make a fresh start and govern fairly and honestly.[20] Their dedica-

---

Asia (Studies in Third World Societies, Vol. 44, Williamsburg, Va.: College of William and Mary, 1994).

[19] For a detailed discussion, see my *Nongfuhui yu Taiwan jingyan* (Taipei: Sanmin shuju, 1994).

[20] See Chen Cheng, *Ruhe shixian gengzhe you qi tian* (Taipei: Zhengzhong shuju,

tion in this effort ultimately produced positive results.

Their devotion to the task was matched by a lack of objections from their Taiwanese counterparts. The local Taiwanese policymakers—members of the first Temporary Provincial Assembly (1946)—were the cream of Taiwanese society. About half of them held university or graduate degrees; even those schooled in the cultural tradition of China held a cosmopolitan point of view. Many came from landowning families endowed with vast financial and political resources. They all enjoyed high social esteem—they were truly the leaders of their society. Consequently, in the beginning they felt free to voice numerous objections to land reform—after all, they were representatives of the old landowning intelligentsia.

Suddenly, the situation took an ugly turn. During the notorious 228 incident of 1947, many of these intelligentsia *cum* landowners were assassinated and thus removed from the political arena. In his memoir, one Taiwanese intellectual described how hushed and lifeless the government business office had become, in contrast to its pre-February 28th vibrancy; it had become an entirely different world.[21] The dark, ominous atmosphere in which land reform was conducted effectively silenced the landowners' objections. It was reported that the first and second general meetings of the first Temporary Provincial Assembly had enjoyed nearly full attendance; in contrast, daily attendance at the third general assembly averaged around 16 or 17 members (once, attendance reach a high of 21).[22] Tycoon landowner Lin Hsien-tang exiled himself to Japan, asserting, "I seem to hold somewhat dif-

---

1954), p. .93.

[21] Han Shih-chuan, *Liushi huiyi* (Taiwan: Han Shih-chuan xiansheng sishisan zhounian juanji weiyuanhui, 1996), pp. 86–87.

[22] Cheng Chih, *Taiwan shengyihui zhi yanjiu* (Taipei: Huashi chubanshe, 1985), p. 122.

ferent opinions about the government's '375 Reduction of Land Tax' and especially the 'Buying-up of Surplus Grain among Big Families.'"[23] Lin died in September 1956 in Japan, his death signaling the end of the old period. There were no further objections from Taiwanese landowners—thus, the February 28 Incident was the second cause for the success of the land reform program.

The third cause for the success of the land reform was widespread public discontent over the unfair distribution of arable land resulting from the old Japanese policies. Statistics dated April 10, 1939 indicate that 224, 931 families cultivated less than 1 *jia* each, a total area of 103, 412 *jia*, and 3,576 families cultivated more than 10 *jia* each, a total area of 106,887 *jia*. In contrast, 579 families cultivated more than 20 *jia* each, a total area of no less than 68,410 *jia* (*jia* = .97 hectare). The report indicated that 53.1 percent of farmers cultivated only 14.96 percent of land, whereas 0.13 percent of the farmers cultivated 9.9 percent of the land. These statistics revealed not only major landowners renting out parcels of land, but a concentration of land in the hands of a few, with minute segmentation of the rest of the land for the vast majority of farmers.[24] This was a legacy of the Japanese occupation.

More than 60 percent of farmers were tenants or half owner-cultivators during the era of Japanese rule. Oppressed by colonial policies and by the capitalists, farmers in Taiwan were eager to see the land situation changed—as soon as possible. Discontent over unfair land distribution was the third factor leading to the success in instituting land reform.

---

[23] Yeh Jung-chung, ed., *Lin Hsien-tang xiansheng jinianji* (Taipei: Privately published, 1960), Vol. III, p. 109.
[24] Chou Hsien-wen, "Riju shidai Taiwan zhi nongye jingji, *"Taiwan Yinhan jikan,* 8:4 (1956), p. 91.

Building an Infrastructure

Another factor in Taiwan's rapid modernization, as well as its rapid development of agriculture, was the construction of an infrastructure during the fifty-one years of Japanese colonial rule.[25] The Japanese government oversaw major civil engineering projects, including irrigation, electrification, railways and seaports. Initial achievements in these areas impressed Liang Chi-chao (1873–1929), who visited Taiwan and tried to understand how they had happened: "The same sun and moon, the same mountains and rivers . . . Why such accomplishments by the Japanese?"[26] Chen Yi, governor of Fujian province, was similarly impressed during his visit in 1935 to attend the "Commemorative Exposition, the Fortieth Anniversary of Japanese Rule." To draw upon the "Taiwan experience" under the Japanese occupation, Chen Yi invited the Japanese engineer who had designed the Chianan dam, Hada Yoichi, to observe the waterways of Fujian, so he might formulate "Plans for Developing Fujian."[27]

The Japanese achievements also impressed members of the JCRR during their visits to Taiwan in 1949. In the first issue of *Working Reports of the JCRR,* which appeared in 1950, members recalled their difficulties in coping with the agrarian situation in Mainland China.[28] They praised the achievements in Taiwan un-

---

[25] On the Japanese colonial experience as a factor in postwar Taiwan development, see Hyman Kublin, "Taiwan's Japanese Interlude, 1895–1945," in Paul K. T. Sih ed., *Taiwan in Modern Times* (New York: St. John's University, 1973), pp. 317-58; Ramon H. Myers and Mark R. Peattie, eds., *The Japanese Colonial Empire, 1895-1945* (Princeton: Princeton University Press, 1984); Thomas B. Gold, "Colonial Origins of Taiwanese Capitalism," in Edwin A. Winckler, et al., eds., *Contending Approaches to the Political Economy of Taiwan* (New York: M. E. Sharp, Inc., 1988), pp. 101–120.

[26] Liang Chi-chao, *Yinpingshi wenji,* Vol. 4, p. 14.

[27] Kogawa Katsumi, *Taiwan o ai shida Nihojin* (Matsuyama: Aoyama Tosho, 1989), pp. 260–261.

[28] *Chungguo Nongcun fuxing lianhe weiyuanhui baogao* (October 1, 1948–January 15, 1950), p. 12. Hereafter cited as *Baogao.*

der Japanese rule.[29] Not only did Taiwan have a sound infrastructure for agricultural and industrial development, it was blessed with a comprehensive transportation system. Taiwan also had effective agricultural organizations, including the Irrigation Association (*Shuilihui*) that facilitated the tasks of agricultural construction by coordinating with local organizations, such as the farmers' associations.[30]

The "Taiwan miracle" was possible largely because of this infrastructure built up by the Japanese colonial rulers. Unfortunately, some of these constructions were destroyed by American bombs during World War II and were rebuilt only with much difficulty by members of the JCRR.

The Japanese Legacy: Problems

The Japanese contribution to the Taiwan experience was not problem-free: Japanese colonialism and capitalism produced a trauma of *oppression*—the feeling that Taiwan being pushed into a dependent, marginal position—among the Taiwanese.

Japan built up an infrastructure for modernizing Taiwan for one overriding purpose, expressed in the slogan: "Industrial Japan, agrarian Taiwan." This phrase carried two implications: Taiwan existed on the margins, in the shadow of *capitalist* Japan, and was dependent on and colonially subservient to *imperialistic* Japan. Taiwan suffered both economic colonialism and political oppression. She, indeed, was held prey, "Under Imperial Japan," as indicated by the title of Yanaihara Sadao's classic study *Nihon Teikokushugi ka no Taiwan*.

The economic development of Taiwan under Japanese occu-

---

[29] Ibid.
[30] *Baogao*, p. 39.

pation was tightly controlled and carefully managed in order to serve Japan's needs. During the 1940s, numerous sugar-manufacturers were merged into four major ones, including the Taiwan Sugar Company (*Taiwan Sato Kabushiki Kaisha*), which ran forty-two sugar mills and fifteen alcohol factories; its private railroad had 2,900 miles of track.[31] The total area covered by its installations was over one-eighth the amount of cultivated land in Taiwan. In Yen-shui Kang and Hua-lien Kang prefectures, the sugar company occupied 9,248 *jia*—more than one-fourth of the area of cultivated land in those counties.

Japan's other important achievements in Taiwan included: reform of the currency system (1904); a complete land survey (1905); an islandwide railroad system and the opening of seaports in Keelung and Kaohsiung (1908). These achievements were undertaken under the control of the Japanese capitalists.[32] As Yanaihara points out, Taiwan was made capitalistic under the policies of economic colonialism solely in order to benefit Japan.[33] Internationally, Taiwan was made marginal and subservient to the capitalistic "centers" (prewar Japan, postwar United States) for which it produced low-cost goods. Domestically, the influx of capitalism restructured and opened up the traditionally closed farming communities, turning their agricultural land and labor into salable commodities at the mercy of commercial markets at home and abroad. According to statistics, the ratio of cash income to agricultural income jumped from 39.8 percent (1958) to 89.3 percent (1986), while the ratio of cash payments within total agricultural expenditures jumped from 59 percent (1958) to 92.9 percent

---

[31] Yamanbe Kentaro, "Riben diguozhuyi yu zhimindi," *Shihuo Monthly*, trans. by Cheng Chin-jen, N.S. 2:1 (1972), p. 48.
[32] Yanaihara Tadao, *Riben diguozhuyixia di Taiwan* trans. by Chou Hsien-wen, (Taipei: Pamier shudian, 1985), p. 26.
[33] Yanaihara, op.cit., p. 12.

(1986).[34]

Commercialization of agricultural toil and lands did not occur as precipitously in Mainland China as in Taiwan. This was borne out by John L. Buck who studied 16,456 farm families in 156 counties in 22 provinces on the Mainland from 1929 to 1933. Amano Motonosuke (1901–1980) also analyzed the extent of comercialization of agricultural products based on documents provided by Buck. Amano's report shows the extremely low rate of commercialization of agricultural products (foodstuffs).[35] In sum, traditional Taiwanese agricultural enterprises were transformed under the impact of imperial capitalism.

The second problem attendant with Japanese development of Taiwan was the infiltration of Japan's political colonialism, which began with a census and registration (1905) of the Taiwanese population. A land survey was conducted from 1898 to 1904 and a survey of forests and fields from 1910 to 1914 in order to enact land control legislation. The Currency Reform Act (1904) laid the foundation for the modern monetary system. The railway system ran from Keelung in the north down to Kaohsiung (1908). The great Chianan dam was constructed (1920–1930). An electric power station was built at Sun-Moon Lake (1920–1935). All these projects were undertaken under the careful planning and supervision of the colonial government. Such official infiltration into Taiwan's economic-industrial development continued after World War II through land reform, the reorganization of farm associations, the Irrigation Association (*Shuilihui*), the grain-fertilizer barter system, and others. These various regulations and reorganizations demonstrate how government worked to shape the formation of

---

[34] *Agricultural Development in the Republic of China on Taiwan* (Taipei: Council of Agriculture, 1988), p. 32.

[35] Amano Motonosuke, *Chugoku Nogyou Keizailon* (Tokyo: Ryukei Shusha, 1978 revised edition), Vol. 3, p. 9.

industry in pre and postwar Taiwan.

2:4 The JCRR and Its Role in History

Besides the Japanese government, another organization that influenced the rural Taiwan experience was the Sino-American Joint Commission on Rural Reconstruction (JCRR), which signaled the beginning of the positive poswar Taiwan experience.

The Principles of the JCRR

The JCRR was officially inaugurated in Nanjing on October 1, 1948. Drs. Raymond T. Moyer and John Earl Baker, appointed by the President of the United States, two other American members and three illustrious Chinese members, Chiang Meng-lin, Yen Yang-chu and Shen Tsung-han, who were appointed by the Chinese President, composed the first JCRR. This Commission ranked among the most important contributions made by the United States to development in postwar Taiwan. The JCRR recruited agricultural experts for membership through testing and personal interviews.[36] The JCRR thus obtained technical experts with doctorates from the United States who had their own ideas for solving Taiwan's agrarian problems.[37] They helped to implement the charter of the JCRR as outlined by Chiang Meng-lin, "to apply all the JCRR's efforts in conformity with historical, political and social developments of China."[38]

The JCRR declared, on October 15, 1948, their five main

---

[36] Huang, Chun-chieh, *Zhongguo Nongcun fuxinglLianhe weiyuanhui guoshu lishi fangwen jilu* (Taipei: Institute of Modern History, Academia Sinica, 1992), pp. 153–170. Hereafter as *Fangwen jilu*.

[37] Ibid.

[38] Chiang Mon-lin, "Shiying Zhongguo lishi zhengzhi zhi shehui beijing zhi nongfuhui Gongzo," in *Nongfuhui gongzo yanjin yuanzhe zhi jiandao* (Taipei: Council of Agriculture, Executive Yuan, 1990), p. 27.

aims in working to revitalize Chinese agrarian communities:[39]

1) To improve the living conditions of farmers;

2) To increase production of foodstuffs and other important products;

3) To develop labor resources so as to build up local communities, and then the entire country;

4) To assist in establishing, strengthening, and promoting various organizations, new and current ones, at the prefectural, provincial, and national levels;

5) To provide opportunities for young, democratic intelligentsia (and others who desire to help) to join in these tasks.

In addition, six principles for putting these aims into effect[40] together with five policies for concrete work were announced. All these pronouncements and policies embodied some basic ideas enunciated by JCRR's first chairman, Chiang Meng-lin: do not engage in a big build-up and compete with local organizations; rather, try to understand farmers needs at the grass-roots level; promote production while at the same time taking care to promote social justice, and work with local organizations.[41]

Initially, the JCRR stressed two main characteristics in its efforts: pragmatism and dynamism.

---

[39] *Baogao*, p. 3.
[40] Ibid.
[41] See Chiang Meng-lin's letter to Raymond T. Moyer (Chairman of JCRR, 1948–1951), ed. in *Zhongguo Nongcun Fuxing Lianhe Weiyuanhui shiliao Huibian* (Taipei: Sanmin shuju, 1991), pp. 45–51. Hereafter *Huibian*.

The JCRR insisted on combining theory and practice in its work, which was to be of real benefit to crop and livestock yields and to farm living conditions. They thus emphasized progressivism and efficiency.

Progressivism: The early JCRR leaders believed their work had to be carried out in piecemeal fashion taking care of one part of a project then another, one step at a time, for the whole is merely the sum of its parts. And their work did proceed in this way—no matter whether the project was irrigation or fertilizer promotion—which coincided with Karl Popper's (1902–?) conception of "piecemeal social engineering."[42] The JCRR thus was opposed to "utopian social engineering."[43] Li Chung-tao, JCRR Chairman, between 1973 and 1979, described this method well,[44]

> Our beloved Mr. Yu Kuo-hua laughingly said that we act like a petty little pediatrician and nudged us to tackle big projects instead. But the fact of the matter is that we had to devote a long time before coming up with a Four Year Project or a Ten Year Project . . . We simply had to tackle small projects piecemeal, one at a time, to really benefit our dear farmers. This was something like waging a war; we fight small battles, one at a time and sometimes in order to fight this battle we must fight it on another front, as another battle. As we tackle the production problem, we encounter problems of distribution and environmental protection. We then have to decide that production must come first; we first make money to fill

---

[42] Karl R. Popper, *The Open Society and Its Enemies* (Princeton: Princeton University Press, 1933), Vol. 1, p. 42. Chiang Meng-lin also knew Hu Shi, a scholar-activist of the May 4th period, who—following the American pragmatist philosopher John Dewey—had advocated taking the piecemeal approach of solving one problem at a time.
[43] Popper, op. cit., Chapter 9.
[44] *Fangwen jilu*, pp. 7–16.

our bellies then we can talk about improving livelihood before facing the environmental problem. So what Mr. Shen said about production strategy is correct. It must be tackled, and with immediate efficiency.

This spirit of progressivism, shared by all technocrats, was the JCRR's first emphasis in its efforts.[45]

Efficiency: As Chiang Meng-lin insisted,[46] the JCRR worked for the greatest results in the shortest time because of the dangers of national unrest and internecine warfare at the time. This stress on efficiency, however, caused them to neglect certain longstanding agrarian problems. This shortcoming was shared in common by otherwise excellent governmental technocrats.

The JCRR also stressed dynamism in its efforts. This had two aspects: (1) activity at the grass roots and (2) freedom from political constraint.

The JCRR initiated their projects at the grass-roots level. As Chiang Meng-lin said, the JCRR first tried to "listen to and understand the needs of local farmers, instead of telling them what their needs should be." JCRR members often visited local villages and listened to their practical problems. Chang Hsun-shun characterized JCRR workers as "pushing their projects at the grass roots," and not trying to impose theories learned from foreign lands upon the farmers.[47]

The JCRR was independent of official control with its members being appointed by two national presidents of the ROC and the United States; and were not beholden to any department in ei-

---

[45] *Huibian*, p. 494.
[46] *Baogao*, pp. 84–90.
[47] *Huibian*, pp. 130–132.

ther government. Free of political burden but armed with its problem solving approach, the JCRR could operate freely like a special fighting unit in the army but on the agricultural front.[48]

To what extent did this pragmatic, dynamic JCRR play the crucial role we would expect it to in the initiation of the postwar Taiwan experience?

The JCRR's Role in History

The JCRR had a difficult role to play. On one hand, it was a government agency; whatever it did represented the position and activity of the government. On the other hand, it insisted on promoting social welfare among agrarian villages and strictly adhered to political neutrality. For example, the JCRR did not take sides in the September 1952 land ownership disputes between tenants and the Taiwan Sugar Company which had been instigated by American land reform expert Wolf Ladjinski.[49] The problem as to whether or not to abolish regulations on the fertilizer-grain barter system was hotly debated in 1959 between the Agricultural Economics Section and the Plant Production Section of the JCRR. No resolution was reached until September 1972, when the JCRR was abolished by the government.

In fact, the JCRR was mainly an advisory organization and just provided financial and information resources to assist people in agriculture; it refrained from involvement in disputes over power or profit. In some respects this was where the JCRR's strength lay, but it also led to some shortcomings. On one hand, the

---

[48] For more detailed discussion, see my *Nongfuhui yu Taiwan jingyan*, Chapter 1.
[49] For a study of the problems with land reform in Taiwan during the 1950s as revealed in Wolf Landjinski's Letter to Chiang Kai-shek, see my "Guangfu cuqi Taiwan tudi gaige guocheng zhong di jige wenti: Lei Cheng-chi hanjian jiandu," in my *Zhanhou Taiwan ti zhuanxing jiqi zhanwang* (Taipei: Zhengzhong shuju, 1995), pp. 101–130.

JCRR managed to keep itself from being politically or economically polluted during its thirty years of operation. On the other hand, its value-neutrality rendered it incapable of standing up for the farmers at key points. Furthermore, as mentioned, its stress on efficiency led it into a short-range mindset, so it was unable to attend to Taiwan's long-term, sociocultural problems.

The JCRR assisted in the development and modernization of agriculture in Taiwan, especially by helping the full owner-cultivators with Sino-American expertise and American financial aid, thus laying the foundation for rapid industrial development in the mid-1960s. Sadly, this application of the fruits of agricultural development to foster industrialization was to spell the demise of the traditional Chinese agrarian culture. The JCRR was not positioned to stem this unfortunate tide.

2:5 Conclusion

It is with mixed emotions that I summarize the story of the postwar Taiwan experience from the perspective of agriculture.

The Japanese construction of an infrastructure, combined with the ROC's land reform policies, did much to facilitate the rise of Taiwanese agriculture and then to usher in modern Taiwan.

The rise and modernization of Taiwan's agriculture was created with the seeds of its own downfall, led by two forces: capitalism and infiltration. Its hard-won profits were forfeited for the sake of nurturing Taiwan's industrialization, at the same time that profits were being weakened by an influx of foreign farm products. The JCRR was the government's last-ditch attempt to stem the tide, to halt the demise of agriculture and promote an agrarian culture.

In short, the rise of agriculture contributed to the rise of industrialism and the rise of industrialism contributed to the fall of agriculture and the emergence of modern Taiwan. Politics has been a checkerboard (with sides repesenting pro and con) of connections to this drama under Japanese colonialism, the ROC, and the JCRR. Such is our story, the postwar Taiwan experience viewed from the vantage point of Taiwan's agrarian history.

If there is a lesson to this story, we can find it in Daniel Bell's suggestive rumination on the Western experience over the past 150 years to the effect that the institutions of economy, politics and culture tend to come into conflict with one another. That is, drives for economic efficiency, political equality and cultural self-realization are often at odds with each other. The story of the West during these past 150 years has been the drama of such conflicts.[50] Our story here is largely the same, and our task is similar. We are challenged by the historic task of coordinating these three, often contradictory demands: efficiency, equality and self-realization. The rise and fall of agriculture that provided for the modernization of Taiwan can be viewed as Taiwan's mighty, historic struggle *toward* harmonizing and developing these three conflicting yet inescapable demands of humanity. The struggle remains to be completed, the vision of a grand harmony remains to be envisioned and drawn up.

---

[50] See Daniel Bell, *The Cultural Contradictions of Capitalism* (New York: Basic Books, 1976), pp. XXX–XXXI.

3

Transformation of Farmers' Social Consciousness (1950–1970)

3:1 Introduction

We shall now trace the shift in farmers' social conciousness (that is, their outlook as expressed in social interaction) from the social consciousness characteristic of a moral economy to that characteristic of a political economy. This change was initiated by government policy infiltration into the farming society and by changes in their relations of production.

Specifically, we claim that Taiwanese farmers' attitudes toward landowners were influenced, perhaps shaped, by social conditions, which changed dramatically after the Japanese occupation of the island began in 1895. These changes came in three stages: monopoly capitalist production of sugar and rice initiated by the Japanese; the land reform and reformation of farmers' associations by the Kuomintang (KMT) government in the 1950s; and the dissolution of farm villages in the face of the economic boom and rapid urbanization of the 1970s. Such social changes as these led to changes in farmers' social consciousness. First, the arrival of the Japanese shook the moral economy and social relations based on kinship of traditional Taiwanese society. Next, exploitation by the Japanese provoked and then suppressed political activism. Finally, the position of the landowners was diminished as the values of capitalism, especially individualism and the profit motive, started to permeate rural Taiwan.

We shall highlight the changes in rural social relations and social consciousness by focusing on the distinction between traditional moral economy imbued with social feelings and the profit-oriented individualism of modern capitalism. This admitted simplification underlines the crucial impact of the shift to modern capitalism and the toll that change took on farmer social consciousness as their villages crumbled and gave way to urbanization. While farm villages are not a panacea to the ills of modern society, the sudden collapse of the former certainly intensifies the gravity of the latter.

Since the Japanese occupation began in 1895, Taiwan underwent a twofold change visible in the basic economic strata of agriculture. First, Taiwan was brought under the aegis of capitalism. Taiwan, on the periphery, has been made to serve two masters, namely, Japan in the pre-World War II period and the United States in the postwar period. The closed village community was opened up to capitalist production and commercialization. Agricultural land and labor, which had previously been sacred family inheritances, were converted into salable commodities to become investments for profit. Following World War II, Taiwan, along with other Southeast Asian and developing nations, was drawn into serving what Eric R. Wolf calls North Atlantic capitalism.[1]

Second, beginning with the Japanese occupation, offical power started to permeate Taiwanese society; this infiltration was accomplished by the investigation of traditional society and by control of land distribution. The KMT land reform of the early 1950s is a powerful example of the infiltration of government into society. This example of governmental control can be compared to the development experience under colonization of other Southeast Asian regions,[2] as well as to the situation in rural China in the nineteenth century.[3] Still, the commercialization of agriculture in

---

[1] See Eric R. Wolf, *Peasant Wars of the Twentieth Century* (New York: Harper & Row, 1969), p. 276.
[2] Cf. James C. Scott, *The Moral Economy of the Peasant: Rebellion and Subsistence in Southeast Asia* (New Haven and London: Yale University Press, 1976).
[3] Cf. Kung-Chuan Hsiao, *Rural China: Imperial Control in the Nineteenth Century*

3. Transformation of Farmers' Social Consciousness (1950–1970)

Taiwan forms a sharp contrast with Mainland China,[4] particularly with the "involuted" villages of Hopei and northwest Shandong.[5] Such comparisons, of course, cannot be expected to yield direct correlations.

We shall trace changes in the farmers' social consciousness in Taiwan since 1945. The term "social consciousness" refers to the social dimension of human value systems and is expressed in four main attitudes toward people and society; in particular, toward,

1. Relationships among individuals;

2. Relationships between individual and community;

3. Relationships among communities; and

4. Society at large.

The nature of these relationships, as well as the attitudes held, vary with the social status of the individuals involved. For example, "relationships among individuals" for farmers include relations between the farmer and the landowner and among the farmers themselves, as well as the more usual relationships of family, friends, teacher-student, and so on. In the case of Taiwanese farmers, "relationships between the individual and the community" refer especially to relationships between farmers and the farm associations. Thus, the meanings of these relationships are unique to

---

(Seattle: University of Washington Press, 1960).

[4] The commercialization of farm production is revealed by the rising proportion of cash receipts/expenses in total farm receipts/expenses. The percentages of cash in total farm receipts and expenses in 1958 were 39.8 percent and 59 percent, respectively. However, the former became 90.5 percent while the later 91.8 percent by 1987. See *Agricultural Development in the Republic of China on Taiwan* (Taipei: Council of Agriculture, 1988), p. 32.

[5] See Philip C. C. Huang. *The Peasant Economy and Social Change in North China* (Stanford, Calif.: Stanford University Press, 1985), p. 304.

agricultural society.

Moreover, these relationships are somewhat interdependent. For instance, the ostensibly individual relations between the farmer and the landowner develop within a context that includes individual-community relationships and, frequently, kinship relationships, and cannot be considered outside of this context. Thus, "each such peasantry—Haiti, Jamaica, etc.—is the product of specific historical events; each functions within state systems that are different in character and in the sort of pressure they pose upon rural citizens, each faces a markedly different future."[6] Because of the complexity of the topic, this study will focus on just two aspects of rural social consciousness in the period following the Kuomintang takeover, specifically, changes in farmer attitudes toward,

1. Landlord-farmer relationships; and

2. Farmers' associations.

These two attitudinal changes typified the trends in the evolving farmer social consciousness and they were associated with two instances of land reform, one in the 1950s and the other in the 1970s and 1980s. In addition, the more data (both primary and secondary) exists that are relevant to these two questions than to other aspects and permit a more detailed investigation.

---

[6] Sidney W. Mintz, "A Note on the Definition of Peasantries," *Journal of Peasant Studies*, no. 1, 1973, pp. 91–106.

3:2 Farmers' Social Consciousness in The Early Period of Retrocession

A. Historical Background

In order to understand the landowner-farmer relationship during the land reform of the early 1950s, we must consider the trend towards capitalism and concentrations of land into the hands of the few in Taiwan under Japanese imperialism.

Following her occupation of Taiwan in 1895, Japan carried out a monetary reform (1904) and an investigation of land (1905), constructed a railroad system traversing the island from north to south and opened the harbors in Keelung and Kaohsiung. All of these efforts, as Yanaihara Tadao has shown, were designed to turn Taiwan into a capitalistic society so as to facilitate its exploitation.[7]

Japanese capitalists controlled the four large sugar companies, fifteen alcohol distilleries with a private railroad system stretching 2,900 miles and rice production.[8] These modern sugar operations occupied 78,601 *jia* (*jia* = .97 hectare) of land which, combined with leased farmland, totaled 103,838 *jia* (1926 statisics). This was more than one-eighth of the arable land of Taiwan. In Hualien Kang District, Yen Shui Hang Sugar Company possessed 78,601 *jia*, more than one fourth of the entire cultivated land of the Hualien Kang District. Every one of the sugar companies were controlled by Japanese capitalists.[9]

The rice economy in Taiwan also followed this trend toward

---

[7] Yanaihara Tadao, *Riben diguo zhuyixiadi Taiwan* trans. by Chou Hsien-wen, (Taipei: Pamier Book co., 1985), p. 13.
[8] Yamanabe Kentaro, "*Riben diguo zhuyi yu zhimindi*," trans. by Cheng Chin-jen, *Shihuo Monthly*, n. s. 2:1 (1972), p. 48.
[9] Yanaihara Tadao, op. cit., p. 26.

capitalism,[10] giving the rise of capitalism under the Japanese a multidimensional significance in Taiwan history. As Yanaihara Tadao pointed out,[11] these developments transformed the feudal society of Taiwan into a modern capitalistic society, rife with class and ethnic tensions.

Backed by the strength of Japanese rule and capital, the Japanese held prominent positions in the bureaucracy and served as capitalists and as bank and company employees; most farmers and laborers were Taiwanese. Between these two groups were two contending groups of middle class merchants and industrialists, one Japanese and the other Taiwanese. Naturally, the Japanese middle class allied itself with the elite class of officials and capitalists. In addition to these antagonisms between ruler and ruled, and between the capitalist and farm and laboring classes, were other ethnic tensions provoked by differences such as those found in language, culture, national origin and attitude to life.

These ethnic and class struggles intensified the suffering of Taiwanese farmers, and prompted the development of their group farm consciousness. On June 28, 1926 they formed the Association of Taiwan Farmers with branch offices throughout the island; the association spoke out against capitalistic enterprises and provided assistance for local opposition to the Japanese. This was the first noteworthy expression of Taiwanese farmer group consciousness prior to the Kuomintang takeover.

The second major trend of the Japanese occupation was the concentration of farmland into relatively few hands. The number of small landowners decreased and the number of large landowners increased. Between 1921 and 1932, the number of large land-

---

[10] Kawano Shigetani, *Riju shidai Taiwan migu jingji lun.* trans. by Lin Yin-yen, (Taipei: Bank of Taiwan, 1960), p. 2.

[11] Yanaihara Tadao, op. cit., pp. 99–100.

owners increased. Between 1921 and 1932, the number of households that owned less than one *jia* declined from 259,642 (64.08 percent) to 201,913 (59.26 percent) while the number of holdings larger than 50 *jia* increased from 572 (0.14 percent) to 775 (0.23 percent).

In terms of the acreage of tillable land, the 224,931 households tilling less than one *jia* had land holdings totaling 103,412 *jia*, while the 3,576 households with more than 10 *jia* held land totaling 106,887 *jia*. In addition, most of these lands were held by households with over twenty *jia*, with 579 households holding an amazing 68,410 *jia*. In other words, 53.10 percent of farmers held just 14.96 percent of the land, while 0.13 percent of farmers owned 9.90 percent. A large part of the farmland was concentrated in a few hands, while the majority of farmers worked small, inefficient plots.[12]

Land ownership was a primary concern of Taiwanese farmers during the Japanese occupation. As a result, the land reform of the early 1950s received widespread welcome from the farmers.[13]

B. The Landowner-Farmer Relationship in the Farmers' Social Consciousness during the 1950s

The retrocession of Taiwan to Nationalist China in 1945, following World War II, had a tremendous psychological impact on

---

[12] Chou Hsien-wen, "Riju shidai Taiwan zhi nongye jingji," *Taiwan Yinhan qikan*, 8:4 (1956), p. 91.
[13] For details on the 1950s Land Reform, see: (1) Martin M. C. Yang, *Socio-Economic Results of Land Reform in Taiwan* (Honolulu: East-West Center Press, 1970); (2) Tseng Hsiao, "Theory and Background of Land Reform in Taiwan," in James R. Brown and Sein Lin eds., *Land Reform in Developing Countries* (Hartford, Conn.: University of Hartford Press, 1968), pp. 324–346; (3) T. H. Shen, "Land Reform ad Its Impact on Agricultural Development in Taiwan," op. cit., pp. 347–366; (4) C. F. Koo, "Land Reform and Its Impact on Industrial Development in Taiwan," op. cit., pp. 367–379; (5) S. K. Shen, "Administration of the Land Reform Program in Taiwan," op. cit., pp. 380–443.

Taiwan's farmers. Arthur F. Raper's report, based upon a survey of 1,176 farm households in sixteen rural villages throughout Taiwan, concluded that:[14]

> Generally speaking, the Taiwanese regard retrocession as the beginning of a new era in which peoples' lives will be improved. This attitude manifests itself most clearly in the following facts: Local leadership find people to be stronger in freedom and autonomy; people are more cared for by local officals, the positions of whom are, in turn, filled by more common folks; fertilizers and bean-cakes are delivered on time to every destined farmer, whose taxes are lowered and now has official contracts; not a few farmers have purchased land during those forty-one years; the farmers also welcomed to put into effect the land reform act of "tillers own land" (land reform policy) of 1952, etc. Besides, the mortality rate of the people has dropped as their educational level climbs, and the number of those who possess modern equipment (except for radios) has increased. All this has exerted a tremendous influence on farmers and their lives. People's work efficiency and accomplishments are in large measure decided upon by their psychological attitude.

As in other countries,[15] the 1950s land reform in Taiwan was implemented more for political considerations than for purely economic reasons. The land reform program was implemented through a three-step policy that started in 1949; this included a rent reduction program, sale of public land to cultivators and tenants and the Land to the Tiller Program.

---

[14] Arthur F. Raper, *Taiwan muqian zhi nongcun ji jianglai zhi zhanwan* (Taipei: JCRR, 1953), p. 223.
[15] Elias H. Tuma, *Twenty-six Centuries of Agrarian Reform* (Berkeley and Los Angeles: University of California Press, 1965), Chapter 12.

3. Transformation of Farmers' Social Consciousness (1950–1970) 61

A major reason why land reform was able to win widespread support from the farmers was that it was in concert with their own aspirations toward the retrocession. At the same time, however, many documents attest to an increase of tensions between landowners and farmers as a result of the land reforms.

Farmers reported to government observers of the land reform that some landowners (such as those in Yunlin County) used various methods to reduce their land in district records to zero before the enactment of the reform to avoid losing all of their lands. Farmers proposed that the government institute a policy that identified and rewarded the landowners who cooperated with the reforms while punishing those who sought to subvert the land reform.[16] As the following eyewitness report shows, these tensions sometimes resulted in violence:[17]

> We found in Yunlin County a very bad landowner. He did not obey the government's Land to the Tiller policy nor did he heed government arbitration efforts to reduce the rent. He even hired some vagabonds and beat up his tenant Mr. Li. Later the district government sent a Mr. Kuo, head of the Department of Land, to advise and negotiate with him, but he again instigated some thugs to beat Mr. Kuo. Fortunately Mr. Kuo was keen enough to extricate himself from the situation and reported the matter to the police station nearby. Officers then arrested those ruffians and sent them to the court for arraignment. Many farmers angrily protested that the investigation and arraignment should have been extended to the landowner himself; and indeed I feel that the farmers are right and the landlord should be interrogated.

---

[16] Teng Hsueh-ping, *Taiwan nongcun fangwen ji* (n. p., 1954) p. 135.
[17] Ibid.

Many incidents of this sort took place. Many Kaohsiung farmers complained to a government observer that the lands collected for redistribution were little while those kept by the original owners were extensive. As this observer reported in 1954, the city of Kaohsiung included over 10,500 *jia*—7,000 of which were arable. Of this arable land, 3,756 *jia* were privately owned and 2,540 *jia* were privately leased; the government had collected only 1,022 *jia*, kept 810 *jia*, and exempted 704 *jia*. Thus, 50.8 percent of the land was either kept or exempted, while the tillers received less than 42 percent of the land. Kaohsiung farmers felt it was unfair for any landowner to be allowed to keep over 100 *jia* of land. When some landowners claimed some land for buildings, which never materialized, tillers requested the government to develop a decisive plan for the city of Kaohsiung that did not leave any loopholes for landowners to keep their excess land holdings. They also requested loans to allow farmers to purchase land.[18]

Stories of this sort were not limited to Kaohsiung farmers; it was typical of tensions between landowners and farmers throughout Taiwan. Such tensions persisted into the 1960s. In 1959, the JCRR invited economists and political scientists to follow up on Raper's 1952 report and assess the situation in rural villages. The actual project was initated by scholars from National Taiwan University and supplemented and completed by scholars from the Hong Kong University. In the subsequent report, E. Stuart Kirby described relations between landowners and farmers in the following terms:[19]

> All 18 villages still have tenant farmers, except for mountainous Jen Ai Village (which has none). The enforcement of 375 Rent Reduction has resulted in a gen-

---

[18] Teng, op. cit., p. 108.
[19] E. Stauart Kirby, *Rural Progress in Taiwan* (Taipei: JCRR, 1960).

3. Transformation of Farmers' Social Consciousness (1950–1970) 63

eral increase of agricultural production while the levying standards remain as before, making it easier for farmers to pay taxes on time although we still see some lingering ones paying taxes only after the landowners' urgings. One more important difference from the past is that farmers are now in possession of written contracts.

Unfortunately, the landowner-farmer relationship had become "frigid and forced," the landowners having to give away their land to the farmers in conformity with the "Land to the Tillers" policy. Landowners initially were indignant and antagonistic to their tenants; such sentiments had only recently subsided. According to the report at a discussion held among the local leaders, the landowner-farmer relation in twelve villages had become a mere formality, a cold contractual relation in which warm "feelings" were a thing of the past; the relation in five other villages was even worse.

In the past, on every festive occasion farmers used to bring presents to their landowners, whom they sometimes volunteered to favor with extra labor so as perhaps to win special treatment. Landowners, in turn, lent them buffalo and money, or looked among relatives and friends for other jobs for farmers, or rewarded them with extension or even cancellation of rent for fields. This warm convention (based on custom and tradition) vanished after implementation of land reform act.

In 1957 and 1958 fieldwork in a village in the Changhua district, anthropologist Bernard Gallin also found that relations between farmers and landowners had become "frigid and forced":[20]

---

[20] Bernard Gallin, *Hsin Hsing, Taiwan: A Chinese Village* (Berkeley and Los Angeles: University of California Press, 1966), p. 95. After the Land Reform, many landlords, losing their lands and having no training necessary for taking new jobs, were drown in the whirlpool of history. Gallin reports some sad cases. See his "Land Reform in Taiwan: Its Effect on Rural Social Organization and Leadership," *Human Organization*, xxx: 2

With the tenant's security on the land protected, he no longer had to kowtow to his landlord or attempt to maintain good Kan-ch'ing. Today it is common to hear a tenant, formerly courteous to his landlord whether he liked him or not, actually curse him when he comes in his own wagon to collect and load the tenant's land rent. (The tenant formerly delivered the rent to the landlord.) On one such occasion in Hsin Hsing, K'ang, a landlord from another village, came to pick up his rice rent. In Mandarin, the name is pronounced K'ang, but in the local Taiwanese dialect, it is pronounced K'ung. But K'ung in Taiwanese also means stupid. The Hsin Hsing tenant, while watching the landlord load the rice into his wagon, laughingly repeated over and over for all to hear, "K'ung K'ung is here for the rent." It was obvious to everyone, including the landlord, that the tenant was punning on his name. While the others stood around and laughed, the landlord just continued his work without a word.

Given these tensions, clashes between landowners and farmers were inevitable and, in fact, they occurred frequently throughout the island. Starting on July 30, 1946, a Committee on Land Rent was established in every village to arbitrate over rents and other land matters. These committees had nine elected members and two members appointed by the local government; the elected members included two landowners, two owner-cultivators and five tenants, while the appointed members were the district magistrate who served as the head of the committee, and the officer responsible for land matters at the district government who served as the committee's secretary. The selection of the nine elected members was initiated at the grass-roots level. Farmers would elect their

---

(1963), pp. 109–112.

various representatives who, in turn, elected the nine committee members.[21] Because during the 1950s farmers participated more regularly than did landowners, the committees functioned quite effectively.

The type of arbitration followed by the Committee on Land Rent is historically significant in Chinese contexts. It is different from what is commonly referred to as government intervention and arbitration. As Hsiao Kung-chuan points out,[22] in reconciliation of disputes in rural China during the nineteenth century, the disputants often bypassed government agencies. The reconciliations were worked out in a non-authoritarian and voluntary way and formed an integral part of the social order. Arbitrators were people who were respected and accepted by people on both sides of the dispute; the process did not rely on statutes or abstractions but rather was aimed at satisfying the interests and needs of all parties concerned while remaining in accord with opinions of the elders. In traditional rural China, even under an authoritarian regime when formal arbitration broke down, voluntary negotiation took over to supplement governmental procedures.

Such arbitration was rooted in the kin-based social structure that was fundamental to traditional rural society. In this situation, it was relatively easy to arbitrate disputes by "community compacts" (*xiangyue* 鄉約). Zhu Xi 朱熹 (1130–1200) of the Southern Song edited and revised the following portion of the community com-

---

[21] For the regulations governing the organization of the Committee of Land Rent, see *Organization Regulations of Committee of Land Rent in Cities and Countries*, kept in the Academia Historica, edited in *Tudi gaige shiliao* (Taipei: Academia Historica, 1988), pp. 338–339. For a discussion of the role of law in the 1950s Land Reform in a broader perspective, see Herbert H. P. Ma, "The Role of Law in the Land Reform of Taiwan," *Soochow Law Review*, no. 1 (Nov., 1976), pp. 1–16.

[22] Kung-chuan Hsiao, *Compromise in Imperial China* (Seattle: School of International Studies, University of Washington, 1979).

pacts of the Lu brothers of the Northern Song:[23]

> In general, the village contract is fourfold: mutual exhortation over virtue and profession; mutual regulation of mistakes; social intercourse according to decorum and customs and mutual assistance in distress. People shall recommend a virtuous elder as village headman, flanked by two assistants of learning and good conduct. These three shall take turns being on duty for a month. Three registered records shall be kept and anyone willing to enter the contract shall be registered with a written document to that effect which shall be kept by the person on duty until his month is over, when he shall report to the headman and turn it over to the next person on duty.

Such community compact, arising from tradition, formed a model for Chinese intellectuals interested in the reconstruction of farming villages. During the early years of the Republic of China, Liang Sou-ming 梁漱溟 (1892–1988) advocated the formation of a new structure for farm villages based on just such a community compact; he was eager to exclude governmental interference in this area.

Sadly, following the end of the World War II, village contracts based on local autonomy were no longer possible in rural Taiwan. Instead, the government-sponsored Committees on Village Rent and Farming replaced village contracts as the major instrument for resolving tensions between landowners and farmers. Prior to this however, Taiwanese farming villages under the Japanese underwent a transformation similar to that described by Max Weber, from communities based on familial relationships to communities based on contractual relationships.

---

[23] Zhu Xi, *Chu Wengong wenji* (Sibu congkan cubian soben edition), juan 74, p. 13.

In fact, the enactment of land reform in the 1950s represents another such infiltration of governmental power into farm villages, reshaping the economic order while knitting together "state" and "society." At the same time, the socioeconomic structure of Taiwanese farm villages underwent a gradual transformation into capitalism. An example of this transformation can be seen in Gallin's account of his 1956–1957 field study:[24]

> As the population increase continued in recent decades, and an already developing problem of land scarcity became even more extreme, it gradually became both necessary and possible for increasing numbers of rural villagers to migrate to the growing cities to find work to supplement their insufficient income from the land. This migration has broadened the villagers' urban contacts and relationships beyond the village while the villagers have become increasingly more dependent upon and involved with the greater market economy. This has become especially true as patterns of land use have changed in response to all of the changing conditions, so many villagers are increasingly shifting from what was primarily a subsistence form of agriculture to what is now participation in the market economy of the country. Therefore, there has been an acceleration of the impingement on the village by the outside world.
>
> As the villagers have begun to extend their activities and interests beyond Hsin Hsing, the village's influence on the lives of its members has deteriorated even further. The increase in activities beyond the village means that the proportion of their total activities and hence their involvement within Hsin Hsing is decreased. While the *tsu*

---

[24] Bernard Gallin, *Hsin Hsing, Taiwan*, p. 270–272.

continues to perform many of its functions within the context of the village, when its members—by necessity—become more involved beyond the village even the *tsu*'s role must be affected. The still relatively small and rather localized Hsin Hsing village *tsu* have very limited influence or means to support their members in their needs and relationships beyond the village. And, as the villagers seek to establish outside sources of solidarity and security, the *tsu* are even further affected.

This description of a Taiwan farm village differs significantly from the closed world of the semi-familial relations within the farming villages of Hebei and Shandong provinces discovered by Philip C. C. Huang.[25] The Village Rent and Farming Committees which appeared during 1950s were not only a product of the decline of traditional clan relations in farming communities, they reflected the transformation of farmers' social consciousness in Taiwan. Gallin's statement that "the villagers have become increasingly more dependent upon and involved with the greater market economy," describes the shape of village society hewn by the axe of capitalism. Taiwanese farm villages in the 1950s had already been opened to the market economy and were not closed villages any longer.

Traditional farm villages operate according to the ideas of moral economy and subsistence ethics, based on norms of reciprocity and the right to subsistence and abiding by the principles of "safety first" and "mutual assistance in distress."[26] The effect of replacing a morality grounded in community relations with a political economy based on calculation of benefits[27] can be seen in

---

[25] Philip C. C. Huang, op. cit., p. 304.
[26] James C. Scott, *The Moral Economy of the Peasant: Rebelition and Subsistence in Southeast Asia* (New Haven, Conn. and London: Yale University Press, 1976).
[27] For a discussion on political economy among Southeast Asian farmers in general,

3. Transformation of Farmers' Social Consciousness (1950–1970)

the tensions between landowners and farmers in Taiwan. Since Taiwan farm villages can be regarded as an "experimental station," their experiences in the transition from moral economy to political economy provide indications of what lies in store for the rest of rural Chinese society.

Two main factors can be cited in the tensions between landowners and farmers in the 1950s: the exploitation of farmers by landowners and an increase in the farmers' sense of security, which was a result of the land reform. Countless instances of landowners exploiting farmers can be given. What follows are five examples of the mechanisms used by landlords to exploit farmers while maintaining their positions and profits.

First, landowners took advantage of the fact that their contracts with the farmers were oral rather than written to alter the terms of those contracts as the implications of land reform became apparent. As Gallin found in his survey of Changhua villages,[28] landowners routinely added rent to farmers' house and created other charges to supplement the anticipated loss of income from field rents. Furthermore, landowners reinforced the farmers' belief that past oral contracts, combined with their own diligent efforts, were sufficient to fulfill the conditions of land reform and allowed them to till "their land" as before. Then, when no one appeared in court to claim the right to lease the fields, the landowner could claim that the land was his own and that he tilled it himself. When the farmer came to dispute this claim, the landowner would say that the farmer was merely an employee of his. Thus, many landowners retained their claims to the land.

Second, some landowners cleverly registered their fields un-

---

see Samuel L. Popkin, *The Rational Peasant: The Political Economy of Rural Society in Vietnam* (Berkeley and Los Angeles: University of California Press, 1979).
[28] Gallin, *Hsin Hsing, Taiwan*, p. 94.

der several names, each showing holdings small enough to be immune from the restrictions of the land reform policy. That this was a widespread phenomenon is evidenced in a telegram (housed in the archives of Academia Historica in Taipei), dated December 3, 1947, sent by the Taiwan Garrison Headquarters to the Taiwan Provincial Government. The telegram states that a landlord-tenant dispute in Hsinchu County resulted in violence in which the farmer died.[29]

Third, many landowners raised rents to offset the new restrictions on land rent. As this petition sent to the Taiwan Provincial Government indicates, "the bitter situation (of petty tenants) can not be described by pen and paper. . . . If the government does not take any legal sanction the common tenants, having no lands to till, will become the jobless who stand in the starvation line."[30]

Fourth, usury was frequently practiced. For example, on the east coast in 1953, farmers of the Yu Li District were required to pay interest equal to the principal they had borrowed. One farmer, having a bad year, borrowed 2,000 *jin* (1 Taiwan *jin* is equal to 0.6 kilogram), but was required to write that he owed the landowner 4,000 *jin*; this meant that at the harvest, 4,000 *jin* of rice had to be given to the landowner as payment of both the principal and interest. Later the landowner demanded payment with interest, of 4,000 *jin* of rice. A lawsuit ensued and the court ruled in favor of the landowner who could afford an attorney. This was a typical case; landowners who had time and money to prepare always won in court.[31]

The fifth and final example is similar to but more serious than the simple case of usury cited above; it concerned the sale of green

---

[29] See *Tudi gaige shiliao*, pp. 352–523.
[30] Ibid., p. 355.
[31] Teng Hsueh-ping, op. cit., pp. 86–87.

3. Transformation of Farmers' Social Consciousness (1950–1970)

sprouts. The price for 10,000 kg of rice sprouts was NT$ 4,000, while the price for 10,000 kg of rice was NT$14,000. On this scheme, farmers borrowed a certain weight of rice sprouts and paid back the value of an equal weight of harvested and dried rice. Farmers' losses could go as high as 300 percent.[32] It is no wonder that "farmers labored throughout the year, only to see all their profit go into the landowners' hands."[33]

The widespread exploitation of farmers by landlords using methods like these increased tensions between them. The second major contributing factor to these tensions, however, was the sense of security farmers had gained from the land reform. As stated above, Japanese colonization pushed rural Taiwan into capitalist markets that led to the concentration of land into the hands of a few landowners. This situation increased the suffering of the farmers at the hands of the landowners. Due to the lack of secure rights to till the land, farmers brought their harvested crops to the landowners' doorstep in an obsequious manner, hoping to maintain good relations, and hence keep access to the land.

Also, prior to the land reform, holdings were so small that farmers typically could not envision any chance for advancement. This can be seen in the holdings of five typical farming families residing in Kung-min Village, Hsi-tun Township, Taichung City, in 1953.[34] The family of Lu Ah-chih included six persons and tilled 1.5 *jia*; the family of Chiu Fu-li included fourteen persons and tilled 0.65 *jia*; the thirteen members of the family of Lin Chin-lin tilled 1.1 *jia*; Lin Chiu-shui's family of fourteen tilled 1.2 *jia*; and the family of Huang Tsu-hsiang, comprising ten persons, tilled 0.9 *jia*. Each of these families complained that "the land is small; the

---

[32] Ibid.
[33] Quoted from an offical letter from Taiwan Provincial Government dated June 23, 1955, ed. in *Tudi gaige shiliao*, p. 740.
[34] Teng Hsueh-ping, op. cit., p. 27.

people many; the harvest is not enough to live on; life offers no prospect of improvement."[35]

After land reform, farmers' lives improved. Consider the case of a Mr. Ho Yen in 1953. After land reform, his household included only two persons cultivating 0.8 *jia,* which yielded a harvest of 8,000 *jin* of rice. They paid 1,800 *jin* for fertilizer, 1,000 *jin* for field tax, 2,000 *jin* for the land, NT$300 for water, house tax, and other fees. This left them with a surplus of 2,500 *jin* of rice they could sell, with other grains and cattle. This gave them extra money at year's end as well as a better life.

The several steps of the land reform programs, such as the Sale of Public Lands Program, the Rent Reduction Program and the Land to the Tiller Program, gave farmers a feeling of security. They no longer needed to kowtow in worry about an unexpected breach of contract or about the land being leased to someone else. This sense of security thus became another contributing factor in the rising tensions between landowners and farmers.

C. *Farmers' Social Consciousness During the 1950s*

The second dimension of farmers' social consciousness, their self-awareness as a group, is wider in range. Due to lack of space and problems of documentation, however, we must focus our discussion on the relationship between farmers and their associations.

We begin with a description of the historical background of farmers' associations and their reorganization. During the Japanese occupation, farmers' associations were limited by the conditions of colonization and exploitation in their ability to advance their positions.

---

[35] Ibid.

Following retrocession, in 1950, the Mutual Security Agency Mission to China and the JCRR jointly invited Professor W. A. Anderson, a rural sociologist from Cornell University, to come to Taiwan and examine the status of Taiwan farmers' associations.

Meanwhile, in August 1952 the Executive Yuan under its Temporary Policy for Improvement of Various Levels of Farmers' Associations issued a ruling that there should be two types of members in farmers' associations. Regular members were those who derived more than half of their total income from the profits of farming; they had voting rights, as well as the right to be elected to association offices. Associate members derived most of their income from other sources; they had no voting rights and only restricted rights to hold elected positions in the associations.[36]

In 1953, acting in accord with a proposal of W. A. Anderson, the Taiwanese government and the JCRR reorganized the farmers' associations, so they were controlled entirely by farmers, who enjoyed equal representation. The power of these associations rested in two assemblies, one of member representatives and the other of executives, which were composed entirely of farmers. They based their decisions and directed their operations wholly according to the needs and wishes of the farmers. The executive director was selected from and answerable to the assembly of executives; he made all appointments and oversaw operations. This corrected the mistakes of the past when all power was concentrated in the director's hands.[37] As a result of this sweeping reorganization, Taiwan-

---

[36] For a general account of evolution of farmers' associations, see T. H. Shen, *The Sino-American Joint Commission on Rural Reconstruction: Twenty Years of Cooperation for Agricultural Development* (Ithaca and London: Cornell University Press, 1970), pp. 70–76; on the Anderson's reform, see Joseph A. Yager, *Transforming Agriculture in Taiwan: The Experience of the Joint Commission on Rural Reconstruction* (Ithaca, N.Y. and London: Cornell University Press, 1988) pp. 125–146.

[37] Cf. Kuo Min-hsueh, *Duo mubiao gongneng di Taiwan nonghui* (Taipei: Taiwan Commercial Press, 1977), pp. 10–17.

ese farm associations were able to expand the services they offered in a variety of areas including sales, agricultural extensions, cattle insurance and savings and trusts.

As reported by Kuo Min-hsueh, the reorganization clarified membership qualifications, distributed responsibilities evenly and fostered a sense of cooperation among farmers. This contrasted sharply with the regulations governing Taiwan Farmers' Associations instituted by the Japanese in December 1908. Under those rules, the farm associations had only two main areas of operation, purchasing rice for the government and distributing fertilizer. Now the associations became genuine farm cooperatives, serving a wide variety of member needs while fostering a sense of autonomy and mutuality.[38] In addition, farmers themselves elected all of the association representatives and executives.

The membership of farmers also dramatically increased. In 1949, an island-wide survey showed the degree to which the landlord class had dominated the business of farm associations. In the one hundred associations surveyed, landlords held 39.7 percent supervisory positions or seats on the boards of directors, while owner-cultivators held 34.9 percent and semi-owner-cultivators held just 0.9 percent.[39] In 1952, Raper's report on sixteen villages revealed that the leadership positions were still in the hands of landowners and big farmers. Most of the heads of villages, of boards of village representatives, of farming associations and of women's associations were wealthy merchants.[40]

Kirby's 1960 report (using the same methods as Raper's)

---

[38] Kuo Min-hsueh, *Hezohua nonghui tizhi* (Taipei: Taiwan Commercial Press, 1982), pp. 29–33.
[39] Department of Agriculture and Forestry, Taiwan Provincial Government ed., *Investigation Report of Agrarian Organizations in Taiwan Province* (Taipei: Taiwan Provincial Government, 1950), Mimeographed copy, p. 21–22, Table 9.
[40] Raper, op. cit., pp. 168–169.

showed that number of members of farmers' associations in various villages had increased by more than 23 percent, from 589,299 to 726,681. In village districts where the power of the farmers was strong, the percentage of regular members (active cultivators) was greater than the two-thirds required by the membership regulations; for example, in Hsin Pu the regular members accounted for 79 percent of the membership, in Chao Chou 77 percent, in Chung Pu 75 percent, and in Hsi Hu 75 percent.[41]

Enforcement of the Land to the Tiller Program of 1953 also saw an increase in the percentage of farmers holding executive positions. Where owner-cultivators had held 82 percent of these positions in 1953, they held 85 percent in 1957, while at the same time the percentage of executive positions held by tenants shrank from 17 percent in 1953 to 13 percent in 1957. For instance, owner-cultivators held 61 percent of comptroller positions in 1953, increasing to 64 percent by 1957. Meanwhile, associate members decreased from 12 percent in 1953 to 11 percent in 1957.[42]

These statistics indicate a dramatic intensification of the farmers' feelings toward belonging to and identifying with their associations. This conclusion is substantiated in the 1952, 1955 and 1959 reports of Kuo Min-hsueh. In these reports, Kuo found that farmers considered the farm associations as belonging to the farmers, or to the common members, rose from 1.7 percent in 1952 to 56.1 percent in 1955 and again to 79.5 percent in 1959. The percentage of those who acknowledged themselves as members of the associations increased from 20.7 percent in 1952 to 85.6 percent in 1955, and to 94.2 percent in 1959. Also, the percentages of those who held stock in the associations increased through the years. Similarly, the percentage of farmers who participated in

---

[41] Kirby, op. cit., p. 85.
[42] Ibid.

meetings increased from 27.6 percent in 1952 to 57.2 percent in 1955, and to 82 percent in 1959.[43] Farmers who knew that association boards of directors were elected by farmers increased from 20.7 percent in 1952 to 66.5 percent in 1955 and to 80.2 percent in 1959. Finally, those who knew that the members' representatives were elected also increased from 32.8 percent in 1952 to 72.4 percent in 1955, and 82.7 percent in 1959.

This increase in the farmers' sense of identification with their associations was due to the strict regulation of membership, making the associations truly farmers' groups and to the expansion of the services to the services they offered. Kuo Min-hsueh reports that the percentage of farmers who replied affirmatively to the question, "Have you, during this year, received any visits and services from service personnel of your Farmers' Association?" rose from 27.6 percent in 1952 to 46.1 percent in 1955, and up to 74.2 percent in 1959.

Perhaps because of the variety of services offered by the associations, many farmers expressed a desire to become association members. Their wishes were often reflected in the statements of their representatives. For instance, in 1954, Lin Chin-sheng, a member of the Taiwan Provincial Assembly, proposed to Chin Yang-kao, then Head of the Department of Agriculture and Forestry, that, "qualifications for membership should be tightened to admit only those who are truly farmers. At present, many farming folks are unable to become members, while some members till only vegetable gardens of a fraction of an acre."[44] This keen interest in the membership of farmers' associations reflected the farmers' feelings for their associations. This was the second aspect

---

[43] Kuo Min-hsueh, *Taiwan nongye fazhan guiji* (Taipei: Taiwan Commercial Press, 194), p. 148.

[44] Taiwan Temporary Provincial Assembly, *Taiwan linshi shengyihui gongbao* (Taipei: Taiwan Temporary Provincial Assembly, 1954), p. 1445.

3. Transformation of Farmers' Social Consciousness (1950–1970)

of social consciousness among Taiwan farmers in the 1950s, which went along with the first aspect, the tension between landlords and tenants.

Unfortunately, farmers' associations had also been organizations for implementing government policy, channels whereby official influence could infiltrate farming villages. This has been the case ever since the first association was established in San Hsia Township, Taipei County, in 1899. The Kuomintang takeover of Taiwan and reorganization of the associations did not change this, although the associations now belonged to the farmers themselves.

No wonder disputes and wrangling often occurred between farm associations, which are really organizations of the government, and farm cooperatives, which are genuinely organizations of farmers. In the early years of Kuomintang rule, the writer Wu Cho-liu served in the Social Department of the Provincial Government and investigated one such dispute in the Taichung area.[45] In this case, the association's distribution of fertilizer in exchange for rice was a clear example of an association being used as an official instrument in the "developmental squeeze"[46] of agricultural resources.

This testifies to the double character of the development of farmers' associations, which reflected both the Taiwan farmers' sense of identity and the infiltration of governmental influence into

---

[45] Wu Cho-liu, *Taiwan lianqiao* (Taipei: Taiwan Wenyi chubanshe, 1987), pp. 240–241.

[46] For "developmental squeeze," see Teng-hui Lee, *Intersectoral Capital Floes in the Economic development of Taiwan, 1895–1960* (Ithaca, N.Y.: Cornell University Press, 1971); Micael H. H. Hsiao, *Government Agricultural Strategies in Taiwan and South Korea: A Macrosoclogical Assement* (Taipei: Insititute of Ethnology, Academia Sinica, 1981), pp. 55–56. For a study of this rice-fertilizer bartering system, see Samuel. P. S. Ho, *Economic Development of Taiwan, 1860–1970* (New Heaven: Yale University Press, 1978), p. 153 and pp. 180–184.

farming communities.

3:3 Farmers' Social Consciousness in the 1970s

A. Development of the Attitude to Joint Management

From the mid-1950s onward, Taiwan experienced rapid industrialization which went hand-in-hand with the decline in the economic importance of agriculture. I dealt with these changes in another work,[47] so I will not discuss them here.

What we are concerned with here is the concomitant change in social consciousness among Taiwanese farmers. The tensions between landowners and farmers that had developed during the 1950s gradually dissipated in the 1970s; this was due primarily to economic development, urbanization and the influence of the mass media.

Research reports in 1964 and 1978 on eight villages in Mu Cha, Shen Ken and others in Taipei County, concluded that, as the impact of fourteen years of steady economic improvement set in, residents experienced a lower degree of social intercourse. At the same time, their attitudes toward education and marriage of their children became more pragmatic and civilized, while their attitudes toward geomancy and the gods were shaken; the one exception to this latter point was ancestor worship, which held on.[48] These results were typical of changes experienced throughout Taiwan.

The most significant development since the 1970s, however, has been in farmer attitudes towards joint management. This new

---

[47] Liao Cheng-hung et. al., *Guangfuhou Taiwan nongye zhengci di yanbien lishi ji shehui di fenxi* (Taipei: Academia Sinica, 1986), Chapter 1.

[48] Chu Chien et. al., *Taiwan nongcun shehui bianqian* (Taipei: Taiwan Commercial Press, 1954) pp. 190–191.

form of management was developed in response to declines of arable land and in the size of the agricultural labor force, combined with a rise in the average age of farmers. In the early 1970s, the government established workshops on joint management and in 1980, enacted the Second-stage Land Reform which stressed the expansion of large agricultural operations. The plans were put into effect in one village in each of five counties of Taoyuan, Taichung, Yunlin, Tainan, and Pingtung. In July of 1980, this was expanded to an additional five areas in Taoyuan, Hsinhua, Yunlin and Chiayi. Two similar plans were put into effect in 1982 and 1983. These plans all involved some form of joint management, where the landowners entrusted the agricultural operations of their lands to a management team.

Farmers responded to these operations enthusiastically, as can be seen in this journalist's report from January 1971:[49]

> Recently the Department of Agriculture and Forestry planned a joint management operation in an area of 100 *jia*, inundated fields in Lun Tzu Shang near Hsiu Shui Village. Every farmer in and around the area warmly welcomed the plan. Farmers in Hsiu Shui Village wondered aloud why the government did not choose their area. The plan is a new idea. Each farming household still owns their plot of land; they offer their fields for joint farming and managing without asking questions until harvest. After the yields are counted up, each farming household receives their fair share of the harvest.

The enthusiasm spread all over Taiwan. The idea of joint farming was not entirely new, however; joint farms had been in existence in Taiwan during the early years of the Kuomintang re-

---

[49] Wu Feng-shan, "Jintian di Taiwan nongcun xilie baodaon," *Rili wanbao*, Jan. 9, 1971.

gime. According to a 1951 report issued by the Land Reform Investigation Group, there were 132 community farms in Taiwan. The most highly organized of these was Chiu Ju in Pingtung County. Originally, the Japanese regime had established this community for retired military personnel. Its thirty-eight households farmed 230 *jia* of which less than one-fifth was inundated fields; the rest were dry fields. The village had wide roads, tidily arranged houses and well-kept yards. With a tasteful dotting of trees and shrubs providing shade all around, this community was truly an idyllic farming village.

After the Japanese pullout in 1945, this village was converted into Chiu Chu Joint Farm in late June 1947. Over one hundred households were regimented into this joint farming operation. Initially they worked primarily according to schedule, with secondary priority allotted to daily chores; management thus was difficult and efficiency was low. In 1950, they shifted their priorities so the daily chores received primary attention while the schedule was relegated to a secondary position. As a result of this change, they achieved high efficiency.

Their community was highly democratic. Ultimate power resided in the people's assembly, which was divided into monthly assemblies and an annual assembly. The nine executive members were elected at the annual assembly. These executives met on the sixth of every month to examine the gains and losses of the previous month's operations, and to plan the next month's business. Their decisions were submitted to the head of community for implementation. The people's assembly also elected three comptrollers who met every other month. In addition, there were six other administrators who came under the aegis of the executives; these included the head of the community, the accountant, the manager and the clerk. People were able to enter and leave the joint farm as they wished.[50] This type of joint-management farm community gradually disappeared with the implementation of the Land to the Tiller Program, only to reappear gradually during the 1970s as a response to the unfavorable farm economy.

Data concerning farmers' consciousness and attitudes toward joint farming are scarce. We are forced, therefore, to hazard some hypotheses on the basis of secondary materials. In 1984, Tsai Hung-chin circulated some results from research conducted in 1980 on government-sponsored joint farming. In analyzing these studies, we find that, since the 1970s, farmers have changed from traditional family-centered consciousness to a profit orientation.

For example, among his sample of 500 households, Tsai reported that when asked which factors would induce them to participate in joint farming, farmers saw market factors as having more significance than issues of family. Their most important considerations were the potential for mechanization, followed by the shortage of labor and the difficulty of recruiting workers and by the promotion of agricultural knowledge and skill in the third. The demands and needs of relatives, friends and neighbors were regarded as having the least significance in the decision.[51]

When asked about possible factors that could lead them or others to join joint management group farming, those sampled selected their own shortage of labor as being most important, the lack of reliability of others in the community next and finally their own shortage of land. When asked why they cited lack of labor as a factor inducing them to entrust the farming to others, they indicated that the question of the profitability of prices and the profit-

---

[50] Teng, op. cit., pp. 278–279.
[51] Tsai Hung-chin, *Nongchang gongtong weiduo ji hezo jingying zhuzhi gongzo xuduan wendi zhi diaocha yanjiu*, Mimeograhed copy (1984), p. 28, Table 3-11.

ability[52] of self-farming were the two most important factors.[53]

This shows that the farmers of the 1970s were profit-oriented, that their interest in joint farming was motivated by profit rather than by family relations. It must be admitted, however, that other reports indicate that the traditional culture and clan values exerted a great influence on farm cooperative efforts and that the influence was greater among the more rural communities. Rice paddy communities were more cohesive than livestock-raising communities. In all these communities, those farmers who did come together shared a surname or some kinship relations.[54] In the final analysis, however, profit came to replace kinship relations as the basic factor in the farmer attitudes toward joint management.

This corresponds to a change in farmer attitudes toward agriculture itself. Since retrocession, land lost the sacred character it once had for Taiwan farmers and became secularized; in like manner, farming lost its character as a vocation (in the Weberian sense), and became instead, merely another way to make a living.[55] Such attitudinal changes towards land and farming have much to do with farmers' attitudes toward joint management.

B. Farmers' Alienation from Their Associations

The alienation of farmers from their associations has, as its root, the second reform act of the associations in 1974. This act initiated two changes. The first involved changing the shares farmers had purchased in their associations into "investments in the enterprise." With this change, the government nullified all of

---

[52] Tsai, op. cit., p. 31, Tables 3-14 and 3-15.
[53] Tsai, op. cit., p. 32, Table 3-16.
[54] See Liao Cheng-hung and Huang Chun-chieh, *Zhanhou Taiwan nongmin jiazhi qü xiang di Zhuanbian* (Taipei: Lianjing chuban gongsi, 1992), Chapter 4, pp. 29–44.
[55] Ibid.

3. Transformation of Farmers' Social Consciousness (1950–1970)   83

the privileges and responsibilities toward the association that were represented by the shares. What remained of the relationship between farmers and associations was now only unilateral trade.

The second change was in the method by which the chairman of the board of directors was chosen. Previously, the individual holding this position had been selected by popular election. Upon the implementation of the reform act, the chair was selected by the government and appointed by the association. Although both of these changes were instrumental in alienating farmers from their associations, the question of the method of how to selection the chair of the board was the more significant. Most of the criticisms of the reform act were aimed at the selection and appointment of officers by the top governing levels.[56]

The severity of the alienation was evident everywhere. For instance, in December 1979, a journalist reported on the complaints of the chairman of the board of directors about the farm association in Heng Shan Village. According to the chairman, "Previously, the chairman of the board of directors was the farmers' 'big brother,' they would believe whatever he said. Now, the chairman says one thing, and the farmers immediately return with a rebuttal. You tell them to turn east, and they reply, 'Why not west!'"[57] In the same year, a working member at Hsin Wu Village expressed a similar sentiment from the other side. "Most farmers have already lost their trust and interest in the work of the association."[58]

The disorder and inefficiency due to the system for selecting

---

[56] Liao, Huang and Hsiao, op. cit., pp. 198–201.
[57] Chu Hung-lin, "Dui nongmin yinyou xindi renshi," *Zhongguo shibao*, Dec., 6, 1979, p. 3.
[58] Hung Chin Chu, "Tingting nongmin zenmo shuo," *Shibao zazhi*, no. 92 (Sep., 1981), p. 23.

officials further led to the farmers' sense of alienation from the associations. This was well expressed by a member of the Taiwan Provincial Assembly on June 27, 1978:[59]

> The organization of the farmers' associations can be said to be half belonging to the government, half belonging to the people; it can also be said to be neither governmental nor of the people. The association work and services are extremely disorganized. Besides, the organization of the associations is extremely vague; which level of organization belongs to which is never set down clearly. Everything is mired in bureaucratic entanglements.

Even implementation of the system for selecting leaders was in disarray. One Taiwan Assemblyman spoke to this in June, 1981:[60]

> Being selected by the selection committee as the top grade executive director of the association does not guarantee being appointed by the association. For he who was judged to be a second-rate executive director may get the appointment and keep the job, in the executive meeting over which he has control. And control is obtained by "lobbying" those executives with drinks and vacations, the expenditures of which run from several tens of thousands of NT dollars to several hundreds of thousands, some even up to more than a million. This is obtaining votes by "competition in spending."

This sort of administrative chaos inevitably led to the com-

---

[59] Taiwan Provincial Assembly, *Taiwan shengyihui gongbao* (Taichung: Taiwan Provincial Assembly, 1979), p. 977.
[60] Taiwan Provincial Assembly, *Taiwan shengyihui gongbao* (Taichung: Taiwan Provincial Assembly, 1982), p. 92.

plete alienation of farmers from their associations.

3:4 Conclusion

This chapter has documented the transformations that occurred in farmers' social consciousness and attitudes. First, we examined the situation that resulted from the land reforms of 1950s, which saw the ascendancy of owner-cultivators and the decline of landowners. We considered the ensuing tensions between these two groups and identification farmers developed with their associations. These two phenomena were definitive of social consciousness of Taiwan farmers in the 1950s.

Later, with the agricultural crises of the 1970s, we saw an enthusiasm for joint management and enterprises, accompanied by a shift from the traditional value system towards an orientation for profits. Eventually, however, corruption in the system for the selection of association officers led to the alienation of farmers from their associations; this corruption involved both buying votes and using power to secure positions. Thus, the rise and fall of identification with joint enterprises influenced the social consciousness of farmers during the 1970s.

Now, let us consider the historical significance of these vicissitudes of the farmers' social consciousness in Taiwan. This chapter began with two trends that have been operative in Taiwan since 1895—capitalism and the official infiltration into society. These two trends reflect each other. They explain the tension between landowners and farmers, the farmers' devotion to their associations in the 1950s, as well as rise of farmers' profit orientation in their joint management enterprises and their eventual alienation from their associations in the 1970s.

Capitalism presupposes a market economy. Everything is produced and traded on this basis. This system of economy is different from the farming society of pre-twentieth century China and from Taiwanese farming villages of the Ming and Qing dynasties. Taiwan's transformation into a capitalist system brought about wholesale changes in the traditional cultural system and intense social dislocations.

In the traditional farming society, the leadership was made up of gentry and landowners, who were farmers, or the "earthbound," as Fei Hsiao-tung phrased it.[61] Their resource was immovable land. Once capitalism entered the villages, however, the leadership started to shift towards those who controlled liquid resources (i.e., money). These were the merchants. Then, the traditional basis of "moral sentiments" or "feelings for each other" also gradually disappeared from the relationship between landowners and farmers.[62] For instance, Fried gives an example (cited by Wolf) of a farm village in Anhui province in 1949, where the mutual feelings between landowner and farmer had disintegrated to the point that military force was required to collect the rent.[63]

This sort of social dislocation occurred not only in farming villages of Mainland China but also in modern Japan. The dislocations in Japan, however, did not result in revolution but rather in the rise of fascism.[64]

---

[61] Fei Hsiao-tung, *Peasant Life in China: A Field Study of Country Life in the Yangtze Valley* (London: G. Routledge and Sons, 1939).

[62] These "warm feelings" may have been mostly just oil in the utilitarian engine of business transaction. These feelings may even have been necessary in the traditional village transactions, to cover up deep-seated antipathy to the landlord. Later, such antipathy surfaced as traditional village transactions gave way to capitalism where such "warm feelings" were no longer needed.

[63] Eric R. Wolf., op. cit., p. 285–286. For Morton Fried's study, see his *Fabric of Chinese Society: A Study of the Social Life of a Chinese Country Seat* (New York: Praeger, 1953).

[64] Barrington Moore Jr., *Social Origins of Dictatorship and Democracy: Lord and Peasant in the Making of the Modern World* (New York: Beacon Press, 1966), pp. 228–313.

3. Transformation of Farmers' Social Consciousness (1950–1970)

The disintegration of the old order also allowed for the infiltration of both government and capitalism in farming society. In the forty years following the World War II, these combined factors were responsible for the differentiation of class among farmers and for changes in the social consciousness of farmers. In the case of the growing influence of capitalism in Japan following the war, class differentiation in Japanese farming society led to an increase in the number of both large and small landholders and a decrease in the number of middle-class farmers.

The same holds true for postwar Taiwan. The expanding influence of market capitalism was directly related to the tensions between landowners and farmers in the 1950s. The leading role played by the government in land reform and in education is especially noteworthy.[65]

In fact, this active intrusion into rural society on the part of the government had been a common factor in Taiwan since the beginning of the Japanese colonial period. As Shiomi Shunji points out, during the first twenty-five years of Japanese rule, the police force was responsible for implementing economic policy[66] and continued to play an indirect but influential role during the latter part of the occupation. Since the Kuomintang takeover, farmers' associations have been more or less completely under government jurisdiction, and have been used to implement government policies. Thus, the strong commitment felt by farmers for their associations during the period of the land reform in the 1950s collapsed with the onset of the agricultural crises of the 1970s, precisely because

---

[65] Bernard Gallin, "Rural Development in Taiwan: The Role of the Government," *Rural Sociology*, XXIX: 3(1964), pp. 313-323. And, "Land Reform in Taiwan: Its Effect on Rural Social Organization and Leadership," *Human Organization*, XXX: 2(1963), pp. 109–112.

[66] Shiomi Shunji, "*Jingcha yu jingji*", trans. by Chou Hsien-wen, in Chou, *Taiwan jingji shi* (Taipei: Taiwan Kaiming Bookstore, 1980), pp. 947–983.

of the increasingly politicized character of the associations. Thus, the farmers' associations functioned as a barometer for measuring changes in the social consciousness of farmers.

4
Transformation of Confucianism (1950–1980)

In the whirlpool of postwar Taiwan, the economic, industrial and political upheavals provoked the writing of a new chapter in the history of Confucianism. Several eminent Chinese Confucian scholars reflected and wrote in Taiwan, in political and spiritual exile from the mainland. Nostalgic "grafted" mainland Confucians and critical homegrown Taiwanese Confucians, both put forward ideas leading to a more cosmopolitan perspective and fresh historical reflections in Taiwan. All this led to an intellectual maelstrom that tested and renewed traditional Confucianism. Below, we consider the characteristics of Confucianism in postwar Taiwan (Section 4:1), then its methodology (Section 4:2) and finally the process of propagating Confucianism in Taiwanese society, that seismic spread of the Confucian pathos and the ensuing intellectual whirlwing (Section 4:3).

4:1 The Characteristics

At the outset, we must pause to note two main characteristics of Confucianism in postwar Taiwan before proceeding to investigate its methodology in the next section.

Scholars in Taiwan do not just examine objective accounts of Confucianism; they try to hammer out an identity of their own through their Confucian studies, in the light of the uncertainty of the present. Their Confucian scholarship is thus an existential engagement in this cultural endeavor. They grasp Confucianism less as a bundle of propositions to be examined than an existential value-system whereby they, *qua* investigators, cultivate their own personal identities while at the same time enriching themselves culturally to meet challenges of modern urban industrial society.

Mou Tsung-san 牟宗三 (1909–1995) is a case in point. He expressed deep feelings when he emigrated from Mainland China in 1949, as follows:[1]

> Just ask where one's country is, where one's home is, [and one is plunged into a vertigo of cultural vacuum]. I have only the Chinese cultural life-blood, the ideals of Confucius and Mencius, to sustain my self-identity. Fortunately, we still have our living space in Taiwan. A friend of mine, Hsu Fu-kuan 徐復觀 (1902–1982), founded the *Democratic Journal (Minzhu Pinglun* 民主評論*)* upon arriving in Taiwan. I contributed many essays to it in the spirit of my own journal, *History and Culture*. Now I have crystallized my radical reflections in *The Philosophy of History*. Tang Chun-i 唐君毅 and Hsu Fu-kuan are also actively undertaking an unprecedented cultural hermeneutic.
>
> The five or six years when the Communist Party was going from Chengfu to the Great Wall were also my period of unbearable pathos, wherein I completed *Critique of Cognitive Mind,* a work of pure speculative philosophy; the approach was converted to "concrete understanding" when I came over to Taiwan, where I systematically pondered the direction that the essence of China, the very core of our culture, *should* take, i.e., the path that the life of our people should follow. My pathos was infused and transmuted into my *logos*.

Factual investigation was thus joined to value concerns, as the scholar at the same time sought to confirm his cultural identity.

---

[1] Mou Tsung-san, *Wushi zishu* (Taipei: Erhu chubanshe, 1989), pp. 128–129.

4. Transformation of Confucianism (1950–1980)

This feeling of loss of identity in helpless solitude recorded by Confucian scholars in Taiwan was equally experienced by Chinese scholars overseas. Exiled from Mainland China during the Communist takeover in 1949, many Chinese scholars in the United States suffered a deep cultural nostalgia: "Three disasters, and I still remain alive;/Ocean waves crossed over again,/and my locks are now silvery." During their struggle to explicate Chinese scholarship abroad, they "Dreamed of sufferings of the fatherland a myriad miles away/Under a lone lamp of long distressed night." They pined for the arrival of spring in mainland China: "Turning at a hidden cliff, I looked far and long,/Plum petals flying, mingled with snowflakes over the chilly pond" (all selections from Dr. Hsiao Kung-chuan's 蕭公權 poetry).

The Cultural Revolution of the '60s plunged China into long-term pandemonium, and affected scholars abroad beyond measure: "How could I embrace anti-Confucianism?/Having been adrift in a lone skiff east of the *Dao*" (Yang Lien-sheng's 楊聯陞 poem, 1982). Their profound dedication to Chinese scholarship, shaken to the core, crystallized in numerous deep scholarly monographs. Such pathos colored the lives and thoughts of Chinese scholars exiled in Taiwan and abroad.

The second characteristic of Confucianism in postwar Taiwan is that this existential approach was provoked by the turbulence of the postwar years. Reacting to identity crises and sociopolitical collapse, these scholars launched valiant responses, hoping that by probing the Confucian tradition they could meet the crisis with powerful proposals for cultural renewal.

Concerned about the fate of China, Confucian scholars in Taiwan plunged deeply into Confucian studies for a native system by which to interpret and, perhaps, to reform the world anew. Two outstanding figures in this project were Chien Mu 錢穆 (1895-1990) and Hsu Fu-kuan (1902–1982).

Chien Mu expressed his attitude toward the history of Chinese thought in the foreword to the 1977 edition of his *Chinese Intellectual History*, first published in 1951:[2]

> People without ideas cannot survive on their own. Ideas have their inevitable origins, their life. Ideas without origin or life are mere baby babbles; they are not ideas. Today, the world of Chinese ideas, sadly, has contracted the disease of baby babbles. My book indicates the deep origins of Chinese ideas and thereby seeks to revive and express their true spirit. I do hope my book will enable the reader to understand the following: understanding the essence of Chinese ideas, one can become adept at using them; learning widely about the past, one can better understand the present. Then, the reader can start to realize that the Chinese have bright prospects and are amply capable of blazing their own trail. I wish that my dear reader would not simply stop at toying with past problems and themes.

Professor Chien has inquired into the history of Chinese thought in this pragmatic spirit ever since 1937 when his groundbreaking *The History of Scholarship in China in the Past Three Hundred Years* was published.[3]

Hsu Fu-kuan, whose scholarship was often opposed to that of Chien, also shared his realistic concerns in the study of the history of thought in China. Hsu said in the foreword to his *History of Chinese Theories of Human Nature: Pre-Qin Period* (1962):[4]

---

[2] Chien Mu, *Zhongguo sixiang shi* (Taipei: Taiwan xuesheng shuju, 1983), p. 3.

[3] Chien Mu, *Zhongguo jinsanbainian xueshu shi* (Taipei: Taiwan Commercial Press, 1972), 5th ed., Vol. I, Preface.

[4] Hsu Fu-kuan, *Zhongguo renxinglun shi: Xian-Qin pian* (Taipei: Taiwan shang-wu yin-shu-kwan, 1969), p. 1.

4. Transformation of Confucianism (1950–1980)

> Without a satisfactory history of philosophical thought in China, we cannot tackle such exigent problems as, comparisons of Chinese and Western cultures; the significance of Chinese culture for modern China and for the modern world; the position Chinese culture occupies among world cultures, and so on. The reason is that, before tackling these problems we must first understand *what* Chinese culture is, and this is something we cannot grasp in a piecemeal way. We must systematically go into main themes in our rich culture inheritance; and, only then, from such thematic researches, can we proceed realistically to formulate an overall solution of the problem.

He refined this practical approach to research in his later work, *History of Thought During the Two Hans*, Vol. 3 (1979):[5]

> My work over twenty years has convinced me of the truth of Croce's remark that, in fact, there exists only contemporary history; he meant that all histories are grasped from the present point of view. Without the anti-Chinese pressure of the 1950s, without the anti-Confucian pressure of the 1960s, would not have had the key to understanding the ideas of the Greats of antiquity; never would I have been able even to initiate such a laborious attempt. Jiang Qing 江青 and her henchmen had modeled their Legalist fight against Confucianism after the *Yantielun* 鹽鐵論. Scholars Guo Moro 郭沫若 and Feng Youlan 馮友蘭 also took part in this fight. Together, they unjustly attacked "*xianliang* literature," Confucius, and the Confucians. Thus provoked, I had to write essays

---

[5] Hsu Fu-kuan, *Liang-Han sixiang shi* (Taipei: Taiwan xuesheng shuju, 1979), Vol. III, pp. 3–4.

concerning the political, social, and cultural problems discussed in the *Yentielun*, giving thorough solutions to them. This is a vivid example.

This exemplifies what Feng Youlan expressed in his poem of 1982, "Alarmed at radical changes in *Dao* and its arts?/Please inquire into past events, the ups and downs."

Concerns over the present situation still continue to motivate Confucianism studies conducted by the new generation of scholars today. But, the locus of the "present situation" has shifted from Mainland China to Taiwan. In fact, young Confucians complain that, even after the forty years since the old scholars went into exile from the mainland, a *Taiwanese* Confucianism worthy of the name has yet to appear.[6]

Young Confucians in Taiwan today urge that Confucian studies be linked to their society, reflecting the time-honored Confucian dedication to safeguarding the people and the land. They strongly urge that focus of received Confucianism on the mainland should now be shifted to the Taiwanese society in which they actually live, thereby opening up new territory in Confucian studies.

4:2 The Approaches

To reiterate, Confucian research in postwar Taiwan has been characterized not so much by new contents as by new methodologies, or at least by a new senstivity to the methodologies by which research is undertaken, all in light of the new postwar situation in which Taiwan-based Confucians find themselves.

---

[6] Yang Ju-pin, "Renxing, lishi qiji yu shehui shihui shijiecong yuxian di renxinglun kan Mou Tsung-san di shehui zhexue," *Taiwan shehui yanjiu jikan*, Vol. I, no. 4 (Winter, 1988).

Various *methodologies* are applied in Confucian studies in Taiwan on the basis of favored intellectual approaches. The threee main approaches taken in postwar Taiwanese Confucianism include: 1) historical, 2) philosophical and 3) sociological.

1) Historical Approach: This research approach seeks to explicate the contents and development of Confucianism in light of its historical background. Such research involves examining phenomena vertically with respect to development in history, and horizontally with respect to spirit of the age. Chien Mu and Hsu Fu-kuan are most typical here. They are joined by scholars abroad who publish widely in Taiwan, such as Hsiao Kung-chuan (1897–1981),[7] Wing-tsit Chan 陳榮捷 (1901–1994)[8] and others. To simplify our account, here we only consider Ch'ien and Hsu.

Chien Mu was a giant of twentieth-century Chinese studies; notably he wrote copiously on Chinese historiography. He continually stressed the close ties between historical studies and the actualities of human life from his early *Outlines of Chinese History* (first published in January, 1940) through the Taiwan publication of *Chinese Historical Spirit* (1951, 1976), *Introduction to Historiography* (1969), and *Classics in Chinese Historiography*. *Outlines* (1973) is known for Chien's reinterpretation of Chinese history in presenting the identity of the Chinese people and country during the Sino-Japanese War;[9] it forms a powerful illustration

---

[7] Cf. Huang Chun-chieh, "Hsiao Kung-chuan yu Zhongguo zhidai renwen xueshu," in *Ruxue chuantong yu wenhua chuanxin* (Taipei: Dongda tushu gongsi, 1983).

[8] Cf. Huang Chun-chieh, "Chen Jung-chieh (Chan Wing-tsit) xiansheng di xuewen yu zhiye," *Newsletter of Institute of Chinese Literature and Philosophy, Acadmia Sinica*, Vol. I, no. 1 (March, 1991), pp. 39–42, and my foreword to Wing-tsit Chan (ed.), *Zhongguo zhexue wenxian xuanbian* (Taipei: Zheliu chubanshe, 1992), which is the Chinese translation of his *Source Book in Chinese Philosophy.*

[9] For a discussion of Chien's historical scholarship, see: Hu Chang-chih, *Lishi zhishi yu shehui bianqian* (Taipei: Lienjing Publishing Co., 1988), pp. 133–144 and pp. 234–252.

of the realistic-historiographical approach.

Chien repeatedly emphasized that history of ideas and intellectual history must be studied in close connection with the social background. He wrote:[10]

> We must emphasize self-cultivation and popular praxis; academic studies must be understood from the academician's own practical living. Neglect the person and the understanding of that person's scholarship stays superficial, irrelevant.

Chien's most representative work was his massive magnum opus, *New Critical Anthology of Zhu Xi's Works* (*Zhuzi xin xuean* 朱子新學案; 1971). He worked on this study from his retirement from New Asia College, Hong Kong in the summer of 1964 until November 1969. It consists of five volumes (more than 2,000 pages), detailing Zhu Xi's (1130–1200) concepts and thought, quoting extensively from Zhu Xi's *Wenji* and *Yulei*. Chien describes his methodological approach in the conclusion to *Overview of Zhu Xi's Learning*:[11]

> One must seek to understand the great tradition a great thinker takes over before one can understand that thinker. I have systematically arranged Zhu Xi's selected words so that the reader can understand them by just reading them in context, without explanation. This follows Zhu's hermeneutical method of teaching and understanding the Classics. I cannot suppress my occasional admiration, however, in the text. I hope the reader will not accuse me of flattery; it is all too reasonable that birds of a feather flock together (as is written in the *Book of Poetry*). My

---

[10] Chien Mu, *Zhongguo lishi yanjiufa* (Taipei: Sanmin shuju, 1969), p. 72.
[11] Chien Mu, *Zhuzi xin xuean* (Taipei: Sanmin shuju, 1971), Vol. I, pp. 234–235.

incidental elaborations are meant to help the reader appreciate Zhu's creative excellence against the background of our great tradition. As was said of old, one must know the person and discuss the situation (Mencius); being clear about the man and the age are particularly essential for understanding Zhu Xi.

Chien's "great tradition, great background" means to study Zhu Xi as an essential part of the entire cultural tradition. Zhu had wanted to study the great thinkers of antiquity, to comprehend them and harmonize their views so as to grasp the threads of similarity that run through them all; Zhu never wanted to promote his own views. This was the traditional spirit of Chinese scholarship. Chien's methods of studying Confucianism result in his depicting it less as a conceptual game played in an ivory tower than as a system of vital ideas for confronting real life problems.

Hsu Fu-kuan fully shares this approach despite his differences from Chien concerning, for instance, the character of despotic rulership in Chinese history.[12] Hsu emphasized that, "A system of ideas can be grasped only by tracing its developmental process; its character can be grasped only by comparison with others. All of our analytic-synthetic efforts must be extended in these two directions—development and comparison."[13] "Development" and "comparison" are the methods of studying Confucian ideas in the context of history. One cannot treat an idea as an isolated entity in abstraction from a total context. Hsü describes the historical character of Confucianism as follows:[14]

> Confucianism is a cluster of ideas that seeks to bear re-

---

[12] Hsu Fu-kuan, "Liangzhi di miwang–Chien xiansheng di shixue," in *Rujia zhengzhi sixiang yu minzhu riyu renquan* (Taipei: Bashi niendai chubanshe, 1979).
[13] Hsu Fu-kuan, *Liang-Han sixiang shi*, Vol. II, p. 2.
[14] Hsu Fu-kuan, *Rujia zhengzhi sixiang yu minzhu riyu renquan*, pp. 39-40.

sponsibility for humanity by confronting real human life head-on. Here one cannot escape into nature, emptiness, conceptual games, much less into foreign settlements. The Confucians can only stand firm amidst the nitty-gritty of human life, shouldering the destiny of human survival and development. They may be forced to adapt to a long period of despotic pressure, or bend and twist under a burden of political trends. Prolonged twisting can lead to forgetting the original Confucian spirit, expressed in "turning all under Heaven to the public," "precious are the people, negligible is the ruler." But this cannot be helped in the actual historical process.

But these bendings and twistings are distortions of Confucianism under the load of despotism; Confucianism in itself has never been an instigator of despotism. In fact, even during the dark days of despotic pressure, Confucianism functioned as a modifying, mitigating force, giving people confidence and direction, thus helping our people to weather it all. This power is that of rationalism rooted in human moral nature, the power explicated by the pre-Qin Confucians.

To study Confucianism, we must peruse the textual materials in hand to probe its inner recesses, to grasp its original "essence." Then, we have to understand how its purpose, its spirit, has been molded by actual conditions of the ages into its present shape. We must trace the historical realities, the vicissitudes, of the upward struggles Confucianism has undergone through despotic warping and corruption.

Hsu's historical attitude yielded deep insights in his Confucian studies.

Chien and Hsu engaged in a holistic, realistic methodology. They believed that an idea is best understood in the total cultural context, its total historical structure, in which that idea is a composing element; the significance of this "element" can be ascertained only in its "position" (Hsu) as a "part" (Chien) of that total historical structure. Attending to the developmental history of Confucianism, the position of the Confucians is thereby posited in the context of the whole intellectual history of China.

Following this holistic historical approach, we see various lines of problem-proposals as directions taken in Confucian studies in postwar Taiwan. Three main lines can be cited:

a) How did Confucianism develop amidst consolidation of vast political centralization and the commoner clan system in the Han period? All of Hsu's writings after the 1970s can be said to answer this problem by considering sociopolitical structures of the Zhou-Han dynasties and probing the *Hanshi Waizhuan* 韓詩外傳, *Xinxu* 新序, *Shuoyuan* 說苑, *Shiji* 史記, and so on. Hsu's essays on these themes are included in the three volumes of the *History of Thought in Two Hans*.

b) How did Zhu Xi synthesize Sung Confucian scholarship with that of the Han and Tang periods? What were his ideas in structural detail? Although in *New Critical Anthology of Zhu Xi's Works*, Chien sought to provide detailed objective descriptions,[15] he also included his views and answers to these problems.

c) How did the Confucian ideas on world management (or statecraft, *jingshi* 經世) and the socioeconomic situation influence each other? What were their ideas on world management? How were these ideas related to the Classics?

---

[15] Chien Mu, *Zhuzi xin-xuean*, Vol. I, p. 235.

World management (or statecraft) is one of the main themes in the history of thought in China; the expression—*"jingshi"*—has been in circulation since the pre-Qin period. Zhuangzi in chapter 2, *"Qiwulun* 齊物論*"* wrote, "As for the records of managing the generations of people of the former emperors during many springs and autumns, the holy man argues about what is right and does not dispute." And, again in *"Waiwu* 外物*,"* Chapter 26, "Without hearing about the manners of the present rulership, one is far from engaging in managing the world."

Confucians have always discussed how best to manage the world. Throughout his life, Confucius was uneasy because he was very eager to bring peace to the world; Mencius, too, went forth with tens of carriages and hundreds of followers from ruler to ruler to propound this ideal; for his part, Xunzi exhorted learning, promoted rituals and honored the rulers, all for this ideal. These seminal Confucian thinkers all devoted themselves to cultivating the people so as to change the world by scholarship and education.

When the world was unified under the Han regime, Confucians were brought into the government and Confucian ideals of managing the world were widely implemented. Han Confucians pursued "versing oneself on the Classics, thoroughly applying them [in the world]"; Song Confucians emphasized both "Classical hermeneutics" and "managing affairs"; Qing Confucians advocated "managing the world, becoming thoroughly useful." From the nineteenth century, as China faced crisis after crisis from the Western powers, the ideals of managing the world took on a new complexity; as Liu Kuang-ching pointed out, these ideals turned into the promotion and development of agriculture, industry, and commerce.[16]

---

[16] See K. C. Liu's preface to *Jinshi Zhongguo jingshi sixiang yantaohui lunwenji* (Taipei: Academia Sinica, 1984).

The ideal of world management and its connection with the intelligentsia has been a topic of academic discussion in Taiwan since l980. Yu Ying-shih published a book in Taipei in August 1980, entitled *Essays on the Chinese Intelligentsia Class: the Ancient Times*, in which he examined interactions between intellectual history and the history of society and analyzed academic ideals and their social function in Chinese history. At the First International Symposium on Sinology sponsored by Academia Sinica in August 1980, there was a panel on the role of intelligentsia in Chinese history.[17] Subsequently, in August 1983, the Institute of Modern History at Academia Sinica sponsored a Seminar on the Ideal of World Management in Modern Chinese History (i.e., since the eighteenth century). In March 1986, National Tsing Hwa University sponsored a conference on the ideals in Chinese intellectual history to examine critically the Confucian ideals, especially their linkage to the actual sociopolitical environment. Liu Kuang-ching said:[18]

> Confucianism consistently emphasized world management. This ideal includes philosophical and ideological components, that is, social thoughts, rituals and customs, ideas concerning education, administration, politics; it is closely linked to actual situations. Ideas reflect and influence reality, sometime more, sometimes less. Too high an ideal takes longer to have an impact on society; unrealistic dreams may not be realized at all. Some ideals, however, managed to be rooted in society; changing them is well nigh impossible. Analyzing various relations between ideas and reality gives us better discernment into life.

---

[17] All papers presented to this panel were published in *Zhongyang yanjiuyuan guoji hanxue huiyi lunwenji* (Taipei: Academia Sinica, 1981), *Lishi kaogu* section, Vol. II.

[18] See *supra*, note 18.

This kind of research easily draws the attention of concerned historians. Such research interests also happened to coincide with research being conducted abroad at the time. In January 1986, Robert Hymes of Columbia University and Conrad Schirokauer of the City University of New York jointly organized a Conference on Song Statecraft: Ideals and Actions, in order to look into connections between the environments and ideas on world management in the Song dynasty.

In Japan, Yamanoi Yu 山井湧 and Mizoguchi Yuzo 溝口雄三, both of Tokyo University, pay special attention to the socioeconomic background of the development of ideas in history. Their interest draws on the deep and broad Japanese research being conducted on the socioeconomic history of China, especially in the agrarian societies of southern China during the Ming and Qing dynasties. Professor Yamanoi, for instance, claimed in his *Studies in the Intellectual History of the Ming and Qing Dynasties* (1980) that it is important for us to dig into the socioeconomic roots of the ideas in the Song and Ming, that is, to bridge social history with the history of ideas, if we want to understand the ideas of the period. Thus, there has been mutual influence in this line of inquiry among scholars in Taiwan, Japan and the United States.

2) *Philosophical* Approach: The second methodological characteristic of Confucian research in postwar Taiwan has been the attempt to establish the philosophy of Confucianism in the spirit of what Tang Chun-i called "philosophizing according to the history of philosophy." The most noteworthy examples are three: Fang Tung-mei's 方東美 (1899–1977) metaphysical direction Tang Chun-i's idealistical direction and Mou Tsung-san's Kantian direction. Prevalent in Taiwan also are many publications of Lao Sze-kwang 勞思光 (1927–) and Liu Shu-hsien 劉述先 (1934–), both long-time residents of Hong Kong; their approaches aim at

philosophical understanding. Lao Sze-kwang employs what he calls a "Key-problematique approach,"[19] which aims at a reconstruction of a given philosophical theory. Liu Shu-shien's approach to Chinese philosophy may be characterized as a synthesis of those of Fang, Tang and Mou. I will skip a host of writings by their students, and concentrate on the three scholars based in Taiwan.

What is the method of research that is called "philosophizing according to the history of philosophy?" Tang explains it in this way:[20]

> [Since] philosophical truths are expressed in the words of a philosopher [who is in time], those truths are expressed in various modes in the order[ly process] of history; to depict systematically how these modes came and went is to "philosophize according to the history of philosophy." Such comings and goings constitute the common flow of historical vicissitudes; within this flow must be mutual similarities and differences.[21]

> Different philosophies are like different houses in and out of which people go. In their goings, they must meet occasionally. These meetings are where philosophies communicate one with another. As we watch them meet and depart, we see, in our historical impartiality, their differences in similarities and similarities in differences. It is in these flows of philosophical truths that we see the [historical] continuity of ancient and modern wisdom. To see it, we follow various genetic relations of ideas, up

---

[19] Lao Sze-kuang, *Xinbian Zhongguo zhexue shi* (Taipei: Sanmin shuju, 1981), pp. 1-20, esp. pp.15–17.
[20] Tang Chun-i, *Zhongguo zhexue yuanlun: yuanjiao bian* (Hong Kong. New Asia Colloge, 1975), p. 8.
[21] Ibid., p.7.

and down, down and up.

In short, Tang wanted to watch the "order[ly process] of the history" of thoughts in order to capture the "flow of philosophical truths" and the "continuity of ancient and modern wisdom." This is to seek philosophical wisdom within the order of history. The history of philosophy then is the road to philosophical system, distinct from the historical approach outlines in the previous section. Both Fang and Mou practiced "philosophizing according to the history of philosophy."

Fang Tung-mei (a.k.a. "Thome H. Fang") wrote mostly in English. He taught at National Taiwan University for about thirty years and served as a visiting professor at Michigan State University and the State University of New York. His most systematic work was *Chinese Philosophy: Its Spirit and Its Development* (1981). He lectured on its main themes twice at National Taiwan University (1966–1970, 1970–1973). Upon his retirement in 1973, he compiled these lectures in the above book, which presents a fair representation of the study of Confucianism in postwar Taiwan.

Fang emphasized that while Western metaphysics tends to be transcendent (beyond experience), Chinese philosophy tends to be transcendent in its immanence and immanent in its trans- cendence. The basic writings of Confucianism are, in his opinion, the *Hongfan* 洪範 Chapter of the *Shangshu* and the *Yizhuan* 易傳, especially the latter. Early Confucianism advocated a theory assuring the dignity and the inner value of human nature. He divided Neo-Confucianism from the Southern Song into three main schools: realist, idealist and naturalist. Although distinct, they can be subsumed under the classical tradition of Confucius (551-479 B.C.), Mencius (371-189 B.C.), and Xunzi (fl. 298-238 B.C.), since they all share the following four points in common:[22]

a) They all corresponded with heavenly principle through the myriad of things in the universe—by upholding the heavenly principle, collaborating with the myriad of things, discerning human nature, thereby thoroughly embodying the constancy and transformations of the universe to correspond with nature.

b) The structures of their thought were not homogeneous but miscellaneous—Confucians after the Song inherited various aspects of Chinese culture, and were thus unable to strike out in completely new directions. They also had to mix orthodox Confucian themes with quotations from the Buddha and Laozi.

c) They all thought that spirit and matter are one and man was the natural pivot of the universe—believing that a subtle power pervades nature for universal nourishment.

d) They all upheld a consistent philosophical theory of human nature, that is, the ideal that human nature is supremely goodman is correlated with Heaven, grows in the virtue of centrality, transforms his nature, initiates activities, until arriving at the ultimate good.

Fang's other writings, such as *Collected Lectures of Professor Fang Tung-mei*[23] (1978) and *The Chinese View of Life* (1975),[24] explicate the *Dao* of Comprehensive Harmony in Chinese philosophy, and are similar to *Chinese Philosophy — Its Spirit and Its Development*.

---

[22] Thome H. Fang, *Chinese Philosophy: Its Spirit and Its Development* (Taipei: Linjing Publishing Co. Ltd., 1981).
[23] Taipei: Liming Publishing Co., 1978.
[24] Hong Kong: Union Press, 1975.

Tang Chun-i had previously studied Western philosophy, and had written *Outlines of Chinese Philosophy* (1978),[25] which is reputed to be the best Chinese-language book in the field. In all his numerous writings, he engaged in philosophizing via reconstruction of the history of Chinese philosophy. He commented on Chinese intellectual history and since history has commented on him, there was a hermeneutical circle in his philosophizing.

Tang's reconstructions of Chinese philosophy are collected in the multivolume *Essays on the Origins of Chinese Philosophy* (1966-75), organized in the order of the *Zhongyong's* opening proposition: "[What] Heaven decrees is called [human] nature; to follow [our] nature is called *Dao*; to cultivate *Dao* is called instruction." This series of books includes the *Introduction* (1966);[26] *Origins of Human Nature* (1968),[27] a philosophical anthropology; *Origins of Dao* (1974),[28] a metaphysics of *Dao*--the foundation of human development and the human world; and *Origins of Instruction* (1975),[29] a history of Neo-Confucianism in the Song and Ming periods. This is a reconstruction of the philosophy of idealism and subjectivism, an exercise in philosophizing according to the history of philosophy.

Mou Tsung-san's turning point coincided with his emigration to Taiwan in 1949. As recorded in *My Confessions at Fifty* (1989), this was when Mou came to realize:[30]

---

[25] 2 Vols. Taipei: Taiwan xüesheng shuju, 1974, 3rd edition.
[26] Tang Chun-i, *Zhongguo zhexue yuanlun: daolun pian* (Hong Kong: Dongfang renwen xuehui, 1966).
[27] Tang Chun-i, *Zhongguo zhexue yuanlun: yuanxing pian* (Hong Kong: New Asia College, 1968).
[28] Tang Chun-i, *Zhongguo zhexue yuanlun: yuandao pian* (Hong Kong: New Asia College, 1974).
[29] Tang Chun-i, *Zhongguo zhexue yuanlun: yuandao pian*.
[30] Mou Tsung-san, *Wushi zishu*, p. 28.

My life is no longer grounded in the world; the world has nothing for me now. Just ask: Where is my country? Where is my home? My life is grounded only in the cultural life of the Chinese people, in the ideals of Confucius and Mencius.

He sojourned in Hong Kong and later taught in Taiwan. As Shen Ching-sung pointed out, his writings can be divided into three groups.[31]

Works of the first group are concerned with the reconstruction of the history of Chinese philosophy, the second translate and comment on Kantianism and fuse it with Chinese philosophy; the third analyze, in a fundamental manner, problems of culture and modernity. Mou's most systematic works on Confucianism are *Xin-Body and Nature-Body* (1968)[32] and *From Lu Xiangshan to Liu Jishan* (1979).[33] His views on Chinese philosophy are given in *Features of Chinese Philosophy* (1963),[34] a collection of his early lectures in Hong Kong and *Nineteen Lectures on Chinese Philosophy* (1983),[35] a collection of his lectures at the Philosophy Department, National Taiwan University.

His *Substance of Mind and Substance of Nature* (1968) has as exerted a profound influence in Taiwan in recent years. Most original is his proposal on the three Neo-Confucian schools of the Song and Ming:[36]

a) Wufeng 五峰, Jishan 蕺山 school: This is the ultimate

---

[31] Shen Ching-sung, *op. cit.*
[32] Mou Tsung-san, *Xinti yuxingti* (Taipei: Zhengzhong shuju, 1968), 3 Vols.
[33] Mou Tsung-san, *Cong Lu Xiangshan dao Lui Jishan* (Taipei: Xuesheng shuju, 1979).
[34] Mou Tsung-san, *Zhongguo zhexue di tezhi* (Taipei: Xuesheng shuju, 1963, 1976).
[35] Mou Tsung-san, *Zhongguo zhexue shijiu jiang* (Taipei: Xuesheng shuju, 1983).
[36] Mou Tsung-san, *Xinti yu xingti*, Vol. I, p. 49.

teaching of the "Doctrine of One Root" developed by Zhou Lianxi 周濂溪 and Zhang Hengju 張橫渠 and passed to Cheng Mingdao 程明道.[37] They explicated the concept of Nature objectively in light of the *Zhongyong* and the *Yizhuan*, and explicated the concept of mind subjectively in light of the *Analects* and the *Mencius*. "Manifesting Nature with *Xin*" explains the root of the oneness of *xin* and nature; this is the fullness of the One-Root Ultimate Teaching. The teaching of "Anticipatory discernment, corporal confirmation"[38] was stressed for personal cultivation.

b) Xiangshan 象山, Yangming 陽明 school: This school reversed the direction of the above school. Instead of going from *Zhongyong* and *Yizhuan* to the *Analects* and the *Mencius*, this school subsumed the former pair under the latter, stressing that all things are manifestations, developments, and expressions of the One Xin (heart-mind). It also advocated the teaching of "anticipatory discernment, corporal confirmation" for personal cultivation.

c) Yichuan 伊川, Zhu Xi 朱熹 school: This school studied *Zhongyong*, *Yizhuan* and *Daxue*, stressing the last classic. *Dao*-body and nature-body in the former two classics are converged into an ontological being embodying the principle of "existing without acting." Confucius' *jen* is a principle (*li*); Mencius' original *xin* is a manifestation of breath-energy (*qi*), postnatal self-cultivation by *jing* 敬 (seriousness) and absorption of knowledge are central. "*Xin* 心 turns serene, then *li* 理 turns clear"; the achievability of self-cultivation depends on the "investigation of things, and attainment of knowledge." This school adopted the "comply and obtain" approach.[39]

---

[37] Mou Tsung-san, *Xinti yu xingti,* Vol. I, p. 44.
[38] Mou Tsung-san, *Xinti yu xingti,* Vol. II, p. 476.
[39] Mou Tsung-san, *Xinti yu xingti,* Vol. I, p. 54.

Their complex historical development can now be traced. In the northern Song, Yichuan began to depart from the Lianxi, Hengju and Mingdao; Zhu Xi kept firmly to the new tradition initiated by Cheng Yi 程頤 (Yichuan, 1033–1107). This was the school of Yichuan and Chu Xi, the former a Separate Master (as mentioned in the *Classic of Rites*), whose teachings the latter firmed up into a new school.

The school of Wufeng and Liu Jishan was a tradition directly descended from Masters Lianxi, Hengju and Mingdao, unifying the *Analects*, the *Mencius*, *Zhongyong*, and *Yizhuan* into an objective novelty. The school of Lu Xiangshan and Yangming, in contrast, subsumes *Yizhuan* and *Zhongyong* under the *Analects* and the *Mencius* in order to achieve a subjective novelty. Centered on these four classics, this is the orthodoxy of pre-Qin Confucianism and the great tradition of Song-Ming Neo- Confucianism.

Professor Mou taught at National Taiwan Normal University, National Taiwan University and Tunghai University; the world is awash with his students. His thoughts on Confucianism have exercised a tremendous influence throughout Taiwan; the *E-hu Journal* propagates and develops his views widely. His *Substance of Mind and Substance of Nature* covers Zhou Lianxi, Cheng Mingdao, Hu Wufeng and Zhu Xi in the Sung. In 1979, he published the fourth volume in this series, a book titled *From Lu Xiangshan to Liu Jishan*, which explicates Wang Yangming's doctrine of extending innate knowledge, the Zhu-Wang debates and Liu Jishan's doctrine of "*shendu*, watchful when alone."

Mou's *On Perfect Goodness* (1985)[40] is noted for its meticulous explication of arcane ideas. "Fundamental Truths," chapter one, is a translation *cum* commentary on the "Kaozi" 告子上

---

[40] Mou Tsung-san, *Yuanshanlun* (Taipei: Xuesheng shujü, 1985).

Chapter in the *Mencius*, with several comparisons between Mencius and Kant's views on human nature. In Mou's opinion, Mencius' *si* 思 (thinking) is a more form of practical reason, not speculative reason; hence, Mencius' *xin* 心 (heartmind) is a self-legislating subjective-objective unity, "*xin* as *li* 理 (principle)." Consequently, Mou writes:[41]

> In talking about self-autonomy (self-legislation), Mencius starts with *xin*; meaning is an essential function of *xin*. *Xin*'s autonomy is its freedom. *Xin* is dynamic activity; its active clear consciousness (moving without moving) confirms its practical freedom. Practical freedom is objective freedom; *li* determines its objectivity. Active consciousness involves cognitive intuition with which it confirms itself as free. The function of Kant's conscience is part of the activities of this clear consciousness, independently knowing right from wrong. It is not just subjective receptive capability (which is not perceptual ability); it is the objective foundation of morality. This is a fusion of Kant's conscience with reason. This subjective-objective *xin* is itself *li*, this *xin* is our human nature.

This is an unprecedented contribution to Mencius scholarship.

In sum, Fang Tung-mei, Tang Chun-i and Mou Tsung-san all adopted the method of "philosophizing according to the history of philosophy" in their writings in aesthetics, idealism and metaphysics. At the same time, all of them confronted the political and cultural crises of modern China with Confucian hermeneutics and reconstruction for the grand destiny of Chinese race. Fang's concluding poem to his *History of Chinese Philosophy* expressed well

---

[41] Mou Tsung-san, *Yuanshanlun*, p. 31.

their Promethean thrust: "Tracing ourselves in tribulation; rousing the turbid, raising the translucent."

Sociological Approach: A third methodology applied in Confucian studies in postwar Taiwan is sociological and uses statistics to investigate the relationship between Confucianism and modernism in East Asia, especially in contemporary Taiwan.

Some external factors spurred the investigation. Yu Ying-shih's *Religious Ethics in Modern China and the Spirit of Commercialism* (1987)[42] which was inspired by: 1) lively debates in the 1950s among historians in mainland China over the "sprouting of capitalism," and by 2) Western sociologists recently investigating economic modernization in East Asia in terms of Weber's "Protestant Ethic." The impressive postwar development of the Four Little Dragons of East Asia (Korea, Taiwan, Hong Kong, and Singapore) naturally attracted sociologists and humanists. The "post-Confucian hypothesis" was proposed to the effect that the Confucian business ethic induced these rapid economic developments. This causal interpretation was an extrapolation from Weber's theory of the formation of European capitalism: as the Protestant ethic pervaded Europe to induce its economic prosperity, so the Confucian ethic pervaded East Asia to induce its rapid economic development.

This theory claims that the Confucian tradition has at least four features that helped stimulate the rapid formation of business enterprises in East Asia. These four features include:[43]

a) The Family system facilitated cultivation of self-posses-

---

[42] Yu Ying-shih, *Zhongguo zhishi zongjiao lunli yu shangjen jingshen* (Taipei: Lianjing Publishing Co., 1987).
[43] H. Kahn, *World Economic Development: 1979 and Beyond* (London: Croom Helm, 1979), p. 6.

sion and self-control, respect of education, learning of skills and techniques, responsibility for home and occupation.

b) The ethic promoted self-identification with the group and an inclination to help it prosper.

c) The ethic led to legitimization of class society as a part of one's nature and Nature surrounding one.

d) The ethic regards social relationships as thse of mutual cooperation.

In other words, the factors taken by Weber (in his *Religions in China—Confucianism and Taoism*) as inimical to the development of capitalism in China, such as family cohesion, respect for the power of government and the like, are now regarded as conducive to capitalism. Peter Berger even claimed that Confucian ideals can form a good business ethic and promote productivity. Thus, Confucian ideals of harmony and cooperation perhaps contributed to the rapid development of East Asia.[44] This interpretation reflects the resurgence of Weber scholarship in the West, and is now becoming a fashionable trend in Taiwan, especially among such luminaries as historian Yu Ying-shih, and psychologists Yang Kuo-shu 楊國樞 and Huang Kuang-kuo 黃光國.

These scholars seek out the root cultural tradition responsible for catalyzing development of capitalistic economy in postwar Confucian societies in East Asia. Their sociohistorical standpoint involves five basic research questions:[45]

---

[44] Peter L. Berger, "Secularity: West and East," paper presented to the Kokugakuin University Centennial Symposium on Cultural Identity and Modernization in Asia Countries, 1983.

[45] Yu Ying-shih, op. cit., p. 172.

a) Aside from the apparent economic and institutional backgrounds, was there an identifiable cultural factor involved that enhanced the success of transplanting Western capitalism into East Asia?

b) If the answer is yes, was that cultural factor contributed by Confucian values and ethics?

c) If the answer is yes, what particular elements in Confucian values and ethics most contributed to this rapid economic development?

d) Did these "Confucian values and ethics" as manifested in society come exclusively from Confucianism? Did other traditions, such as Buddhism and Daoism, contribute to the formation of Confucian values and ethics? If they did, what were their specific contributions?

e) Did the ideas of sacred and the secular worlds produce any tension and/or distress in the hearts of the Chinese? How did people manifest this tension or distress?

In *The Religious Ethic of Modern China and the Spirit of Commercialism*, Yu Ying-shih treats the above themes from a historical viewpoint, probing the commercial activities in China until the Ming and Qing periods (sixteenth century). He utilizes newly discovered data, especially from *Selected Collection of Data on Commerce in the Ming and Qing Periods* (compiled by Chang Hai-peng, et al., 1987); on the whole, this body of data supports his claims.

But, the most impressive successes in this area go to the social scientists. Among papers delivered at the "Conference on Confucian Thought and Modernization" (1986) sponsored by the Freedom Foundation in Taipei, the most noteworthy were those by

Huang Kuang-kuo and Yang Kuo-shu.

Professor Huang's *Confucianism and Modernization of Asia* (1988) aims at solving the "the century riddle of Confucianism." Huang came down to the level of individuals and analyzed influences of Confucianism on their social activities. Thus, as a social psychologist he probed the relationship between Confucian ideas and modernization in East Asia. The first part of the book considers the riddle of economic prosperity in East Asia and Max Weber's theory; the second part analyzes the inner structure of Confucian thought; the third part presents his own theory of how Confucian thought is related to modernization in East Asia. He claims that this problem lies beyond philosophical deliberation; the problem must be tackled by the empirical methodology of the social and behavioral sciences—collecting data and critically examining whatever interpretive theories have been proposed thus far.[46]

Huang claims that the Confucian notion of *ren* (benevolence) is basically twofold: transcendental "*ren* heartmind" and natural "cognitive heartmind." The latter is the psychologist's "cognitive mind"; the former is characteristic of Confucianism itself.[47] Much of the book is devoted to explaining the inner structure of Confucian ideas, including *Dao, Ren, Yi* and *Li*. In Chapter Eleven he quotes psychological statistics on education and filiality to show that Confucianism has been a leading directive of the Asian people, a main key to modernization in East Asian countries.

This book manifests a recent achievement of sociological research in postwar Taiwan, but it leaves considerable room for discussion. Huang claimed that "Confucianism itself served as an

---

[46] Huang Kuang-kuo, *Rujia sixiang yu dongya xiandaihua* (Taipei: Zhulin chubanshe, 1988), p. 20.
[47] Huang Kuang-kuo, op. cit., p. 56.

ideology that supported despotism,"[48] that Confucianism "stresses the private realm, but does not abandon the public realm,"[49] and that the greatest weakness of Confucianism is that it stresses family ethic over social ethic.[50] These statements are unsubstantiated, and exhibit the author's insensitivity to the complexity of Confucianism; they certainly provoke various objections. He claims the psychology of Confucian man is entirely social and lacking in profound subjectivity and transcendence. Nonethless, this book remains a milestone among sociological studies conducted in postwar Taiwan.

The progenitor of this sociological approach is psychologist Yang Kuo-shu. Together with Li Yih-yuan 李亦園 of the Institute of Ethnology, Academia Sinica, Yang orgnized a Comprehensive Seminar on personality traits of the Chinese people from the standpoints of sociology, psychology, philosophy and history in 1972.[51] The conference proceedings have exerted a great impact on Taiwan academic circles during the past thirty years.

At present, Yang engages in comparative research on Chinese traditional values, especially organized behavior, social trends, motivations for success and others. Using the standard methods of measurement, he assesses quantitatively the five traditional Confucian value orientations: family-centeredness, humility in one's post, "face" (and honor), relationship, solidarity and cooperation, long-suffering and assiduousness. He found a clear and direct relationship between traditional Confucian values and positive social behavior; the former contributes to the individual's ties to tradition, to the present situation and to motivation for success, while admit-

---

[48] Huang Kuang-kuo, op. cit., p. 305.
[49] Huang Kuang-kuo, op. cit., p. 175.
[50] Huang Kuang-kuo, op. cit., p. 176.
[51] Li Yih-yuan and Yang Kuo-shu eds., *Zhongguoren di xingke: Ke ji zhenghe xing di taolun* (Taipei: Institute of Ethnology, Academia Sinica, 1972).

ting Confucianism is not the only contributing factor in these links. In sum, Yang's research has given initial scientific validation to the post-Confucian hypothesis.[52]

Preeminent in traditional Confucian values is filiality. Few researches on filiality have been conducted in cognitive psychology; most have been done in statistical psychology. Yang thinks four difficulties attend statistico-psychological research on filiality. To obviate these difficulties Yang divides the integral expression of filial behavior into six components to form a cognitive framework for measuring filiality. He selected a sample group of 212 subjects and confronted them—tailoring to their different ages and educational levels—with five stories involving filial dilemmas. Their responses revealed that individual filial cognitive structure changes with education and age. The cognitive structure advances, along with education and age, from heteronomy, unilateral obedience, simple materialist motivation, to autonomy, bilateral mutuality, self-determination and spiritual motivation.[53]

In addition, Yang conducted a survey of 10,000 sample subjects ranging from middle school students, high school students, university students, to ordinary people in society. He found that:[54]

a) All three levels of filiality—cognitive, voluntary and active—have four components: "loving, respecting parents," "obeying parents in self-restraint," "supporting living parents, bringing them honor." Filiality includes possitive feelings of intimacy, respect and negative feelings of self-distancing in awe and

---

[52] Yang Kuo-shu, "Chuantong jiazhiguan, geren yu xiandaihua ji zuzhi xingwei: hou rujia jiashuo di yixiang weiguan yanzheng," *Bulletin of the Institute of Ethnology, Academia Sinica*, no. 64 (1989).
[53] Yeh Kuang-hui and Yang Kuo-shu, "Xiaodao di renzhi jiegou yu fazhan: gainian yu janheng," *Bulletin of the Institue of Ethnology, Academia Sinica*, no. 65 (1989).
[54] Yang Kuo-shu et. al., "Xiaodao di shehui taidu yu cheliang," *Bulletin of the Institute of Ethnology, Academia Sinica*, no. 65 (1989).

fear.

b) The features in mind, Yang designed eight statistical measurement scales on filial knowledge, feeling, volition and action. Applying these scales to the above subjects, Yang found much consistency and validation potential.

c) At the same filial level Yang found a medium intensity of correlation among the above four components of filiality. Within the same component, there was a strong positive correlation between filial knowledge and filial volition, and a weak correlation between filial action and the other two.

d) There is a low negative correlation between positive and negative filial feelings. In addition, filial knowledge, volition and action are conspicuously and positively correlated with positive filial feelings, but only slightly and negatively correlated with negative filial feelings.

Such are the initial findings of sociological and statistical research into Confucianism in contemporary Taiwan society. Confucianism in postwar Taiwan remains actively engaged in its culture, hermeneutics and reconstruction in confrontation with the rapidly changing situation.

4:3 The Propagation

The existential orientation of Confucian studies in Taiwan cannot be overlooked. Rather than describe Confucianism in objective terms, scholars often attempt to stake their own identity on it. They grasp Confucianism less as a bundle of "contents" to be investigated than an existential value-system forged to cultivate the identity of people and culture in this brave new postwar environment. Thus, this essay would be incomplete without a look into *how* this new pathos of Confucianism has been spread, and how it is still spreading in Taiwan society at large.

We see two main channels of transmission of Confucianism in Taiwan: 1) *Official* government propagation through schools, publications and officially sponsored social movements, and 2) the *popular* religious propagation through pamphlets (*shanshu* 善書) issued by folk "phoenix temples." We note that the contents propagated through official channels differ much from those issued through popular channels, just as the great tradition of official Confucianism differed much from the lesser tradition of grassroots Confucianism.

1) Official propagation of Confucianism comes through three main channels: a) the educational system, b) social movements and c) various publications.

a) The KMT government extensively infused national Confucianism into textbooks in schools at all levels. The course curricula "Goals" at the primary school level were issued in 1952, 1962, 1968 and 1975; those at the middle school level in 1952, 1962, 1972 and 1985. All eight versions of textbooks emphasize "stimulation of love of our nation; promotion of our national spirit, the Chinese culture."

Course descriptions for such courses as "Life and Conduct" in primary school and "Civics and Morals" in middle school express the "Goals" of "bravely loving our nation," "stirring up the spirit of nationalism and anti-Communism" and "strengthening national consciousness" no less than six times, and the "Goals" of "exalting Chinese virtues," "practicing Four Cardinals, Eight Virtues" and "laying the foundation for resurgence of Chinese culture" no less than seven times. Clearly, the emphasis is on the promotion of nationalism and traditional Chinese culture for political purposes.[55]

---

[55] Cf. Yang Yih-jong, *"Xiandaihua yu Zhongguoren di jiazhi bianqian: jiaoyu jiaodu di jieshi,"* International Conference on Values in Chinese Societies: Retrospect

The textbook contents stress not modern but traditional values, such as "filiality, friendship and nationalism" (primary school level) and "nationalism, fraternity and family" (high schools). Loyalty to the nation remains the highest priority at all levels.[56]

Textbooks for junior high schools put the greatest emphasis on tributes to the political leader, then on norms of personal conduct, such as solicitude, self-control, kindness and forthrightness. All of these moral slogans are closely tied to political propaganda: solicitude and forwardness are supposed to lead to nationalistic fervor, kindness appears with closeness to the political leader and even self-control has political overtones. Frugality as an ideal (issued in 1968) is linked to the political goal of "national buildup," that is, cultivation of nationalism. Thus, morality is for the sake of political stability.[57] Textbooks for senior high schools in "History of Chinese Culture" devote much space to ancient Confucianism, classical scholarship of the Han and philosophical scholarship of the Song, Ming and Qing periods. The required texts for the seniors, "The Basic Resources for Chinese Culture," include the *Four Books* (the *Analects*, the *Mencius*, the *Great Learning,* and the *Doctrine of the Mean*).

The government secures homogeneity in all these materials by monopolizing textbook design, production and distribution throughout the educational system. In October of 1991, the Taiwan Provincial government distributed reference materials for teaching the basics of Chinese culture (categorized under "The First Stage of Plans to Carry Out 'Teaching Without Discrimination, Teaching According to Talent'") to all teachers, all educational personnel in

---

and Prospect, May 23–26, 1991, Taipei, p. 18.
[56] Op. cit., pp. 18–19.
[57] Cf. Li Li-ching, *Guozhong guowen jiaokeshu zhi zhengzhi shehuihua neirong fenxi*, Master's Thesis (Taipei: Institute of Education, National Taiwan Normal University, 1989), p. 259.

the government, all schools, and all educational organizations in the island. All textbooks are published by the National Bureau of Compilation-Translation (*Guoli bianyi guan* 國立編譯館), and have the official stamp of approval.

b) The Committee on Chinese Culture Resurgence initiated various social movements. The government set up this Committee in July 1967 in response to the Cultural Revolution on the Mainland to propagate the traditional values of Confucianism. But as anthropologist, Li Yih-yuan pointed out, this cultural effort to preserve traditional Confucianism was really taken up in opposition to the Communist regime, with the emphasis on morals, not on aesthetics or intellectual pursuits.[58] From July 1967 to April 1991, this semi-official organization promoted Confucian ethics and morals through several social movements.[59]

i. Committee on Popular Life Assistance set up to infuse Confucian values into people's lifestyles;

ii. Guidelines for People's Life (with pictures and essays) produced for wide distribution among the people;

iii. Guidelines on Etiquette and Ceremonial Customs—to harmonize traditional and modern customs and mores. The ROC President examined this and gave his approval to the Interior Ministry to distribute them to the populace;

iv. Discussion Groups on traditional culture, modern living, manners and customs—inviting domestic and foreign scholars to

---

[58] Li Yih-yuan, "Wenhua jianshe gongzo di rogan jiantao," in Zhongguo luntan bianzhi weiyuanhui ed., *Taiwan diqu shehui bianqian yu wenhua fazhan* (Taipei: Lianjing Publishing Co., 1985), pp. 305–336, esp. p. 309.

[59] For a general report on the activities of this Committee during twenty-five years, see Chen Li-fu, "Zhonghua wenhua fuxing yundong weiyuanhui gongzo shulue," *Zhongyang Monthly*, July 1991, pp. 38–40.

4. Transformation of Confucianism (1950–1980) 121

submit reports and discussions, for publication and distribution throughout the island.

c) Government *publications* on Confucian cultural matters are numerous. The Committee on Resurgence of Chinese Culture organized a Sub-Committee on the Promotion of Scholarly Publications and put out more than forty volumes in the following series: "Chinese Culture Series," "Modern Commentaries, Modern Translations Series" of classics and more than ninety biographies from the Duke of Zhou (d. 1094 B.C.) in the "Biographical Series on Chinese Thinkers."[60]

2) Since the Japanese occupation in 1895, the development of public primary schools throughout Taiwan spelled the demise of traditional "private academies," which were usually focused on the Confucian classics. Taiwanese people now often see the Confucian value-system infused in their life from the lesser tradition of *folk religions* from local temples.

Sung Kuang-yu 宋光宇 undertook a study of the "*Shanshu* (books for good [behavior])" issued by "phoenix temples" that exhort people to be good. He reports that these pamphlets consist mainly of moral persuasion and criticism of social problems, such as lust, the inhumanity of the wealthy, being unfilial and others.[61] These emphases on filiality and belittling wealth reflect Confucian values. *Shanshu* seek to propagate Confucianism by way of folk religion.

Clearly, the government propagates Confucianism as a state ideology, while folk religions propagate Confucianism as the

---

[60] Ibid.
[61] Sung Kuang-yu, "Cong zuijin jishi nian lai di nuanzo yujishi shanshu tan Zhongguo minjian xinyang li di jiazhiguan." International Conference on Values in Chinese Societies: Retrospect and Prospect, May 1991, Taipei.

standard upright lifestyle. The dual propagation of Confucianism in Taiwan continues the historical experience of official Confucianism and popular Confucianism generally in Chinese culture.

4:4 Conclusion

Confucianism in postwar Taiwan is a strange amalgam of cultural pathos among the Confucian scholars, ideological propaganda of the government and religious campaigns for moral living. All these efforts are intended to meet the challenge of the modern situation in Taiwan that saw the replacement of traditional agrarian society with an industrial one implicated with rising division of labor, urbanization and new cacophonies of ideologies unheard of in Chinese history.

Confucianism attempts to meet the challenges of modern Taiwan in its turbulent transitions to the twenty-first century, to industrial, commercial and cultural internationalism and to many sorts of concommitent ecological and sociological problems.

This confrontation between Confucianism and modernity offers positive prospects for both Confucianism and modern life in Taiwan. The transformation of Taiwan involves transformations of the *people,* how they change, and set the task of becoming human. But, how to become truly human entails first understanding what "becoming human" means, for in order to achieve something one must know what it is that one intends to achieve. The "how" is dictated and directed by the "what."

Having survived thousands of years of abuses and misinterpretations, the Confucian spirit proposes being truly human as integral, intersubjective and cosmically intervolved. For Confucianism, humanness entails inalienable dignity, inherent sociality and ecological mutuality, with each facet entailing the other two. As a beacon of human ideals, Confucianism lights the way for the trailblazers for the future of Taiwan. The Confucian scholars' pathos amounts to bringing out this age-old spirit of Confucianism, while at the same time drawing from it vigor and strength for carrying out this effort, becoming thereby truly human while spreading this vision of humanity.

Taiwanese modernity poses a danger and a promise. The danger is that people in Taiwan can be so dazzled by bewildering changes of modernity as to consign Confucianism to past relics and trash, mistaking true Confucianism for the corrupt forms that were misused by officialdom. To treat Confucianism in this way would amount to depriving the Taiwanese of this precious human ideal and incline them to drift away from being human—from themselves—in the maelstrom of modernity; for people lacking an idea of their true self cannot survive. And, these ideas did not come in a vacuum; they are time-tested, wrapped in a rich tradition whereby they have been nourished at their cultural core.

Taiwanese modernity can become a promise. Rootless modernity can shake us to the marrow and provoke cultural nostalgia, so we can cleanse Confucianism of its dross, produce proposals for reconstruction of cultural identity and go on to reinterpret, reform, rectify and strengthen Taiwan itself. Negatively, Taiwanese modernity can serve as an imperative to cleanse Confucianism of its past irrelevances, misuses and misinterpretations, on pain of the disappearance of both Taiwan and Confucianism.

At the same time, positively, Confucianism can be concretized, made relevant and then mobilized for our critical cultural hermeneutics in Taiwan. In order to "tackle such exigent problems as comparisons of Chinese and Western cultures; the significance of Chinese culture for modern China, for the modern world," so as to stand firm in our critical assessment of (and learn from) new ideologies that enter the shores of Taiwan, "we must first understand *what* Chinese culture is, by going systematically and deeply into our rich cultural inheritance."[62]

In short, either Confucianism is sharpened as a hermeneutical guiding power for the critical task of humanizing, restoring and enhancing the cultural identity of Taiwan in the turmoil of twenty-first century transformations, or else Confucianism will perish with Taiwan itself.

After all, tradition is that which has succeeded in cleaning the past dross and nourishing the future; otherwise, tradition would not have been worthy of being handed down. The Confucian tradition is anything but idle conceptual games, played in isolation from the actual situation; Confucianism has been the source of our cultural strength forged in unceasing grapplings with actuality throughout history. The Confucian ideals have managed to take root in society; it would be well nigh impossible to uproot them. We have been nourished by Confucian values; we are what we are today, thanks to the cultivation offered by Confucianism, the "Chinese cultural life-blood."[63] We will have to continue to be nourished by this historic and history-proven tradition. Learning broadly of the past leads to a better understanding of the present.[64]

We must, in view of Taiwanese modernity, delve deeply into the Classics to cleanse Confucianism of past misuses and misinterpretations, and thereby bring out its powerful, exigent, normative vision of socioecological humanity. Only then, can we devise tactics to develop Confucianism as the hope of Taiwan today to the people, whole and untainted. Only then will we "realize that the Chinese people have a considerable future ahead and are

---

[62] Hsu Fu-kuan, *Zhongguo renxinglun shi: Xian-Qin pian*, Preface, p. 1.
[63] See *Supra*, note 1.
[64] See *Supra*, note 23.

amply capable of blazing their own trail."[65] Only thus will "Confucianism in Taiwan today" embody the time-honored, history-tested tradition to "shape and lead politics and society".[66] Here lies *the* promise of postwar Taiwan.

---

[65] See *Supra*, note 2.
[66] See *Supra*, note 6.

5

A Contemporary Confucianist's Postwar Taiwan Experience: The Case of Hsu Fu-kuan (1902–1982)

Confucian scholars in Chinese history often forged their own cultural identities in the context of the turmoil they faced. In the whirlwind of postwar Taiwan history, how did the Confucian scholars who emigrated from the Mainland in 1949 construct their world of thought? We shall consider the existential character of Chinese culture and the cultural character of human existence in China. Chinese culture is shaped by human pathos in reflective and often tragic living circumstances, and the Chinese are integrated meaningfully or dispersed pathetically along with the vicissitudes of their defining college. Thus, Chinese culture and people form a highly tense reciprocity rarely seen in other civilizations.

First, in section 5:1, we see in the following Chinese "cultural impacts (especially in collapse) on persons," how Chinese culture influences and irrevocably shapes human existence. Then, in section 5:2, we show that the existential power of Chinese culture comes from the fact that the culture itself is forged in the strife and struggle of human living; thus, we register the "personal formation of Chinese culture." Finally, in section 5:3, we identify the resultant "distinctiveness of Chinese culture:" Chinese culture is a unity of history and circumstance in personal biography. Chinese culture is reciprocally determinative of and interactive with individuals, and this culture provides us with concrete universal rules for living.

In this inquiry, we consider the case of Hsu Fu-kuan 徐復觀 (1902–1982) and his experience of personal-cultural upheaval in Taiwan. We regard Hsu's life experience as typical of this sort of dynamic convergence of the cultural and the biographical; it provides an epic case of the intertwining of cultural crisis with personal crisis.

5:1 Cultural Impacts on People

We all have to make sense of what we do and who we are, in order to live at all; a senseless life cannot be lived any more than a senseless act can be tolerated. Meaning is our bread of life. We live on meaning; since meaning is purposive, we live *for* meaning as well. Thus, we live on and for meaning; life without meaning and purpose is a living death.

We all know this. What we may not realize, however, is that we create this meaning that feeds and fulfills life, not in a vacuum but within a "culture," that is, the meaning-ambience within which we live, move and have our being.[1]

One of the best ways to depict this pervasive shaping influence of culture for Chinese individuals is to proceed negatively and observe what befalls individuals when culture *collapses* in their lives. Cultural collapse can take two modes: personal failure to shape life with culture and the breakdown of culture itself.

Failure to create meaning through our life activity breeds feelings of "life-vertigo," "life-nausea" and despair. And, this becomes sickeningly serious when the very meaning-matrix, the culture, is itself fragmented, that is, when there is a breakdown of cultural integrity into meaninglessness. This latter case involves cultural crisis, which becomes autobiographical in impact; it becomes an intensely personal crisis to those devoted to the culture. What we glibly call "culture shock" manifests a brief period of radical life-vertigo when one's personal, cultural meaning-matrix

---

[1] See Appendix.

becomes disoriented.

Culture shock becomes acute, serious, pervasive and chronic for Chinese intelligentsia when their culture, a culture that has historical depth, is rendered meaningless and ineffectual in days of political and economic crisis; it is just when cultural guidance is especially needed that the culture is shaken at its foundation to the breaking point. Here, cultural turmoil immediately constitutes disintegration of their life—its meaning, context and integrity.

Emigration to Taiwan after the communist takeover of Mainland China (1949) created this historical cultural crisis for a group of distinguished Chinese intellectuals. In desperation, they tried to find, and then recreate, the structural meaning of life by probing, and thereby *reconstituting*, "Chinese culture" from the roots up.

Hsu Fu-kuan was a distinguished Chinese scholar who emmigrated to Taiwan due to the political-cultural turmoil of civil war in 1945–1949. He was suddenly, personally alienated from his cultural soil and expressed his feelings of uprootedness in tragic nostalgia. He had to undertake the mammoth task of redefining himself by reconstructing Chinese culture in a foreign land. His intellectual history then constituted the history of his reconstruction of "Chinese culture," enriching and rejuvenating Chinese culture.

The unity of culture and personal existence manifests itself clearly in Hsu's creation of his "Chinese culture," which has three interconnected elements: 1) political, 2) agricultural and 3) Confucian. Agricultural soil gives solidity of virtues; political artifice manages them. Classical Confucianism mediates both and mediation is a pragmatic affair. The intense subjectivity (element 1) that forms the basis of Chinese populism (element 2) differs, as Confucianism (element 3) insists, from Western democracy based on an atomistic individualism. Let us proceed to examine these three basic cultural elements one by one.

5:1:1. The first element in the triune structure of Chinese culture as depicted by Hsu is *political*. In China, politics is pervasively important, even for common people. Politics is management of popular welfare, an immediate concern of the people; they are the ones who feel their shoes being pinched by political handling of their affairs. People suffer whenever popular welfare is sacrificed for private royal gain. Politics is thus an immediate barometer of popular suffering.[2]

To understand Chinese culture is understand how much suffering has occurred under the persistent despotism of the supreme royalism that oppressed the traditional agrarian society. The system of absolute monarchy in traditional China began in 221 B.C. when the First Emperor of Qin (r. 246–210 B.C.) achieved the first unification of all Chinese territories.

In Hsu's view, Chinese despotism had five characteristics: a) an incontestable one-man rulership, equivalent to a supreme human divinity on earth; b) this institution resulted from historical and societal factors as well as from royal efforts at fulfilling their ideals; c) the social system was patterned after the Legalist penal system; d) all people were subordinated to the supreme ruler and completely deprived of the rights to self-determination or protest and e) no scholarly autonomy was allowed.[3]

This gigantic political machine was maintained and operated throughout Chinese history. All that conscientious scholars could do under the tight rule was to attempt to mitigate its oppressive measures, which crushed anyone attempting any significant reform

---

[2] Hsu Fu-kuan (hereafter HFK), ZSSL, p. 257.
[3] HFK, LHSS, pp. 63–162.

of the machinery. This Legalist-style system had its nucleus in absolute sovereignty, feeding on the vast Chinese territories and peoples, with legal administrative gadgets backed by the enforcing power of the military. All subsequent Chinese culture, economics and social life were developed within this machinery.

Hsiao Kung-chuan sums up the absolute sovereignty of the ruler thus: it is opposed to (i) populism, rulership by the people and to (ii) the supreme rule of the law, to which even the ruling body ought to be subjected.[4] This absolute autocracy was what has prevented China from changing and advancing to modernity. And Hsu Fu-kuan consistently targeted this as *the* principal object of reform in his writings. And the autocrats were not limited to those of antiquity; they included the Communist Chinese leaders, backed by intellectuals (e.g., Guo Moro 郭沫若) who depicted the early Zhou as a slave society.[5]

Reform begins with probing into the root of corruption. For Hsu, autocracy began with the switchover from the original ideal of populism, "people as the lord of the world," to royalism, "the ruler as the lord of the world." Early Confucians had suggested a solution. The rulers' means of obtaining absolute sovereignty, that is, their talents, their desires, should be directed to work for the desires and satisfaction of the entire world. In other words, the talents and desires of the ruler should be objectified and integrated into the world's talents to satisfy the world's desires.[6]

Under such conditions, the ideal state of political concord, according to Hsu's view of Confucianism, would be achieved. His

---

[4] Hsiao Kung-chuan, *Xianzheng yu Minzhu* (Taipei: Lianjing Publishing Company, 1982), pp. 171–182.
[5] LHSS, pp. 1–62, esp. p.13.
[6] RZYM, pp. 218–219.

idea of the ideal Confucian state included seven characteristics.[7]

First, populist politics is an outcome. The administrative machine becomes centered on popular welfare, with people as the lords and the ruler as their servant. The ruler does not give or take the world; people do. People's "obedience" to the ruler is based on a contractual relationship—the ruler manges social affairs well, so the people feel inclined to obey his "orders."

Second, the ruler who fails to fulfill his contract to rule has abrogated the people's obligation to obey him. People then have the right and responsibility to disobey and rebel against him.

Third, the ruler's supreme obligation is to satisfy the people's needs, the most basic of which are their needs for survival. Consequently, the ruler's requirement is to protect and guarantee the people's lives. "Loving and nourishing the people (*aimin, yangmin*)" is the sole greatest task of the ruler.

Fourth, the ruler's responsibility to observe the people's right to life entails his adherence to the "right-profit distinction" insisted upon by the Confucians following Mencius. "Right" in this context refers to the people's rights; "profit" refers to the ruler's benefits.

Fifth, the ruler exists to satisfy people's needs; thus, all political activities are for the sake of the people, not the ruler. Therefore, the people's obligation to obey the ruler is their obligation not to the ruler *per se* but to join in the communal tasks he mandates to promote community welfare.

Sixth, this sort of rulership consists in the rulership of virtue, rulership with the ruler's personal expressions of virtues.

---

[7] XYZ, pp. 199–200.

And seventh, the "obtaining the world" so much desired by the ruler, is not the main purpose of rulership but its means to the rightful purpose of "loving and nourishing the people."

Two questions remain to be answered: Why should this conversion from royalism to populism take place? How is it to happen? Hsu's answer to the first question constitutes the second element 2) agrarian soil of our souls, while his answer to the second question leads us to the third element 3) Confucianism.

5:1:2. We come now to the second element in Hsu's triune Chinese culture—*agrarian soil*. We treat two themes in the following: a) First, Hsu's ideal political world as depicted above resembles that of contractual communal relationship in the West proposed by Hobbes, Rousseau, Locke and other philosophers. What is distinctively Chinese in Hsu's ideal politics? The answer is that the Chinese political ideal is rulership by virtue, while the West has a politics of competing individualism; b) second, where does this Chinese political ideal come from? The answer is: from the agrarian soil.

a) Hsu's contractual rulership in China differs from that of the West primarily in motivation. Western democracy is based on an individualistic struggle for the rights and interests of private citizens. Individuals are naturally endowed with several inalienable rights—such as rights to life and happiness—for which individuals struggle, and a contractual relationship with the ruler is a means to balance conflicting demands to satisfy their rights.

In contrast, the Chinese ideal ruler's contract with his people is expressed through his virtue (德, *de*) and ritual-décorum-decency (禮, *li*). Here, virtue means the feeling of being unable to bear other people's suffering; decency means behavior appropriate to the situation. In the West, what works is the mutual negotiation among contending parties with conflicting interests and rights. What is supposed to work in Hsu's ideal politics comes from moral self-awareness and compassion, extending individuals' (especially the rulers') family feelings to others' families.[8] Hsu's ideal is based on family-politics; Hobbes' is based on adversity-politics.

In other words, Western politics is that of conflict and negotiation, while Hsu's Chinese ideal politics works by objectification in the public arena of personal moral feelings toward other persons. We can see immediately that Hsu's ideal comes from Mencius' passionate appeal to our inborn feelings for the suffering of others.

b) But, where do the moral feelings come from? Hsu thinks they come from the village life of agrarian *soil*; the following passage reflects his feeling for the home-soil where he was born.[9]

> Agrarian villages are where the Chinese were soil-born and soil-grown. Any individual, any community, any people, when they reach the sorry extent of forgetting what soil they came from, having lost feelings for their originative soil, whence they cease to draw a drop of life juice, then they forget any and all things, divested of feelings for anything, unable to obtain life from anywhere anymore. . . . To be able to persist in one's conviction when danger strikes, to stand firm in the conviction of such virtues as devotion, loyalty, filiality, diligence in tilling, studying and handing down a good family tradition and the like, all these are the deepest and greatest accomplishments of Chinese agricultural villages. Absorbing such agrarian virtues and extending them to politics produces wise skillful officers who make for the age of clean, brilliant politics.

---

[8] XYZ, pp. 53–54.
[9] XYZ, pp. 71–81. The quotation is from pp. 72, 80.

The agrarian soil lies deep in us, constituting the soil-depths of our sturdy virtues and spirit. All the Confucian explications of moral virtues spring from that soil.

This account of agrarian soil came from Hsu's personal nostalgia for his old home, Xishui village in Hubei Province. He was a son of the Great Earth.[10] Hsu told of the psychological damage he sustained; when his came to Taiwan he felt uprooted from the agrarian village where he was born and had grown up. His greatest sorrow was that he could never go back home to smell that home-soil to replenish the spirit had drained out from him.[11]

The agrarian home-soil was where he felt he obtained the original virtues, which armed him to fight for justice in the world. The idyllic cohesion of agrarian society, wherein everyone is concerned about everyone else in a natural and unassuming manner, forms the social-psychological matrix from which Hsu drew his blueprint of what it means to be a "good" person. Culture and its roots are essentially biographical, as exemplified in the seminal intellectual, Hsu Fu-kuan.

5:1:3. But, how could these soil-virtues be elevated to infuse the upper political echelons of society? The answer is: through the mediation of *Confucian scholarship*, which constitutes the third element of Hsu's triune Chinese culture.

The agrarian soil, for all its virtuous beauty, is unobtrusively reticent. It requires Confucianism to provide an expressive voice and proponent, which will promote it to the world of politics. Confucianism is anything but an ivory-tower system of metaphys-

---

[10] Chen Chao-ying quoted Hsu Fu-kuan's own characterization as a "son of the Great Earth." See Chen Chao-ying, "Yige shidai di kaishi—jijin di rujia Hsu Fu-kuan xiansheng," in HFKWT, Appendix 2, p. 362..

[11] HFKZ (4), p.81; HFKZ (II), p.291-94; HFKZ, p. 46.

ics and much less an official ideology convenient for autocracy. For Hsu, Confucian scholarship is a pragmatic, worldly critical force that mediates the agrarian soil-virtues with the world of politics and administration.

As a matter of fact, all of the populist ideals and all of the political defects described above emerge from the words of the Confucians, the mouthpieces of people's basal soil-feelings. It is in this sense that Hsu said that the primary function of Confucianism is to bear and infuse responsibility. Confucians bear the ineluctable responsibility, "Heaven-conferred," for people of all ages; a) for their existential development and b) ceaselessly to advocate such populist ideals as "the world be publicly-shared (*tianxia weigong*)" and "people are precious, rulers are of lesser value (*mingui, junqing*)" to people everywhere.[12]

The two responsibilities—for people's existential development, for populist concord of the world—are in fact one; they are two sides of the same human-cosmic coin. People's development, their growth into integral personhood, consists in calming, settling and integrating feelings (*qing*), reasonableness (*li*), and sincere decency (*li*) until they form a harmonious whole and attain the balanced unity (*zhong*) of a whole person. The person thus cultivated is, in turn, obligated to extend this personal harmony among his personal relations. His family feelings are to be expanded *via* reciprocal interactions with others so that social-political concord will grow naturally and spontaneously. This progression from personal integrity to social harmony is inevitable, though it requires conscientious effort; it constitutes the basis for Confucian pragmatic metaphysics, the personal-political-natural harmony among the heavenly, the earthly and the human.[13]

---

[12] RZYM, pp. 39–40.
[13] HFKJ (I), pp. 277, 279, 303; HFKZ (II), pp. 65–76; ZWL (II), pp. 1–21.

Requiring our full devotion, the expansion from personal integration to political concord is as full of pathos as it is inevitable. This pathos Hsu calls "pathetic awareness (*yuhuan yishi*)". This is the so-called "tragic" element in Chinese culture struggling to realize itself. This struggling to self-attainment bespeaks the vitality of the tragic cultural life of China, as embodied among sincere Confucians.[14]

The phrase "sincere Confucians" is used advisedly. For sincere Confucians must struggle not only against autocratic rulers but also against fellow Confucians in officialdom. The Confucian ideal of moral-political populism was persecuted, oppressed and twisted by powerful autocratic rulers and their Confucian stooges time and again throughout history.

Hsu described three stages of political oppression and corruption that were particularly harsh on Confucian ideals. First, silver-tongued sophists were employed at court to refute arguments of officials and Confucians against royal misrule. These sophists emphasized the august power of imperial rule. The royal withering of this rhetorical path for the scholar-officials effectively destroyed the court advisory system. The second stage, contemporaneous with the first saw the rise of Office of the Masters of Writing (尚書, *Shangshu*) and Palace Master of Writing (中尚書, *Zhongshangshu*) cabinet system. In the third stage, we saw the coming of nepotism, the eunuch chamberlain system and the vassalage system, all of which served to consolidate royal sovereignty.[15] Machinery for political oppression was thus in place.

Cultural collapse due to autocratic corruption redounded to personal miseries among people and their mouthpieces the Confu-

---

[14] ZRL, pp. 20–21; ZSSL, p. 158.
[15] LHSS (I), pp. 203–280.

cians. And, as the miseries worsened to the breaking point, the Confucians themselves collapsed into scheming and perpetrating underhanded maneuvers for their own survival. Confucians under royal patronage arose to quote the Classics in presenting the official line in defense of despotism. Fights and intrigues among themselves to benefit the royalty became widespread. Such so-called Confucians merely strove to survive and even prosper under despotism.[16]

Under such circumstances, all that conscientious Confucians could do was to *limit* the spread of the despotic poison and try to advance Confucian ideals from within royalism. There was no way to restructure the autocratic system itself. And such stopgap measures only further encouraged the rulers to use Confucianism as means to advance *their* causes.[17] The pathetic consciousness attending the Confucian ideals can be partially explained in this. We can feel Hsu's pathos of hope that perhaps in the future: "Ten years, twenty, fifty or perhaps a hundred years from now there must appear a vital renaissance of the Confucian Middle Way!"[18]

Confucianism, the third element in Hsu's triune structure of Chinese culture, is a pathos-filled mediator between the soil-level virtues of humanness and top-level administration of social affairs, promoting grassroots populism so as to spread virtues throughout sociopolitical administration, binding people and rulership together into a harmonious, unity between Heaven and earth.

We have just completed a historical and "biographical" account of the impact Chinese culture makes on people, especially when the culture collapses. This collapse of culture was due to political mismanagement; the pain of common people was expressed

---

[16] ZSSL, pp. 263–277, esp., p. 277.
[17] RZYM, p. 66.
[18] ZSSL, pp. 263–277, esp. p. 277.

in the Confucians' scholarly protests. The Confucians therefore tried their best to refashion Chinese culture. A prime example of this was Hsu Fu-kuan's reconstruction of Chinese culture. Life could be made meaningful by Hsu's triune "Chinese culture." Political artifice permeates life from the top of the social ladder; agricultural soil pervades life from the bottom of our being; Confucianism mediates and integrates the two.

Unfortunately, as power corrupted, political administration was narrowed into one-man manipulation and disasters ensued throughout Chinese history. Confucianism struggled heroically to restructure culture so as to rectify political life and render popular welfare morally meaningful via virtuous political administration by spreading the grassroots moral feelings. All this exhibits the intertwining of culture with the personal existence through which cultural impacts are radically, tragically, felt.[19]

5:2 Personal Formation of Culture

If Chinese culture makes an ineradicable existential impact on individual people, then people do make their decisive marks on this culture. This is the second aspect of the mutuality of the cultural and the biographical in China.

We saw in section above that whenever political disaster struck in Chinese history, the intelligentsia were shaken to their cultural foundation and rose up to protest and redress the top-level evil, in scholarly expressions reflecting the ancient primal shouts of Confucius (551–479 B.C.), Mencius (291–289 B.C.?) and others, of the soil of innate virtues exhibited in agrarian villages. It was

---

[19] Wang Kuo-wei 王國維 (1877–1927) responded to cultural crisis with suicide; Liang Sou-ming 梁漱溟, Mou Tsung-san 牟宗三, T'ang Chun-I 唐君毅, Chien Mu 錢穆, and Hsu Fu-kuan responded with their respective passionate reconstructions of Chinese culture.

thus that Confucians came to refashion and rejuvenate Chinese culture, exercising their influence on the culture. We elaborate on this aspect—influences on culture by primal Confucians—in the following.

How individuals exert influence on culture is graphically illustrated in the preceding by Hsu Fu-kuan's reconstruction of triune Chinese culture. In this section, we provide two more examples of this: 1) how Chinese cultural ideals are variously expressed by individuals in different life situations and 2) how those ideals coagulated into a culture in which reflective, creative individuals can realize themselves as paradigmatic individuals.

5:2:1. People in different life situations characterize Chinese cultural ideals variously. Chinese culture has biographical origins. Personal culture formation can be seen concretely in various expressions of key notions according to the person who expresses them.

Let us compare Hsu's impressions of various notions with those of his contemporaries. Autocracy for Hsu is synonymous with ruler-sovereignty in societal affairs, which is a means to enhance the supreme authority of the ruler. Autocracy is despotism,[20] the main culprit responsible for the corruption of Chinese culture and miseries of all sorts. And despotism (for Hsu) originated in one-man rule, the autocratic system established with the First Emperor of Qin.

For Chien Mu (1895–1990), in contrast, autocracy is "a democracy in the Oriental-Chinese style." The hegemonic violence of vassalage, feudalism and aristocratic rulership disappeared in the Qin; plutocratic oppression was forbidden from the Han, mili-

---

[20] LHSS (I), pp. 281–294.

tary juntas exerted light rule throughout Chinese history; thus, Chinese imperialism hardly deserved the epithet "despotism" in the one-man rulership of the court, where many scholar-officials thronged to advise the rulers in light of Confucian scholarship. Autocracy in China turned out to be the rule of wise commoners, forming a peculiar "Chinese democracy."[21]

The difference between Hsu and Chien sprang from their different life-experiences. From early life, Hsü had been active in circles of political power and in and out of party politics. His writings reflect his sense of pathos toward the corrupt atmosphere of the times,[22] his personal experience of the political vicissitudes of the 1940s. In contrast, Chien all his life had been a pure academician, going from one educational institution to another, enjoying prestige for his publications and public addresses. All Chien saw was viewed through the lens of historical documents.[23]

The second example is the notion of "tragic consciousness" (*yuhuan yishi*). It was taken by Hsu, in his genetic, historical, pragmatic approach, as a typical spirit in the intelligentsia's struggle to propagate Confucianism. In contrast, Mou Tsung-san (1909–), with his speculative, metaphysical frame of mind, took this consciousness as one of the three ingredients of "moral consciousness" typical of Chinese philosophy.[24] Tragic pathos for Hsu was the originative power of culture via protest; for Mou it was a structural ingredient of culture, a part of its autonomy.

---

[21] Chien Mu, *Guoshi dagang* (Taipei: Taiwan Commercial Press, 1980, Revised 7th ed.,) I, Introduction, pp. 14-15; *Shijie jushi yu Zhongguo wenhua*, (Taipei: Dongda tushu gongsi, 1985), pp. 246–247.
[22] HFK, HFKWLHC, pp. 2, 304-05; CKJHLS, Preface, p. 1.
[23] For Chien's autobiography, see his *Shiyu chayi* (Taipei: Dongda tushu gongsi, 1983).
[24] Mou Tsung-san, *Zhongguo zhexüe di tezhi* (Taipei: Taiwan xüesheng shuju, 1963), p. 12.

The third example is Mencius' notion of "treading-forth bodily-form" (踐形, *jianxing*). In his intensely pragmatic stance, Hsü focused on the "treading" and interpreted the notion dynamically as our struggling objectification of moral subjectivity in the world.[25] Tang Chun-i's (1908–1978) predominantly metaphysical exposition, however, emphasized the "form" in Mencius' notion, taking "treading form" as the locus for manifesting our moral life, where there is a final unity of body and heart-mind.[26]

Finally, Hsu's stress on the unity of fact, notion and value inclined him to respect *li*-metaphysics (理學, *lixue*), and to despise textual criticism as an empty "thoughtless" exercise of ivory-tower academia.[27] In contrast, Hu Shih's 胡適 (1891–1962) pragmatic positivism inclined him to prefer scientific textual investigation to speculative metaphysics.[28]

Thus, the key notions have been variously defined and described, upheld and opposed, according to different personal experiences and inclinations. Key notions in culture are shaped creatively and biographically; they are intensely, variously, personal in origin, tint, flavor and atmosphere.

5:2:2. Key notions of culture are intensely biographical in origin. Once this trend is generalized, it is a matter of course that personal formations of cultural notions coagulate into "Chinese culture" which is often crystallized in paradigmatic individuals.

---

[25] ZRL, pp. 185–186.
[26] Tang Chun-i, *Chungguo zhexue yuanlun (yuandao pianyi)* (Taipei: Taiwan xuesheng shuju. 1976), pp. 239–240.
[27] LHSHS (III), p. 619.
[28] Hu Shih, "Fan lixue di sixiangjia—Dai Dongyuan," in Yu Ying-shih et. al., *Zhongguo zhexue sixiang lunji, Qingdaipian* (Taipei: Mutong chubanshe, 1976), pp. 229–240, esp. p. 238.

Hsu thus declared,[29]

> Apart from Confucianism, no Chinese culture can be discussed. Apart from Confucius, no Confucian culture can be discussed. Confucius represents no private opinion but the entire 'historic culture' of China since the legendary emperors Yao and Shun. Without Confucius we have no beacon to illuminate the destiny of China. The destiny of China lies with Chinese culture; the destiny of China lies with Confucius.

Thus, Hsu identified Chinese culture in its entirety with one sole person, Confucius.

For Hsu, such a historical and cultural reflection was not idle speculation but the something that welled up within from heartfelt indignation over the trends of the times. He identified with Croce's dictum, "All history is contemporary history" and went on to push it to the extreme; that is, all historical formation stems from "myself."[30] This is a creative interpretation of Mencius' declaration, "All ten thousand things are there in me,"[31] with Hsu taking "things" to be things cultural and historical.

Hsu's historical writings often consist in biographies of key historical individuals, as Sima Qian's 司馬遷 (145–86 B.C.) historical writings did as well. As we study historical individuals in their concrete traits, situations and behavior, Hsu said, we can see that historical situations are made up of the good within evil, the evil within the good, in all their vivid particularity.[32] History is grounded in historical personage and nothing else.

---

[29] HFKZ (I), p. 279.
[30] YHFK, ZSSL, Preface to Second Edition, p. 3; HFKW (II), p. 2.
[31] *Mencius*, 7A4..
[32] LHSS (III), pp. 422.

Hsu's thoughts about Chinese culture bear one distinctive mark of his philosophy: they express Hsu's personal culture as a recognizably authentic version of Chinese culture.

Consequently, the historic situation of political crisis can be judged by studying the characteristics of key individuals in the situation. For instance, Hsu worried about Deng Xiaoping's lack of acquaintance with the historical spirit of the expression "the world be publicly-shared."[33] Culture is characterized, crystallized, summarized, and made alive in paradigmatic individuals. History is intensely personal; culture is intensely biographical: culture is forged by individual persons.

5:3 The Distinctiveness of Chinese Culture

Cultural impact is earthshaking for individuals; personal impressions in a deep sense, in turn, etch forth culture. We have seen the most intimate reciprocity of Chinese culture and the personal; in fact, the cultural *is* the intensely personal. Culture is not a simple noun, an entity to be objectively bandied about but something lived, thus something adjectival, the "cultural," with performative personal force. This cultural force can now be characterized in four ways:

First, the cultural consists in the historical and the situational, crystallized in the biographical. By the biographical is meant that the situational-historical ambience in which personal life is lived significantly, whose meaning is discovered, seen-through, interpreted and shaped by one's situated intuition, one's lived heart-mind. To live humanly is to be culturally oriented.

Second, if "culture" is taken as a repository of cultural forces, this culture interacts with individuals and depends for its formation

---

[33] HFKZ (II), PP. 208-16.

on such interaction. An individual in turn is a particular projectory of biographical history unified significantly by culture, so much so that when culture collapses individuals have to rise up to reconstruct it. There is a reciprocal shaping, a mutual constitutive molding, between culture and individuals.

Third, we saw in the above a particular reflective individual, Hsu Fu-kuan, who, in his times of personal crisis, forged his version of triune Chinese culture to regain his own personal integrity. The result was Chinese culture modernized, with its focus redefined and sharpened. This happened because Hsu put new emphases on key ideas of Confucianism, thereby proffering a novel configuration of traditional Chinese culture.

Finally, if the *repository* of the cultural "culture" were to be taken as the concrete universal, an unexpected vista opens. The cultural universal in China exerts direct impact on daily life, on the integration or disintegration of individual lives. Conversely, reflective, private, existential living has an immediate formative bearing on the cultural universal. To act and think responsibly for oneself is *eo ipso* to bear responsibility for the whole culture.

The traditional conundrum in the West of how to relate the universal to the concrete is matter-of-factly resolved in China. In China, culture is the meaning-matrix of all our activities, and to solve problems of culture is the basic first step to solving problems in politics, economics, education and other areas.[34]

Thus, we see in Chinese culture a novel existential blend, a cultural chasm between the individual and the communal whole, the particular and universal form, but not between the part and the whole. This cultural chasm opened routinely in Chinese history,

---

[34] See Appendix, pp. 154–156, below

and has found its pathetic expressions in cultural crises, which are personal crises, as in the person of Hsu Fu-kuan.

It is in this situational, biographical sense that Chinese culture is peculiarly existential and Chinese people are peculiarly cultural. Chinese culture is as much shaped by reflective and often tragic individuals in their daily lives as the Chinese people are integrated meaningfully or disintegrated pathetically with the ups and downs of their culture. Culture and humanity are in reciprocal interaction, shaping each other to an extent rarely seen in other civilizations.

Appendix

That culture provides people meaning-matrices for living is shown in intellectuals at junctures of sociopolitical crisis. We here consider four prominent examples—Liang, Chen, Hsu, and Chien.

As early as 1921, Liang Sou-ming said,[35]

> What makes a particular cohesive sort of people today is entirely the result of its culture from its past. The West owes its peculiar qualities today to its culture. So does India; so does China, and nothing else.

In 1935 he elaborated on this point, saying,[36]

> Political problems and economic ones cannot but come together; to solve one sort of problem we must solve the other sort as well. We all know it. In fact, it is self-evident that, for China to get out of political problems or economic ones, we cannot do so apart from solving cultural problems. For, since all problems arise out of the

---

[35] Liang Sou-ming, *Dongxi wenhua jiqi zhexüe* (Taipei: Hongqiao Bookstore, 1957), p. 204.

[36] Liang Sou-ming, *Zhaohua* (Taipei: Longtian chubanshe, 1979), p. 144.

common background of culture, their solutions depend on nothing other than solutions of problems of culture. Solutions of all Chinese problems, without a doubt, must contain new cultural elements and must be determined by the cultural history of China.

And again, in summing up his view, he said,[37]

> The failure of China is her failure in culture; the victory of the West is naturally their victory in culture.

Chen Hsu-ching was another intellectual who worried about the future of China. Although his view on the problem of cultures in China and the West differed entirely from that of Liang, he also claimed,[38]

> The China problem is basically the problem of its entire culture. To refashion Chinese politics, economics, education and so on, we must begin with the basics; we must begin reconstructing our culture. Thus, we must think together on the topic, 'the future of Chinese culture,' in order to discover the true future of China.

Hsu Fu-kuan inherited this legacy of "China problems as problems of Chinese culture," emphasizing that the problems of culture are not just intellectual games but concern the very survival of peoples, nations, the world.[39]

---

[37] Liang Sou-ming, *Zhongguo minzhu jiqiu yundong zhi zuihou juewu* (Taipei, n. d.) p. 86.

[38] Chen Xujing, "Zhongguo wenhua zhi culu," in Lo Congqu ed., *Cong xihua dao xiandaihua* (Beijing: Beijing daxue chubanshe, 1990), p. 370.

[39] ZSSL, p. 261.

For his part, Chien Mu said in 1952,[40]

> All problems stem from the problems of culture; all sorts of problems can be solved by solving the problems of culture. This declaration served as the guiding principle in all of his subsequent writings. Each of these four intellectuals exhibits dramatically the persistent fact that culture is the meaning-matrix, the universal in terms of which we orient ourselves in concrete living.

---

[40] Chien Mu, *Wenhuaxue dayi* (Taipei: Zhengzhong shujü, 1952), p. 2..

Appendix

Abbreviations Of Hsu Fu-Kuan's Works

ZRL:	*Zhongguo jenxinglun shi*, Taipei: Taiwan Commercial Press;
ZSSL:	*Zhongguo sixiang shi lunji*, Taipei: Taiwan xuesheng shuju, 1967;
ZSSL (II):	*Zhongguo sixiang shi lunji: xupian*, Taipei: Shibao chuban gongsi, 1982;
ZWL:	*Zhongguo wenxue lunji*, Taipei: Taiwan xuesheng shuju, 1974;
ZWL (II):	*Chung-kuo wenxue lunji: xupian*, Taipei: Taiwan xuesheng shuju, 1981;
ZYJ:	*Zhongguo yishu jingshen*, Taipei: Taiwan xuesheng shuju, 1984;
HFKZ:	*Hsu Fu-kuan zawenji*, Four vols., Taipei: Shibao chuban gongsi, 1980;
HFKZ (II):	*Hsu Fu-kuan zawenji: xuji*, Taipei: Shibao chuban gongsi, 1981;
HFKW:	*Hsu Fu-kuan wenlu*, Four Volumes, Taipei: Huanyu shuju, 1971;
HFKWC:	*Hsu Fu-kuan wencun*, Taipei: Taiwan xuesheng shuju, 1991;
XYZ:	*Xueshu yu zhengzhi zhi jian*, Taipei: Taiwan xuesheng shujü, 1980;
RZYM:	*Rujia zhengzhi sixiang yu minzhu ziyu renquan*, Taipei: Bashi Niandai chubanshe, 1979; Taiwan xuesheng shuju, 1988;
LHSS(I):	*Liang-Han sixiang shi: juanyi*, Taipei: Taiwan xuehsheng shuju, 1974 (previously published as *Zhou Qin Han zhengzhi shehui zhi yanzhe*, from Hong Kong: Xinya Yanjiusuo, 1972);

LHSS(II): *Liang-Han sixiang shi: juaner*, Taipei: Taiwan xuesheng shuju, 1976;

LHSS(III): *Liang-Han sixiang shi: juansan*, Taipei: Taiwan xuesheng shuju, 1979.

Part 2

Prospect

6
The Development of Taiwanese Consciousness: Retrospect and Prospect

6:1 Introduction

A noteworthy phenomenon in Taiwan society after the lifting of martial law in July of 1987 was the sudden volcanic eruption of "Taiwanese Consciousness." Its formation and development is an important theme in the intellectual history of Taiwan. "Taiwanese consciousness" here refers to the Taiwanese people's characteristic spirit and tone of sentiment[1] in their struggle for self-identity, as exhibited in their quest to form a sense of whom the "Taiwanese people" are, and indeed what "Taiwan" itself is. To trace the development and metamorphoses of Taiwanese consciousness is a complex and challenging project.

In the following, we shall outline this development process and offer suggestions on its future. We shall proceed as follows: after this introduction, we analyze (in section 6:2) the four stages of the development of Taiwanese consciousness. In section 6:3, we indicate the persistent generic trait of this consciousness as "protest". In section, 6:4, we offer suggestions on what route "Taiwan Consciousness" should take in the twenty-first century.

6:2 Stages of Development of "Taiwanese Consciousness"

"Taiwan Consciousness" is a widespread and most complex phenomenon. Initially, the consciousness differed among people according to differences in social, political and economic strata. The ruling elite class during the Japanese occupation had one sort

---

[1] The *Oxford English Dictionary* defines "ethos" as "the characteristic spirit, prevalent tone of sentiment, of a people or community; the 'genius' of an institution or system." I adopt "Taiwanese consciousness" in this essay to emphasize the conscious dimension of the Taiwanese "ethos".

of consciousness about Taiwan, while the classes of the common people exhibited others. The capitalists in the post-war era have a Taiwanese consciousness that is distinct from that of the proletarian class. Although the various contents of Taiwanese consciousness share a lingering nostalgia for the Taiwan soil, the consciousness itself is far richer and more complex than mere nostalgia.

We can discern four main stages in the development of Taiwanese consciousness. (6:2:1.) In the Ming (1368-1644) and Qing (1644-1911) dynasties, the Taiwanese had consciousness only of the local districts in Mainland China whence their people originated. Hence, they had "Zhangzhou 漳州 consciousness," "Quanzhou 泉州 consciousness," "Minnan 閩南 consciousness," or "Kejia 客家 consciousness." (6:2:2.) After the Japanese occupied Taiwan, "Taiwanese Consciousness" arose as a collective awareness[2] of an occupied people. This consciousness, which lasted from 1895 to 1945, was in essence ethnic and social status awareness. (6:2:3.) After the post-war Retrocession of Taiwan in 1945, the Taiwanese were keenly aware of themselves as people of "this province". This sense of "provincial consciousness" was heighten- ed by the bloody 228 Incident of 1947, when they protested against the Kuomintang, the ruling party whose constituents were mostly people from Mainland China. (6:2:4.) After the abrogation of martial law in 1987, Taiwan embarked on the road to democracy. Under the slogan, "New Taiwanese," which represents a new mode of thinking, the people's self-consciousness emerged as a form of protest against Mainland China as the PRC authority applied pressure to Taiwan in various ways. We will proceed to trace this history of Taiwanese consciousness as protest.

The Ming-Qing Period

Through the Ming dynasty (ruled Taiwan 1661-1683) and into

---

[2] I shall use "consciousness" and "awareness" interchangeably.

the Qing dynasty (ruled Taiwan 1683-1895), up to the mid- nineteenth century, the Chinese migrants to Taiwan hailing from Guangdong and Fujian provinces spontaneously expressed their nostalgic sentiment by identifying themselves as, "we the Zhangzhou 漳州 People" or "we the Quanzhou 泉州 People", and identified one another in those terms.

This form of local consciousness involved two factors. One, the Chinese immigrants from different provinces settled in different parts of Taiwan. Two, this was largely due to their language differences. Differences in language and locality contributed to forming their sense of local identity and self-consciousness.

People from the coastal provinces of Guangdong and Fujian had been migrating to Taiwan. The rate of migration picked up when the Dutch encouraged it for agricultural development in the 1630s. By 1650, there were 25 to 30 thousand Chinese families in Taiwan, about 100,000 people in all.[3] The migrants were predominantly fishermen, traders, farmers and hunters.[4] After coming to Taiwan, they lived in separate localities. A document from the period[5] claims that equal numbers of Chinese immigrants from Guangdong (called "Kejiaren 客家人") and Fujian provinces (called "Minnanren 閩南人") occupied southern Taiwan while more Kejia villages occupied the regions north of Touliu (斗六). Generally speaking, Minnan people came over first to occupy the fertile flatlands of Taiwan, while Kejia people, braving risks, came later to inhabit the mountainous regions, to till such areas as the disease-infested downstream of the Tamsui River and the mountainous region north of Pan-hsien (Changhua today). Besides these

---

[3] Cf. Kuo Shui-tan, "Heren jutai shiqi di Zhongguo yimin," *Taiwan Wenxian*, Vol. 10, No. 4 (1959), pp. 11-46, esp. 20.

[4] *Op. cit.*, p. 21.

[5] *Fukien Tongzhi Taiwan Fu: Taiwan wenxuan congkan*, 84 zhong (1960), Vol. 1, No. 19, "Fengsu (Customs)," p. 208. This information is quoted from *Chong cuan Fujian Tongzhi*, juan 58, "Chiayi hsien (Chiayi Prefecture)".

historical circumstances, another important factor leading Kejia from Guangdong to settle in the northern mountains was their peculiar environment and lifestyle back in Mainland China.[6]

Accordingly, peoples from various parts of China settled in different parts of Taiwan, where they fostered "Kejia consciousness," "Zhangzhou-consciousness," "Quanzhou-consciousness," etc., respectively.

Besides differences between earlier and later migrations and the special mountain based lifestyle of Guangdong Kejia people, another factor for separate habitations and different identities among Chinese immigrants in Taiwan was language and dialect differences. In 1903 (that is, Meiji 明治 36, Guangxu 光緒 29), the Japanese colonial government undertook an exhaustive census of the Taiwanese, broken down according to the languages they spoke. 1,200,000 people spoke the Zhangzhou dialect; 1,100,000 people spoke the Quanzhou dialect; 100,000 spoke the Ko-chia dialect; while 40,000 people spoke other Chinese dialects.[7] The names of localities often reflected the respective languages spoken there.[8] Thus, people who spoke the same dialect sought to gather into a community and form a common group consciousness.

How did such group consciousness in common ancestral origin, language and habitation concretely express itself?[9] There

---

[6] Cf. Hung Li-wan, "Qingdai Taiwan difang fuke guanxi chutan—jian yi Ching-shui pingyuan Sanshan Guowang Miao zhi xingshuai weili," in *Taiwan Wenxian*, Vol. 41, No. 2, June 1990) pp. 63-93; Shih Tien-fu, "Qingdai zaiji Taiwanren di ziji fenbu yu yuanxiang shenghuo fangshi," Taipei: National Taiwan Normal University, Geography Department, 1987; Lien Wen-hsi, "Kejia zhi nanqian dongyi ji qi taidi liubu—jian lunqi kaito fendou jingshen," *Taiwan Wenxian*, Vol. 23, No. 4, pp. 1-23.

[7] Chen Han-kuang, "Riju shidai Taiwan Hanzu siji diaocha," *Taiwan Wenxian*, op. cit., Vol. 23, No. 1 (1972), pp. 85-104, esp. 85.

[8] Chen Kuo-chang, "Cong diming keyi bianbie Quan-Zhang yuqun di fenbu—yi Taiwan diming weili," *Dili Jiaoyu* (Geography Education, Vol. 24, Taipei: Taiwan Normal University, 1998), pp. 1-4.

[9] The most detailed investigation of the ancestral origins of Taiwanese in the Japa-

were two obvious forms of concrete manifestation: group fights and community religions.

Group consciousness in terms of family and ancestral origin manifested themselves in bloody group fights that were fairly common in the early days of Taiwan. In a touching depiction of a fierce conflict over a trivial difference between two families, people killed one another *en masse* under such banners as *"Quan Xing"* (泉興, Quans Arise!) and *"Xing Zhang Mie Quan"* (興漳滅泉, Changs Arise! Crush the Quans!)[10] Upon meeting a stranger, people used not to ask his name or address but merely asked where and which family lineage he was from in Mainland China. Upon ascertaining that he was from the same place and family, they would honor one another as blood kinsfolk. If different, they would call each other *"Gui Quan* (貴泉, honorable Quan)" or *"Gui Zhang* (貴漳, honorable Zhang)."[11] In fact, this sort of group-ancestral consciousness invited a writer's lament on how immigrants from one homeland to those from another homeland could so discriminate against each other.[12] There was yet to be a common unified "Taiwanese Consciousness".

The local group consciousness was also reflected in local community religion. Temples were built wherever people resided, according to lineage, to venerate their respective ancestors. The temeples were named variously, "Baosheng Dadi Miao 保生大帝廟," "Dadao Gong Miao 大道公廟," "Zhenjün Miao 真君廟," "Kaishan Tang 開山堂," "Ciji Gong 慈濟宮," and so on.[13] Some

---

nese occupation era is perhaps *Taiwan zaiji Han minzu xiangguanbie diaocha* compiled by the Japanese colonial government in Taiwan in 1928 (Showa 3). Chen Han-kuang has a report on this document, 1972, *op. cit.*, p. 104.

[10] *Taiwan Zaifangce*, 1:1, in *Taiwan Wenxian congkan* 55 zhong (Taipei: Taiwan Yinhang , 1959), pp. 35-36.

[11] *Op. cit.*, pp. 37-38.

[12] *Tamsui Tingzhi*, juan 19 shang, pp. 417-418.

[13] "Ssu Yu Chih" in *Chong xiu Taiwan xian zhi*, jüan 6, pp. 179-180.

anthropologists regard this sort of group consciousness centered on familial-religious awareness as nearly unique to Taiwan.[14]

The rises and falls of those temples went followed the fortunes of their worshippers. A clear example is Sanshan Guowang (三山國王) temple of Kejia people. Historians have traced the vicissitudes of relationships between Minnan people from Fujian Province and Kejia people from Guangdong, by tracing the ups and downs of the Sanshan Guowang Temple in Hsinchuang, Taipei County. This temple symbolized the zenith of group consciousness among the Chaozhou (潮洲) people of the Kejia group, and the height of their conflict with the Minnan people from Fujian Province.

After their long struggle from the later years of the Qianlong, through Jiaqing and Daoguang periods in the Qing Dynasty, the Kejia people lost their foothold in the region and moved out. At once, the number of temple worshippers dropped radically and the temple became decrepit and finally was burned to the ground.[15]

Research on the Sanshan Guowang temples in the Chingshui prairie, Taichung County, has led to similar conclusions. The two Sanshan Guowang temples on the prairie had moved with their worshippers to the Tungshih (東勢) and Fengyüan (豐原) regions, where temple prosperity declined along with that the worshippers because of the influx of Fukienese immigrants who set up their Baoan Gong (保安宮) at Shalu (沙鹿) and Niu Ma Tou (牛罵頭).[16] These facts suffice to show the correlation between religious rituals and local clan consciousness.

---

[14] Hsu Chia-ming, "Jisi Quan zhi yu ju Tai hanren di shehui di dute xing," *Zhonghua Wenhua fuxing yuekan*, 11:6 (June 1978), pp. 59-68.

[15] Yin Chang-yi, "Minyue yimin di xiehe yu duili—yi keshu Chaozhouren kaifa Taipei yiji Hsinchuang Sanshan Guowang Miao di xingshuai shi wei zhongxin sozo di yanjiu," *Taipei Wenxian*, Vol. 74 (December 1985), pp. 1-27, esp. 23.

[16] Hung Li-wan, *op. cit.*, p. 79.

Such "clan-group consciousness," based on ancestral origin, gradually decreased from the 1860s on. Originally, clan consciousness characterized Taiwan as an immigrant society. From the 1860s, people were gradually assimilated into Taiwan as their native society. Fresh from Mainland China, the immigrants naturally reconstructed an extension of their old society in the Mainland.[17] This "immigrant society" based on ancestral land, clan and family gradually changed into the society based on the "forefathers" who first settled there.[18]

The rise and fall of these "clan fights" can serve as an index to broader societal change. There was a high frequency of these fights from the Chu Yi-kuei 朱一貴 Incident (1721, Kangxi 60) through the 1860s (Tongzhi years). During the peak period of 93 years (1768-1860), they broke out about once every three years. Their frequency diminished gradually after that and from the 1870s no more fights under the banners of families and clans broke out.[19] The disappearance of clan fights indicates that people in Taiwan from the 1870s had begun to identify themselves with Taiwan as a whole. This formation of Taiwanese consciousness was accelerated by the Japanese occupation, to which we now turn our attention.

Japanese Occupation: 1895-1945

The cession of Taiwan to Japan in 1895 introduced a twist in the formation of Taiwanese consciousness. Japanese colonial rule nullified clan differences among the residents of Taiwan, who all became third-rate exploited people under the Japanese. As a consequence, Taiwanese consciousness took on more generalized eth-

---

[17] Chen Chi-nan, *Chuantong zhidu yu shehui yishi di jiegou—Lishi yu renleixue di tanso* (Taipei: Unchen wenhua shiye gongsi, 1998) pp. 159-203, esp. 172.

[18] Chen Chi-nan, *Taiwan di chuantong Zhongguo shehui* (Taipei: Unchen wenhua shiye gongsi, 1987), p. 125.

[19] Chen Chi-nan, *op. cit.*, pp. 95-97.

nic and class expressions.

Taiwanese Consciousness as Ethnic Consciousness: Since the ruler-ruled distinction during the Japanese occupation established an ethnic line of demarcation between the Japanese and the Taiwanese, Taiwanese consciousness took on ethnic connotations.

This ethnic awareness was expressed most typically in cultural activities, the most conspicuous of which were "Hanwen Shufang (漢文書房, Chinese Literary Institutes)" and "Shishe (詩社, Poetry Clubs)", which were set up in protest against the shrewd Japanese policy of linguistic enculturation.

Soon after the turmoil of cession, the number of Shufangs dropped by one half. They rebounded gradually because the Taiwanese intelligentsia was unyielding to Japanese pressure to speak Japanese and educate the young in Japanese culture. In March of 1897, Taiwan had 1,224 Shufangs with 19,022 students; by March of 1898 the number had increased to 1,707 with 29,941 students, vastly outnumbering the official "Kokugo Denshusho (國語傳習所, National Language Education Institutes)."[20]

Having failed to abrogate Shufangs, the Japanese rulers drafted a plan to "improve" on them, by setting up a "scholarship" to train the teachers, setting up new courses in Japanese language, dispatching Japanese teachers there and issuing new Japanese textbooks for them. Again, the results did not live up to expectations.[21] This resistance to Japanese cultural encroachments stirred up Taiwanese consciousness as expressed in ethnic-cultural protest against the occupation.

Another channel of ethnic-cultural protest by Taiwanese intelligentsia was the spread of traditional "Shishe (Poetry Clubs)".

---

[20] Chen Chi-nan, *Taiwan di chuantong Zhungguo shehui*, pp. 95-97.
[21] Wu Wen-hsing, *Riju shiqi Taiwan shehui lingdao jieceng zhi yanjiu* (Taipei: Zhengzhong zhuju, 1992), pp. 314-318.

6. The Development of Taiwanese Consciousness   161

About 200 of them were formed to preserve and propagate traditional Chinese culture. Chen Chao-ying 陳昭瑛 found that, after 1911, spurred by Liang Chi-chao's 梁啓超 (Jen-kung 任公, 1873-1929) encouragement, many Taiwanese arose from these Clubs who committed themselves to participating in cultural and political anti-Japanese movements.

Some literary talents appeared, including Lin Hsien-tang 林獻堂 (1881-1956), Lin Yu-chun 林幼春 (1880-1939), Tsai Hui-ju 蔡惠, and later Yeh Jung-chung 葉榮鐘 (1900-1956), Chuang Chui-sheng 莊垂勝 (1897-1962). They all broke free from the oppressive mindset of resignation to express the spirit of modernity and create a new chapter in the history of Chinese classical poetry.[22]

We must mention a member of the poetry clubs, Lianheng 連橫 (a.k.a., Yatang 雅堂, 1878-1936), who published his magnum opus *Taiwan Tongshi* 台灣通史 (General History of Taiwan) in 1935-36 to propagate the traditional Chinese spirit against foreign invasion. By writing about the history of Zheng Cheng-kung's 鄭成功 (1624-1662) exploitation of Taiwan and transplantation of Chinese culture, Mr. Lien consolidated the spirit of ethnic identity among the Taiwanese.[23]

In addition, the Luan Tangs 鸞堂 (phoenix halls) and Ci Tangs 祠堂 (ancestral temples) kept up the folk tradition of religious Confucianism. The Luan Tangs publicized and spread Confucian doctrines via Shinto-like preaching. The Ci Tangs propounded filial piety and family ethics via ancestor worship.[24] This was another way in which ethnic identity and awareness was upheld.

---

[22] Chen Chao-ying, *Taiwan shi xuanzhu* (Taipei: zhengzhong shuju, 1996), p. 6.
[23] Chen Chao-ying, *Taiwan wenxue yu bentuhua yundong* (Taipei: Zhengzhong shuju, 1998), pp. 290-291.
[24] Chen Chao-ying, *Taiwan yu chuantong wenhua* (Taipei: Zhonghua minguo Zhongshan xueshu wenhua jijinghui, 1999).

Under Japanese colonial rule, the Taiwanese intelligentsia, together with the people generally, was intent on preserving Chinese culture. For instance, a renowned medical doctor from the historic city of Tainan, Wu Hsin-jung 吳新榮 (a.k.a. Shih-min 史民, Chen-ying 震瀛, b. November 12, 1906, d. March 27, 1967) said that his father donated his entire life savings from medicine to support cultural enterprises. His father also devoted himself to editing *Tainan Xianzhi* 台南縣誌 (Local Gazetteer of Tainan Prefecture) and *Naying Wenxian* 南瀛文獻 (Documents on the Land in the South Sea). Such efforts were intense expressions of Taiwanese ethnic consciousness.[25] Wu Hsin-jung's own diary (dated April 10, 1940) says that his "mission" in life was to have his bones buried in Mainland China.[26] He named his fifth son (born September 13, 1946) "Hsia Tung 夏統," short for "Ta Hsia Yi-tung 大夏一統 (Unification of Greater China), in the hopes that his son would become the "true son of the world of China."[27]

In fact, Wu Hsin-jung was not exceptional. Nostalgia for homeland China was pervasive among the Taiwanese during the Japanese occupation. A renowned writer, Wu Yung-fu 巫永福, wrote in an essay memorializing the 228 Incident victim, Chen Hsin 陳炘 (1893-1947), "We Taiwanese in Japanese territory are much better off educationally and culturally than those in Mainland China. Yet, our blood-ties with Mainland China distress us when we hear about the continual defeats of the Chinese troops by the Japanese, step by step, battle after battle. The Japanese government tries hard to change our Chinese names into Japanese ones. But, how could we ever bring ourselves to do so? In fact, in the midst of their Japanization Movement, with your strong support we propagate our resolve in the drama, 'Roar Up, China!' in-

---

[25] Wu Hsin-jung, *Wu Hsin-jung shujian* (Taipei: Yuanjing chubanshe, 1981), pp. 78-79.
[26] *Op. cit., Zhanhou*, p. 91.
[27] *Op. cit.*, p. 20.

spired by a Russian writer."[28] Such daring activity in defiance the oppressive government's Japanization Movement wouldn't have been possible if it weren't for the surge of Taiwanese ethnic consciousness.

Taiwanese ethnic consciousness was expressed by a young Taiwanese working as a guide at the International Exposition in Japan itself. Yang Chao-chia 楊肇嘉 (1891-1976) said he felt an unspeakable excitement in meeting some people from Mainland China:[29]

> Many elite visitors from Mainland China, perhaps because they were sympathetic to my circumstances, gave me some impressive encouragement. They kept urging me to find a chance to visit the Mainland, saying, "Fatherland China needs many capable young men like you to come and work for the reconstruction of our nation." These words impressed me deeply. Yes, we are all the posterity of our forefather Huangdi; it is only natural that we should go back home to our Fatherland, and fight for the construction of our nation. It is shameful to work like animals under the yoke of Japan- ese imperialism. It is wretched and pitiful to be slaves of Japanese imperialism. Such self-awareness of ethnic identity intensely surged up in me.

This ethnic sentiment expressed by Yang in Japan reflected the common sentiment in Taiwan at the time. He also said that

---

[28] Wu Yung-fu, "San yue shiyi Ri huannian Chen Hsin xiansheng," *Taiwan Wenyi* (Taiwan Humanitas, Vol. 105 May-June, 1987), p. 83. This English version is a mere gist of the poetic impassioned original. On Chen Hsin's life and murder, see Li Hsiao-feng, *Lin Mao-sheng, Tan Lin he damen di shidai* (Taipei: Yushan chubanshiye gufen yuxian gongsi, 1996).
[29] Yang Chao-chia, *Yang Chao-chia huiyilu* (Taipei: Sanmin shuju, 1977), pp. 100-101.

during the Japanese occupation:[30]

> Many Taiwanese continued to use their own native language and writings. Many Shihshes, secret Shufangs, Yishus 義塾 (private schools) and various musical groups (in Nanguan 南管, Beiguan 北管, etc.) remained active. Even geishas 藝妓 at the taverns sang Chinese songs and tunes, and vowed to sell arts but not themselves, not to be dirtied by the Japanese. The very few geishas who did business with Japanese people were laughed at as, "*huan-a ke* 番仔雞 (*fanzi ji*, barbarous chicken)," and the few ladies who were married to Japanese were looked down upon as "*huan-a jiugan* 番仔酒矸 (*fanzi jiugan*, barbarous liquor bottle)." They had nowhere to live in Taiwan. I examined the census registry and found that the number of Taiwanese ladies who became Japanese wives would not fill both hands.

When a Taiwanese graduate from Tokyo Imperial University, Yang Chi-chuan 楊基銓 (1918-), went to Yilan to be governor there, people came out to welcome him and show their enthusiastic support. Mr. Yang thought that this was,

> because the people of Yilan had such a strong ethnic pride and awareness. With me serving as their governor, they considered that I, a Taiwanese, had now climbed up above the Japanese oppressors, especially above the cruel Japanese policemen. This fact gave them a sense of relief after long years of bottled up hatred, a sense of vengeance after long years of injustice.

When someone in China proposed forming a Japan-China Alliance, the *Taiwan Minbao* 台灣民報 (Taiwan People's Daily) published a special feature article expressing their great hope. This

---

[30] *Op. cit.*, p. 4.

sort of enthusiastic news report demonstrates the intensity of Taiwanese ethnic consciousness at the time.[31]

Notably, Chung Yi-jen 鍾逸人 (1921-), who led the twenty-seventh Troop against government soldiers during the bloody 228 Incident, had also revolted against the Japanese and was imprisoned by them. While in prison he felt special concern for a fellow Taiwanese inmate. He wrote, "When I learned he was a fellow Chinese, I felt empathy and a sense of fraternity with him. I hated those 'tegao' (特高, Japanese Special Agents) who regularly took him out to 'fix' and torture him. I could not get over this hatred for a very long time."[32]

These specific incidents are sufficient to illustrate that the distinctive component of Taiwanese consciousness during the Japanese occupation was an intense ethnic consciousness.

Before concluding this section, we must stress that this ethnic awareness was more a nostalgic yearning for cultural identity than a desire for political identification, with China. The Taiwanese felt their dignity consolidated and their identity confirmed by the great historic *culture* of old Cathay, and by reassuring themselves they were among her glorious heirs, for their ancestral blood was of Cathay. The ethnic pride that kept them going during the Japanese occupation was Chinese and *cultural*, not political.

Eminent Taiwanese writer, Wu Cho-liu 吳濁流 (1900-1976), reminisced about hearing his grandfather's story of Taiwanese resistance against the Japanese,[33]

> How burning the love of our land, and how intense the love of our fatherland, felt by the Taiwanese! Everyone

---

[31] *Taiwan Minbao,* No. 61, July 19, Taisho 14 (1925), p. 8.
[32] Chung Yi-jen, *Xinsuan liushi nian* (Taipei: Ziyou shidai chubanshe, 1988), pp. 136-137.
[33] Wu Cho-liu, *Wuhuaguo* (Taipei: Qianwei chubanshe, 1988), P. 39.

ponders and yearns after the fatherland. One thing is certain about the Taiwanese love of fatherland. They love not the Qing Dynasty, the foreign Manchurian regime, which was not Chinese. They fought the Jiawu (甲午) Campaign, and lost their Manchurian wars with Japan. Thus, Taiwan is now under Japanese occupation, but, someday, Chinese troops will arrive to recover Taiwan for China. Surely, Chinese will rise up to recover their nation. Old folks always dream that some day the Chinese army will come to rescue Taiwan. Deep in the Taiwanese heart lives this beautiful "Han (Cathay)", this great fatherland of ours.

This passionate description illustrates the ethnic pride at the heart of Taiwanese consciousness during the Japanese colonial occupation.

Taiwanese consciousness during the Japanese era also included class-consciousness, the awareness of social status; for the vast majority of the Taiwanese were colonial subjects to the Japanese colonizers. Thus, their ethnic pride was mingled with class awareness.

The most penetrating analysis of this problem remains Yanaihara Tadao's 矢內原忠雄 (1893-1961) *Nihon Teikoku Shugi Ka no Taiwan* 日本帝國主義下台灣 (Taiwan under Japanese Imperialism).[34] Yanaihara claims that, from the very beginning of the occupation, Japan began to turn feudalistic Taiwan into a capitalist society. Eventually a complex situation resulted, a threefold opposition: ruler-colonizer vs. ruled-colonized (political opposition), Japanese vs. Chinese-aborigines (ethnic opposition), and boss-

---

[34] Yanaihara Tadao, tr. Chou Hsien-wen, *Riben diguo zhuyixia zhi Taiwan* (Taipei: Taiwan yinhang jingji yanjiushi, 1995), p. 48. Yanaihara's sympathy with and support of the oppressed moved his student Chu Chao-yang, as narrated in *Chu Chao-yang huiyilu* (Taipei: Qianwei chubanshe, 1995), pp. 30, 38-39.

employer-employed worker (economic-industrial opposition). These three sets of opposition criss-crossed and competed to produce a typical complex colonial society. Generally, the Japanese monopolized the higher positions of government officials, capitalists, and their professional employees, including bankers and company workers. Of course, they received the backing of the powerful official bodies and capitalists in Japan, while most Taiwanese were farmers and laborers. The middle class featured fierce competition between the Japanese and the Taiwanese. In the liberal professions, the two groups co-existed and some Taiwanese wielded considerable influence. Since Japanese occupied all the government and large-scale financier positions, they lorded over Taiwan politics and economy. In labor and farming, Taiwanese people wielded some power over the relatively weaker Japanese. Industrial and commercial middle-class Taiwanese played the leadership role among the farmers and laborers, while middle class Japanese relied on Japanese government officials and financiers for an edge in their competition with the Taiwanese. This was how the complex three-in-one oppositions played out.

Naturally, Taiwanese resistance manifested itself in class struggle. For instance, when the governor of Taiwan Ito Takio 伊藤多喜男 (r. Sept. 1924 to June 1926) proposed that "the objective of Taiwan governance lies in the 3,600,000 islanders," he was confronted with criticisms by the over 100,000 Japanese residents in Taiwan, whose benefits and welfare they feared were in danger of being overlooked. *Taiwan Minbao* 台灣民報 (Taiwan People's Daily) reported on the matter,[35] which was then reported in the Osaka, Japan newspaper, *Asahi Shinbun* 朝日新聞. Both papers pointed out that the Japanese protested in Taiwan in order to protect their privileges and benefits.

Again, in 1924 a member of the Japanese Congress, Kanda

---

[35] *Taiwan Minbao,* Vol. 3, No. 6, February 21, Taisho 14 (1925), p. 7.

Masao 神田正雄, declared his sympathy with the Taiwanese and regarded their anti-Japanese sentiment as based on their fair desire to participate in governance. This was also reported in *Taiwan Minbao*.[36] The same year, the Taipei Business Association (mostly Japanese) petitioned the government to protect the Japanese residents' interests in Taiwan. In turn, *Taiwan Minbao* criticized the petition as a Japanese move to "demand the government to double the existing favors on them with double discrimination and oppression against the Taiwanese."[37] While congratulating the birth of an Imperial grandchild, this newspaper even dared to attach a word of appeal, "We, the newly 'attached' 3,800,000 islanders in Taiwan, although suffering under constant discrimination and alienation."[38]

Each of these instances exemplify how deeply Taiwanese consciousness was colored by ethnic awareness in those days. In sum, Taiwanese consciousness during the Japanese occupation constitutes its second stage of development, manifesting ethnic awareness and class-consciousness because of the Japanese occupation of Taiwan at the time.

After the Taiwan Reclamation: 1945-1987

Taiwan's retrocession to the ROC coincided with the Japanese surrender that ended the Second World War on August 15, 1945. This date also initiated the third stage of Taiwanese Consciousness, now expressed in opposition to Chinese Mainlander consciousness. This opposition has constituted the provincial[39] tension in the drama of Taiwan demography ever since.

This tension originated in Taiwan's 51 years of separation

---

[36] *Taiwan Minbao*, Vol. 2, No. 17, September 11, Taisho 13 (1913), p. 6.
[37] *Taiwan Minbao*, Vol. 3, No. 14, May 11, Taisho 14 (1925), pp. 6-7.
[38] *Taiwan Minbao*, Vol. 3, No. 83, December 13, Taisho 14 (1925), p. 2.
[39] "Provincial" in the double senses of "belonging to provinces" and "narrowly partisan in a province.".

from Mainland (due to Japanese occupation), and more importantly, the Mainlanders' post-retrocession misrule over Taiwan. "Their" misrule resulted in an imbalance of power distribution and bitter disillusionment among the Taiwanese—ironically, after so many years of intense nostalgia toward "China, our homeland" while under Japanese colonial rule.

Historical Separation: Initially, the Taiwanese were happy about the retrocession of Taiwan in 1945; at last they were now liberated from foreign rule to be rejoined with the Motherland in equality and freedom. This enthusiasm was reciprocated by unilateral praises of visitors of various social strata from Mainland China. Such visitors praised the Taiwanese for Taiwan's prosperity and modernity. It was not only visitors from Mainland China who offered their praises; John E. Baker of the JCRR (Sino-American Joint Commission on Rural Reconstruction), in summarizing the agricultural experts' reports on visits to Taiwan, applauded the solid agricultural infrastructure in Taiwan, the high quality of agricultural products, and the intelligence of the farmers.[40] Educational visitors from Fujian Province were much impressed by the kindness and honesty of the Taiwanese people and marveled at the novelty and wonders of the railroad system.[41] A group of visiting journalists from Nanjing, Shanghai, Beijing and Kunming were impressed by the social security in Taiwan, in contrast with the constant civil strife in Mainland China. Hsiao Chien 蕭乾, a renowned writer and journalist for *Dagong Bao* 大公報 at the time, said, "My flight from Shanghai to Taiwan, then from Taiwan to Kuangchou, excited me to an unbearable degree!"[42] He always felt heartfelt admiration of the good socio-economic conditions in

---

[40] John Earl Baker, *JCRR Memoirs, Part II: Formosa*, Chinese-American Economic Cooperation, February 1952, Vol. 1, No. 2, pp. 59-68.
[41] Ko Piao, "Taiwan chulu," *Lianhe Bao*, October 25, 1951 (Minguo 40), p. 8.
[42] Hsiao Chien, *Rensheng chaifang* (Taipei: Lianjing chupan gongsi, 1990; the first edition published in Shanghai, 1948), pp.249-260.

Taiwan.

Sadly, these feelings of joy and excitement on both sides of the Strait were not strong enough to heal Taiwan's fifty years of separation from Mainland China. Walls of separation between the Taiwanese and the Mainlanders, social, political and institutional, were visible everywhere. Overseas "*goa-seng lang* 外省人 (*waishengren*, outsiders)" from Mainland China always had such impressions as the following:[43]

> Often we were shocked to hear such phrases as "Chinese," "Chinese officers," "Chinese army" as people chatter at the theaters, salons, street corners, making us feel as if we were in a foreign land. And yet, clearly, isn't this land part of our Chinese homeland? Don't we see here, as anywhere else in China, pictures of our Founder Sun Yat-sen and our national flags? Don't we hear spoken our familiar Chinese dialect of Fujianese? Why then do we hear tones of foreignness and alienation? We cannot help feel heavy-hearted, some unspeakable irresistible heat wells up inside us to make us gaze intently at such a speaker, to look closely at him to see if he is really our fellow Chinese! Several times I suddenly and unhesitatingly approach such a person to ask, "Please, where is your homeland?" That person, on hearing the question spoken in the same dialect, would respond at once with an air of incredulity, "We are Chinese," upon which all of us would burst into laughter in intimate friendship. When I would explain to him why I had approached him out of the blue, he would turn ashamed and apologized.

This story describes the prevalent situation in Taiwan at the

---

[43] Chang Wang, "Women duoshi Zhongguoren," *Xinsheng Bao*, June 26, 1946, p 6.

time. Another Chinese "outsider" described a like encounter,[44]

> Often our fellow Chinese, that is, Taiwanese, spontaneously will say, "You Chinese" are such and such, "We Taiwanese" are such and such. Once I saw a visitor at an office looking for an "outsider" staff member. The Taiwanese doorman replied, "Mr. A is not here; he went back home" "Where did he go home? Where is his home?" the visitor asked. "He went home to the Republic of China," was the reply. This was of course not a conscious declaration but a spontaneous expression. What they meant by "China" must refer to "mainland or inland" China. What they meant by "Chinese people" must refer to "inlanders" or "fellow Chinese from outside the province of Taiwan."

Such "spontaneous expressions" were effects of the long historical separation of Taiwan from Mainland China.

Unfair distribution of rights and privileges: Unfair distribution of rights and privileges sped up the formation of "Taiwanese consciousness." Behind the unfairness lay a superiority complex among the Chinese mainlanders who had come over. An "outsider" as early as back in 1946, made the following observation:[45]

> Back during the days of occupation the Japanese regarded themselves as "superior people" over the Taiwanese, "the inferior people." This view invited the intensest of hatred among the Taiwanese. Now, surprisingly, some of us from the Mainland dare to adopt this sort of arrogant attitude of superiority toward the Taiwanese! No wonder the Taiwanese intuitively yet mistakenly feel that their "fellow Chinese people" are really

---

[44] Yao Chun, "Jenyurenzhijian ji qida," *Taiwan yuekan*, no.2 (November, 1946), pp. 64-65.
[45] *Ibid.*, the quotation id from page 57.

no different from the former oppressors, a new bunch of brutal "colonizers." Then, they blame this superiority complex on the new government itself.

A Taiwanese writer, Chang Liang-tse 張良澤 (1939-) recalled[46] that when he was a student at Tainan Normal College, all teachers and school officers from the Kuomintang regime prohibited him from asserting he was "Taiwanese." He had to say, "I am Fujianese." But, when scolding him, they would shout, "You Taiwanese!" to damage his self esteem.[47]

Yang Chi-chuan 楊基銓 (1918-) also encountered the outsiders' superiority complex when he was employed by the government.[48]

> Every action of those Mainland Chinese showed that they were the saviors of Taiwan, the legitimate governors of Taiwanese. People from the Mainland were higher in socio-political position than the Taiwanese. And, they were, without exception, corrupt officials who abused their powers and prerogatives for rampant nepotism, courting profits with their positions, entirely disregarding the regulations. Naturally, this anarchic situation bred inefficiency along with arrogance against the Taiwanese, who simply could not stomach it any longer.

This situation pervaded Taiwan after Retrocession, and plunged the Taiwanese into an abyss of despair.

After all, what the Taiwanese had yearned for with the Retrocession was socio-political equality and freedom. Writer cum journalist, Hsiao Chien, on his visit to Taiwan in January of 1947 praised the superiority of Taiwan's industries, military education,

---

[46] Chang Liang-tse, *Sishiwu zhishu* (Taipei: Qianwei chubanshe, 1988), pp.55-56.
[47] Ibid.
[48] Yang Chi-chuan, *Yang Chi-chuan huiyilu*, p.197..

6. The Development of Taiwanese Consciousness 173

welfare system of factories and advanced modern lifestyle. He concluded his praises with, "The Taiwanese rushed their return home to our land with no other request than to be allowed to taste freedom for the first time."[49] He went on to predict that[50]

> Traditional political centralization in the long history China has become China's terminal disease. Such despotism is even harder to practice in a Taiwan that has been derailed [from China] already for 51 years in politics, economics and culture. Is Taiwan going to be the Ireland of China? Or, is she going to turn inward to become a member of the body of China? How it turns out will depend completely on the style of governance in Mainland China from now on. Never forget that the Taiwanese are always comparing yesterdays with today. Never, for a moment, forget that what Taiwanese people want is not a change of the hands that chain them, no matter how much less tight than before.

Sadly, his prediction was fulfilled *negatively*! The "style of governance" of the Mainlanders did plunge the Taiwanese deep into despair. Of the 21 top-ranking officials in the government headed by Chen Yi 陳儀 (1883-18, June, 1950), only one (appointed deputy head of Education Bureau) was a half-Taiwanese, Sung Fei-ju (宋斐如), who had once served as a professor at Beijing University. There were only four Taiwanese[51] among the city mayors and county magistrates.

Moreover, these Mainlander officials were not of equally high caliber. Many were arrogant in their sense of superiority, openly

---

[49] Hsiao Chien, *op. cit.*, p.257.
[50] Hsiao Chien, *op. cit.*, p.259.
[51] These four Taiwanese were Taipei mayors, Huang Chao-chin (黃朝琴) and Yu Mi-chien (游彌堅); magistrate of Hsinchu (新竹) county, Liu Chi-kuang (劉啓光), and magistrate of Kaohsiung (高雄) county, Hsieh Tung-min (謝東閔).

licentious in their nepotism, kickbacks, partisanship, coercion, extortion and hooliganism. The glorious "Recovery" (接收, *jieshou*) of Taiwan turned into its "robbery" (劫收, *jieshou*), pure and simple. These officials were appointed to appropriate fivefold goods: gold, houses, vehicles, actresses and ladies. Confronted with such public lawlessness, the Taiwanese were in a state of shock, habituated as they were to a dignified law-abiding life. Complaints arose everywhere; anger roiled all over Taiwan.[52] This sort of ethnic banditry was bitterly satirized in an essay titled, "*Hoa-ui Sian-sin^n Iu-Tai Ki* 華威先生遊台記 (*Huawei xiansheng yutaiji*, Mr. Hua-wei's Taiwan Travelogue)," published in the newspaper *Gonglun Bao* 公論報, Public Forum.[53] This essay typified the feeling of "Taiwanese consciousness" against Mainlanders at the tme, whom they called derisively "*A-soa^n--a* 阿山仔 (*A-shanzai*), "from the other mountain,"[54] a perfect expression of Taiwanese resentment at the Mainlanders.

In sum, Taiwanese consciousness in the post-Retrocession era was basically resentful provincial awareness, directly derived from unfair distribution of rights and privileges. Later, however, after decades of studying together, working together, and intermarriage this harsh feeling against the "outsiders" dissipated gradually.

Sadly, following the repeal of martial law in 1987, in the very process of democratization in Taiwan, some politicians tried to play on provincial animosity and manipulate those ugly sentiments for votes.

Notably, the Taiwanese mentality in this period has contained a dichotomy: Taiwanese vs. Mainlander, native vs. foreign, ruler vs. the ruled. In the Taiwanese outlook, there were always two opposed social classes, higher and lower and *they* belonged to the

---

[52] Chu Chao-yang, *Chu Chao-yang huiyilu*, pp.92-93.
[53] Ai Na, "Hui-wei xiansheng yutaiji" *Gonglun Bao* Sep., 23, 1948), p.6.
[54] Yao Chun, *op. cit.*, p.58.

lower. This resentful attitude of antagonistic dualism was carried over into the latest period to the present day.

After Repeal of Martial Law: 1987 to the Present

The repeal of the martial law in July of 1987 launched a new age. The lid of the political pressure cooker was lifted to release socio-economic forces, stifled for 40 long years, in demand of political democratization. The democratic tide then surged, displaying a socio-political achievement unprecedented in Chinese history. At the same time, this post-martial law era saw a penetration of socio-economic influences into politics, constituting the rise of "*heijing zhengzhi* 黑金政治 (black money politics)." Such is the fourth stage of development of Taiwanese Consciousness.

This social, economic and political interpenetration served to repeal decades of resentful threefold dichotomy in Taiwanese consciousness. The bygone age of *provincial* protest and resentment officially ended when Lee Teng-hui, a full-blooded Taiwanese, became President of the Republic of China on the historic date of January 13, 1988. As the new Taiwanese consciousness was emerging, it was given a definitive form toward the end of 1998 when President Lee lifted the hand of Taipei mayoral candidate Ma Ying-chiu 馬英九 and shouted to the crowd, "I am the new Taiwanese!"

By now, this new slogan has been an expression of the accepted sentiment for a decade and a half. The expression "New Taiwanese" is significant on two counts. First, the slogan symbolizes an abolition of the ethnic and sociopolitical walls *inside* Taiwan. Now "we Taiwanese" form one body, whether we are aborigine or immigrant of whatever periods in Taiwanese history. Secondly, this expression of a united, integral Taiwan as a whole now stresses its progressive uniqueness over against Mainland China. This new Taiwanese consciousness can be seen as the blossoming of seeds sown by Taiwanese intelligentsia under the Japanese occupation.

The container of this "new consciousness" however still lacks definite content. The slogan is a cipher, devoid of Taiwanese autonomy and integrity, thus it vacillates in meaning with the winds of the various interpretations different people give to it. Let us now expand on these two points.

The "New Taiwanese" includes those who permanently reside on the Island of Taiwan, whether they are aborigines or immigrants—Fujianese (閩南, Minnan), Guangdongese (客家, Kejia), or recent "outsiders" (外省, waisheng)—who came to Taiwan during subsequent periods of history. Now "we", the New Taiwanese People, are united as one, in opposition to a hostile Mainland China.

This "we Taiwan residents are united as one" sentiment resulted from developments of the past five odd decades. On November 2, 1998, during The Eighth Provincial Assembly, the Governor of Taiwan Province, Mr. James Sung (宋楚瑜), said,[55]

> I, Chu-yu, shall never forget my privileged extraordinary five odd years in the past. My distinguished colleagues have accompanied my car, traversing the highways and byways of Taiwan. Our trek covered 240,000 kilometers, long enough to encircle the globe six times. These territories we covered together were no mere natural scenes of "clouds and moon." They were homes to problems of survival, lives and developments of our dear fellow inhabitants throughout this great Province. In order to respond to their pressing needs as quickly as possible, my distinguished colleagues accompanied me to take over 280 helicopter rides, in which we made several hundred surveys, often under the starry skies, the magnificent

---

[55] *Taiwan Shengyihui gongbao* (Wufeng: Taiwan Provincial Assembly, Dec. 1, 1998), Vol.84, no.14, p.1978.

stretches of mountains, rivers and coastlines. When we climbed to the top of our highest mountain, Yu Shan, we were breathless, stunned, at the indescribable beauties and magnificence of mountains after mountains, streams after streams! I, Chu-yu, was utterly moved beyond description.

Mr. Sung was born in Hunan Province and is an "outsider." However politically colored and loaded this speech may be, we can discern a crucial meaning in it, that we all have gradually melted into a single body after long years of living and working together on this island. This fact of Taiwan as a "melting pot" remains valid, irrespective of where we are from, whether we are native or immigrant, or when we came to this island, whether a long time ago or just recently.

This shared feeling of unity has been strengthened by the continual pressures in the international arena exerted by the Communist regime on the Mainland. The sentiment of unity was ramified in the face of Communist "military exercises" during which missiles were fired over the island on the historic occasion of the first popular election of the president in March 1996.[56]

The clearest exposition of the significance of the "New Taiwanese Consciousness" remains that of President Lee in his speech on the eve of the Celebration of Taiwan Retrocession, October 25, 1998, he said,[57]

> Today, all of us who share this island on which to grow and live are the true "masters and lords" here, whether

---

[56] Cf. Jaw-Ling Joanne Chang, "The Taiwan-Strait Crisis of 1995-1996: Causes and Lessons," in Chun-chieh Huang et. al. eds., *Postwar Taiwan in Historical Perspective* (College Park: University Press of Maryland, 1998), pp.280-303 ; James R. Lilley and Chunk Downs eds., *Crisis in the Taiwan Strait* (Washington. D.C.: National Defense University Press, 1998).

[57] Lee Teng-hui, *Taiwan di zhuzhang* (Taipei: Yüanliu chubanshe, 1999), p.264.

we are native aborigines, or of immigrant families here for several hundreds of years, or whether we came over here a few decades ago. We have all equally contributed to the development of Taiwan. And, we equally share responsibilities for the common future of Taiwan. How to transform our shared love of Taiwan and concern for our fellow Taiwanese brethren into concrete struggles to create a greater future development of Taiwan—this is the inescapable mission of every "New Taiwanese" today. It is the critical and urgent responsibility of coming generations to open up a vast beautiful prospect for our Taiwan.

Then, President Lee in his *Taiwan di zhuzhang* 台灣的主張 (Advocacy of Taiwan), published on May 20, 1999, wrote,[58]

For many centuries, Taiwanese expended immeasurable amounts of blood and sweat to melt and unify many dimensions of various cultural traditions. On this multicultural basis, they have opened up the prospect for a New Taiwanese life of liberty, democracy and prosperity. Now, they progress proudly toward the twenty-first century to create the New Taiwan of the New Taiwanese, who include the aborigines, the Chinese immigrants of 400 years ago and the new immigrants of 50 years ago. This is to say, all those who reside in Taiwan, whose hearts are bound to Taiwan and who are willing to sacrifice and struggle for Taiwan, are the "New Taiwanese."

These New Taiwanese People will establish and certify their Taiwan identity, build their own government after their own wishes and desires and create their own society without provincial discrimination.[59] Again, this notion of New Taiwanese produces a

---

[58] Lee Teng-hui, *op.cit.*, p.271.
[59] Lee Teng-hui, *op.cit.*, p.263.

distinctive sense of unity over against Mainland China.

This "new" notion is not really so new. It has its historical roots in the thoughts of Taiwanese intellectuals during the Japanese occupation. As early as the New Year's Day of 1925 (Taisho 14), Huang Cheng-tsung 黃呈聰, in the newspaper *Taiwan Minbao* 台灣民報, called for the creation of a culture that is distinctively Taiwanese. He urged that people should build on the basis of the indigenous culture of Taiwan, absorbing, organizing and integrating all foreign cultures that had come, to create a new culture appropriate to the distinctive environment of Taiwan.[60]

In the same year, Kan Wen-fang 甘文芳 proposed the creation of a "New Taiwan," that is, to rationally reconstruct our society and create a new model of Taiwan politics and society. Above all, we should do away with our typically narrow perspective, lack of historical knowledge and a rigid view of "truth" as unchanging, etc., of old Taiwan, to which people were so accustomed.[61]

Again, during the war time, Wu Hsin-jung 吳新榮 described in his diary entry dated August 1, 1941, a vision: Situated in Taiwan as his Archimedean point, he looked out at Mainland China and the whole world, and proposed a Taiwan Centrism, which claims that Taiwan is at *the* center of Southeast Asia and so deserves to be called the geographical "holy land".[62]

Such views—the "New Taiwan Culture" theory and Taiwan Centrism—supplied the foundation on which today's ideology of "New Taiwanese" is built.

Thus far, we have considered the formation of the idea of the

---

[60] Huang Cheng-tsung, "Yinkai zo chuangshe Taiwan tezhong di wenhua," *Taiwan Minbao*, Vol.3, No.1 (Jan. 1,1925), pp.7-8.
[61] Kan Wen-fang, "Xin Taiwan jiansheshang di wendi he Taiwan qingnian di juewu," *Taiwan Minbao*, No. 67, Aug. 26, 1925, pp. 15-18.
[62] Wu Hsin-jung, *Wu Hsin-jung ziji* (zhanqian), p.112.

"New Taiwanese" and its historical background. But, *what* is it? What does it mean? What are its contents? Confronted with these questions, all we can do is scratch our heads, for the answers are not yet clear. It remains a slogan empty of content, long on significance, short on substance. An empty cipher pointing at a fuzzy no-one-knows-what, it presents a vacuum attracting politicians and economists who compete to read meanings into it. The situation is full of portents and prospects, like a beautiful new baby. Dangers always attend hopes, especially in the lack of integrity of the "new" in "New Taiwanese." The three following examples suffice to show the range of diverse, sometimes conflicting, meanings this notion can take on in the thinking of different Taiwanese today.

As our first example, the *Yuanjian* 遠見 (Long View) magazine had a special issue (September 1994) devoted to the "New Taiwanese" in which many interpretations of what the notion means to various prominent people in Taiwan:[63]

> The New Taiwanese are those who are able to extricate themselves from the intricacies of the "Great Mainland" mentality and thoroughly identify themselves with the destiny of our corporate unity of Taiwan. (Peng Ming-min 彭明敏, 1923-).
>
> The New Taiwanese can step out of Taiwan's tragic history to face the task of reconciliation between the two sides of the Strait and thus positively stop the waste of energies in ethnic infighting (王津平, Wang Chin-ping).
>
> Old Taiwanese are tragic and intensely exclusive. The New Taiwanese are inclusive, ethnically harmonious, identifying themselves as Taiwanese (Ou Hsiu-hsiung 歐秀雄).

---

[63] *Yuanjian* (Taipei: Yuanjie zazhishe, Sep. 15,1994), p.19.

> The New Taiwanese have no provincial complex, no burden of history. They are progressive and prospective (楊泰順, Yang Tai-shun).

Clearly the empty vessel of "New Taiwanese" accommodates opposed views—one view intent on Taiwan Independence, the other intent on uniting with the Mainland Regime.

Our second example is taken from an interpretation offered by the Central Committee for Cultural Affairs, Kuomintang,[64]

> "New Taiwanese" no longer refers to any particular ethnic group. It is a new humanistic view formed by inclusive caring, integrating everyone into a unified whole. And so, with all walls torn down, everyone living on this piece of land will together welcome "New Taiwanese" of the twenty-first century. And, our situation is actually as described above. Everyone here for decades strove with sweat and struggle, throwing themselves into the labor of Taiwan reconstruction, together witnessed its development, and are staying and growing together in this "living corporate body" called Taiwan. This living unified troop would have been impossible were it deprived of a single component, a single member. We here have no single hero, no worship of individuals, for you and I all have a share in this "Taiwan miracle" that is our corporate achievement. Every individual's unique value within this troop should be manifest; everyone should be treated fairly and endowed with equal rights to enjoy all of this. Each of us also has the duty and responsibility to contribute all his or her heart and strength to face our greater common challenges and welcome the dawn of the new century.

---

[64] Huang Li-ching, "Women duoshi Taiwanren," *Zhongyang Zhonghw yuekan*, Vol.32, No.1 (Jan., 1999), pp.8-9.

We note that these statements on the implications of the "New Taiwanese" are mere lists of vague adjectives without much tangible content that leave room for a variety of interpretations.

One such interpretation, our third example, is that of Kao Hsi-chun 高希均,[65]

> The "New" economic people no longer seek orders by low priced statements, rely on the government for protection of business, seek profits by going at the edge of the law, seek production by neglecting environmental pollution, or rely on families for development. Instead, they seek research and development, bring entrepreneurial conscience into full play, thereby fulfilling their social responsibilities, sharing profits with the employees, and creating progress together with the entire society.

We could go on like this almost forever.[66] Enough has been said to show how empty yet fertile this notion of "New Taiwanese" is, how dangerously self-contradictory and yet, it is precisely because of the risks that it is so full of promise.

6:3 Characteristics of Taiwanese Consciousness

Next we seek to pin down the characteristics of Taiwanese consciousness by considering a methodological question. We have considered the history of development of an *idea* "Taiwanese Consciousness" in the frame of stages of *political* development. Is it justifiable to consider the history of an idea in the frame of political history? Our answer is that this approach is illuminating in this specific history of Taiwan, for here an idea that developed within the developing political context. Concretely, the implications of Taiwanese consciousness developed in *protest* against injustice and

---

[65] Kao Hsi-chun, "Xin Taiwanren: Kaixie Taiwan shengmingli di xinjuben", *Zhongyang zhonghe yuekan*, Vol.32, No.1, pp.36-38.
[66] *Zhongyang zhongho yuekan*, Vol.32, No.1, pp.41-45.

oppression in various stages of Taiwan's political history.

In the history of Taiwan, ideas developed in step with the development of politics. Since the Japanese takeover in 1895, Taiwanese consciousness brewed in bitter conflict with its imperial colonial overlords. Both the sharp ethnic confrontation of Japanese vs. Taiwanese and the class confrontation of the governing vs. the governed provoked the formation of Taiwanese consciousness. Consciousness during that period was a brew of both ethnic and class-consciousness.

Yeh Jung-chung 葉榮鐘 (1900-1956), born during the early Japanese occupation, remembered his experience,[67]

> Japanese bullying and insulting discrimination amounted to giving effective chemical fertilizer to the Taiwanese seedlings of fatherland nostalgia and ethnic awareness, so these seedlings would grow up to be unshakably firm and strong.

No further proof is needed ideology of Taiwanese consciousness.

Similarly, the root cause for post-Retrocession consciousness of the Taiwanese to become fiercely provincial was the Mainland officials turning "retrocession" into "robbery." The Taiwanese dreams for fatherland was smashed, as is expressed movingly in the biting first two lines of Yeh Jung-chung's seven-word poem of August 15,1945, "Fifty years of disgrace and shame/This dawn's Retrocession turns bitter, piteous."[68] Then, came the 228 Incident in 1947 and its aftermath, the White Terror of village cleansing (the so-called "qingxiang 清鄉").

In fact, the governing body constituted only a fraction of

---

[67] Yeh Jung-chung, *Hsiaowu dacheji* (Taichung: Zhongyang shuju, 1997), p.24.
[68] Yeh Jung-chung, *op. cit.*, p.212.

"outsiders", and the White Terror victimized "outsiders" as well. Yet, the prevalent historical context was patterned in this way in the popular mind. The series of oppression undertaken by the Mainlander regime created a habitual identification of Taiwanese as the governed under the "outsider" Mainlanders as the governing. Taiwanese consciousness in this period thus was intensely and exclusively provincial.

Entering the stage of post-martial law, Taiwan underwent democratization and redistributed powers and structures. The former "outsider vs. Taiwanese" dichotomy was deconstructed and reconstructed. A small number of Taiwanese became part of the governing body and "outsiders" now formed the "new party" of the governed. Fierce power struggles ensued, creating extreme social unrest throughout Taiwan.

"New Taiwanese Consciousness" was created and developed in the peculiar historical atmosphere of the post-martial law era. It was designed to heal the social wounds sustained by tensions among social groups in which power redistribution occurred. It was because of this aim that the content of "New Taiwanese" was left blank—to let people of various backgrounds add in their various respective favorite ideals.

Surveying the history of Taiwan since 1895, we notice a definite trait threading the notion of "Taiwanese consciousness": Taiwanese Consciousness has consistently been expressed in protest. During the Japanese occupation, Taiwanese Consciousness was a war cry *against* Japanese imperialism and oppressive colonialism. Taiwanese Consciousness in the post-Retrocession era was aimed at the oppressive discrimination and unjust distribution of powers and privileges by the Kuomintang regime. The "New Taiwanese" movement of the post-martial law era pursued both unity among various social-ethnic groups in Taiwan and opposition against unreasonable oppression by the Mainland Communist regime in the international arena.

In sum, Taiwanese Consciousness consistently has been the consciousness of protest, consolidating the internal group unity to form a united front against "our common enemy," who was first the Japanese regime, then the "outsiders," the Kuomintang, and now the Communist regime in Mainland China. As the Japanese regime's oppression against the Taiwanese fostered Taiwanese unity, so today's oppression by the Communist regime against the "entire Taiwanese people as enemy" will inevitably consolidate and foster the growth of "New Taiwanese Consciousness".

Presently, this thread of protest in Taiwanese Consciousness from Taiwan history has something to suggest to Taiwan in the global arena of the twenty-first century: this consciousness shall encourage a united front in the world of politics of difference, not to protest but to critically coexist and dynamically interrelate.

6:4 Conclusion

In concluding, we take a daring plunge into the future of Taiwanese consciousness. We first summarize this consciousness as basically that of "protest". Then, we consider how "protest" can be turned to positive use in the Taiwan Renaissance for the future of Taiwan. Finally, taking our cues from the European Renaissance, we war ourselves of three risks.

Taiwanese consciousness is really a complex cluster of ideas branching out into a wide range of aspects. It can be regarded as the fruit of Taiwanese struggles toward cultural and political identities, whose tense interdependence is extremely complex. Cultural identity can be concretized only in political identity, which must be based on cultural identity.

This is why we viewed the developments and metamorphoses of Taiwanese consciousness in the concrete context of political turmoil and vicissitudes. Early Taiwan had the local Zhang 漳州 consciousness and Quan 泉州 consciousness. Under Japanese colonial occupation, Taiwanese consciousness was basically ethnic—

Chinese self-awareness against the oppressive Yamato (大和, Japanese) imperial race, incorporating the protest consciousness of the ruled against the ruling elite. History repeated itself under the Kuomintang regime, especially when the 228 Incident in 1947 erupted. Taiwanese consciousness became virulent provincial self-awareness against "outsider" Mainlanders who had become the ruling class. After repeal of martial law in August of 1987, a New Taiwanese Consciousness finally emerged to unite all residents in Taiwan, irrespective of provincial origin in protest against the oppressive Communist regime on the Mainland. We can see that the protest element in Taiwanese Consciousness persists. In the twenty-first century, this element should be transformed into something more constructive.

We must go forward and move beyond the level of struggle and protest, to refashion ourselves—for protesters are reactive and negative, enthralled by the target of their revolt. We must liberate ourselves from the confines of anything beyond ourselves. Fortunately, the slogan "New Taiwanese" did not originate solely in protest against the Communist regime on the Mainland: it welled up spontaneously together with the bursting economic and democratic development of Taiwan. Finally, in the history of Taiwan, we see the dawn of liberation toward authentic self-consciousness, a true Taiwanese Consciousness.

The slogan "New Taiwanese" has given us a good cipher for foretelling the future of Taiwanese Consciousness. Now, we must begin to fill it with substance, for the way to Taiwan's future lies in defining the "New Taiwanese" and enriching its contents.

"New Taiwan" is a cipher to Taiwan's new identity, a promise to its future, an empty vessel yet to be filled with some positive contents. But, what contents? Facing the *challenges* posed to proposed contents and their characteristics; how are we to integrate the diversity of interpretations given for this significant slogan? How are we to fuse these proposed contents into an organic matrix that relates and supports these interpretations and allows them to thrive together? Rightly grasped, these contents could be made more complementary and full of promise.

It is important that Taiwan be guided in the right direction so as to give the idea of "New Taiwanese" positive significance. Our very survival and prosperity depend on how this idea fares. This would be the dawn of a Taiwanese Renaissance that would truly initiate what Hu Shih 胡適 (Shih-chih 適之, 1891-1962) envisioned long ago as a "Chinese Renaissance."

However, as with anything so novel and great, but indicated only in a vague slogan, "New Taiwanese" and "Taiwanese Renaissance" are shrouded in risks. Since these expressions are roughly synonymous, we must specify three cautions regarding "Taiwanese Renaissance," keeping "New Taiwanese" in mind.

First, renaissance is rebirth animated by a youthful bravado, a spirit of revolt of which Taiwan today has enough. We must avoid being rebels without a cause, revolting for revolt's sake. We are already in danger of narcissistic self-pity. We may well end up in self-demise unless we rein in our self-preoccupation.

Secondly, the Renaissance in Europe involved revolt against its immediate past, Medieval theism, as it moved toward humanism. However, this revolt took the form of a "return" to Greco-Roman classicism. After all, renaissance is a "rebirth", not a simple new birth. Yet, the Europeans did not just return to the remote past in a fawning imitative way. They struck out in their own novel directions, particularly in the arts, philosophy and religion (the Reformation). They struck out in the realm of *ideas*, which can be explosives to the future. Thus, true revolt lay in creating new ideas in the realm of arts, philosophy and religion, the new ideas, but rooted in the ancient past. The New Taiwanese would do well to heed this *fact*. They must also revolt against their immediate past by *returning* to their primal cultural legacy, and do so in an entirely *novel* manner. They must discard cheap complaints against the *status quo*, return to the primal spring of Confucianism and Taoism, and refashion them by making fresh new thought-experiments in the arts and facing ultimate concerns in philosophy and religion.

Thirdly, "we the New Taiwanese" have two inheritances from the classical past, Grecian as well as Chinese. It behooves us to learn from Greek humanism mathematical objectivity (sciences) and artistic harmony (humanism). We must learn from Chinese humanism to feel harmony with nature and regard ourselves as part and parcel of the great Parent Nature in order to avoid ecological havoc and sociopolitical holocausts. In short, the New Taiwanese Renaissance should be animated with new visions infused with solid human-cosmic harmony, always alert to the pitfalls along the way.

7

"Mutual Historical Understanding": The Basis for Taiwan-Mainland Relations in the Twenty-First Century

7:1 Introduction

Resolving the Taiwan-Mainland relationship is perhaps the most pressing issue in East Asia in new century. This issue makes people across the Taiwan Strait burn with anxiety and uncertainty. It threatens not only the future of Taiwan and China but also the peace and stability of East Asia as a whole for the foreseeable future. Below, we identify an indispensable basis for resolving the pressing issue of how to repair the relationship between Taiwan and the Mainland China in the most positive manner–the basis we identify lies in both parties in the relationship acquiring a heartfelt historical understanding of each side. Each party requires a better understanding of itself as well as of the other. The argument proceeds as follows.

Section One (7:2) presents our basic rationale for the indispensability of historical understanding for the parties in this relationship: genuine human relationships are established for the sake of, at the very least, not hurting either party involved; not hurting either party involved requires knowing each other well and knowing each other well consists in understanding each other's history. We conclude, therefore, that resolving the Taiwan-Mainland relationship will depend on the mutual historical understanding of both parties for its success.

Section Two (7:3) sketches Taiwan's history, in particular, the key factors, which created Taiwan's present situation, most importantly, its sad history of imperial oppression that spawned an acute yearning for independence. In light of this historical understanding of Taiwan, we criticize quick-fix solution number one: a quick unification of Taiwan with the Mainland. This "solution" would hurt Taiwan (by overriding her hard-earned institutions and autonomy), and it would hurt the Mainland (by sowing seeds of disunity), too, because of China's ignorance of the historical reasons for Taiwan being what it is—for example, Taiwan's separation from the Mainland in political relations and in sentiment for 400 years, while always feeling nostalgia for an "ideal" cultural China, a yearning to "return home" and reunite with the cultural spring.

Section Three (7:4) presents historical factors and events in the Mainland, which shaped her present sentiment toward Taiwan: "Taiwan is part of one China." In light of our historical grasp of Mainland China, we go on to criticize quick-fix solution number two: quick independence of Taiwan from Mainland. This "solution" ultimately would hurt Taiwan. Our neglect of the historical and attitudinal links of the Mainland to Taiwan would only rouse increasing the Mainlanders' hostility, which could result in military action against Taiwan. This would be a violent backlash we in Taiwan could ill afford to face.

Section Four (7:5) sums up our basic claims: each side needs to cultivate a thorough understanding of the historical backgrounds of both parties involved–Taiwan and the Mainland–in order to establish a rational basis for resolving our problems sooner rather than later, and finding a way to create the conditions for harmony and mutual understanding. For each side to understand the history of both Taiwan and Mainland is the *sine qua non* for resolving the Taiwan-Mainland relation satisfactorily in the new century.

7:2 The Importance of Historical Understanding

The present section examines two questions: a) Why is the historical understanding of both Taiwan and Mainland China a *sine qua non* for managing their relationship? b) In what respects do the two popular quick-fix proposals for managing this relationship lack this requisite historical understanding?

a) The Taiwan-Mainland relationship is perhaps the most pressing problem facing Taiwan today. Yet, no one comprehends how to resolve it satisfactorily. Considerable heat and dust have been kicked up over this burning emotional issue, yet heat and dust serve only to cloud our vision, so we cannot see the way to appropriate management of the problem. Two quick-fix proposals are currently in vogue in Taiwan: quick unification of Taiwan with the Mainland and quick independence of Taiwan from the Mainland. These proposals produce more heat and frustration than anything because they are impatient, naïve and lack depth of mutual historical understanding.

Before tackling the main issue, we must underscore the importance of our rationale, that is, that any negotiations regarding relationships between any social groups require, as their basis, some mutual historical understanding of all parties involved by all parties involved, in responding to one common objection that is understandable but misguided.

According to this objection, the situation of these two political groups across the Taiwan Strait is uneventful if not peaceful or amicable and this stable condition, in all probability, will persist into the indefinite future. Therefore, the issue taken up in this essay is just an insignificant side issue, for the stability of the *status quo* and its likelihood of continuation are secure and well established.

First, Ralph N. Clough, in his article "Taiwan-PRC Relations," concluded that in the future, after the economic integration of Taiwan with the Mainland and Hong Kong, Taiwan's economic position will continue to improve internationally, while the Taiwanese identity problem will remain unresolved.[1]

Second, The Council of Mainland Affairs, Executive Yüan, ROC, issued on February 2002 a report of a research. The report concerns opinions of Taiwanese people about the relationship between the two political entities across the Taiwan Strait. It says that no less than 77 percent of the population prefers maintaining the status quo at present; only 1.9 percent wants quick unification with the Mainland, while another 5.5 percent want quick Taiwanese independence.[2]

Two important points must be raised against the above objection: one, concerning two dangers of blind complacency with the *status quo* and two, that the objection misses the basic point at issue altogether.

First, maintaining the present "stable" situation without tackling the issue could involve two risks: maintaining the present stable situation amounts to sitting on a time bomb and neglecting to deal with it altogether. This bomb is the crisis of Taiwan identity, which lies dormant but ready to explode and destroy Taiwan at any moment. An explosive does not need to be big to do damage; 3 percent of the people support radical unification while another 3 percent of the people support radical independence; that is already enough to destabilize the entire situation, now in an uneasy state of repose. If popular sentiments about Taiwanese identity are suppressed and finally killed, then Taiwan *qua* Taiwan is gone; there will be nothing more to be said about "peace" bought at the price of authentic existence itself.

Second, this objection misses the basic point raised in this

---

[1] Ralph N. Clough, "Taiwan-PRC Relations," in Robert G. Sutter & William R. Johnson, eds., *Taiwan in World Affairs* (Boulder, Co.: Westview Press, 1994), p. 233.

[2] http://www.mac.gov.tw/mlpolicy/pos/9101/9101.html

essay: any negotiation regarding a human relationship must be conducted on the basis of mutual historical understanding of every party by all parties involved. This condition, *sine qua non,* has to be enforced on risk of death to the integrity of each party involved. Discussing the two extreme positions is an explication of this point; the relative stability of the situation at the present moment is not relevant to the discussion at hand.

Why is it necessary for each party to have a historical understanding of both parties involved in negotiation aiming at a balanced relationship between two parties? In brief, the rationale goes as follows. i) A human relationship should consist of and be consummated in a mutual thriving, in which no party is harmed; ii) in order not to hurt any side, each party must understand all parties involved in the relationship; iii) every human entity, no matter whether personal, political or cultural, bears a historical background and to know a person, an ethnic group, a nation, a culture, one must understand his/her/its history, which forms the distinctive integrity of that human entity. This is especially, urgently, true of the Chinese world; iv) Therefore, a good Taiwan-Mainland relationship will depend, critically, on both parties understanding the histories of both—Taiwan and the Mainland.

Point (iii) requires some elaboration. To understand a person, we must hear the life story of that person; human integrity consists of the human biography, verbalized or not, which a person always bears in his or her heart. This is especially true of China. Her political identity and cultural integrity consist in her history. In China, politics is cultural and the historical accumulation of her political-cultural experience constitutes her integrity.

Let's go slower. A person is a bundle of personal experience held together by memory through time. This is personal identity across time, one's story self-composed and remembered through time. But, such a holding together of memories of experiences across time is, in effect, historical consciousness. Therefore, personal identity is rooted in one's sense of historical consciousness. Since a society is a collective person, a society's identity consists in its possession of historical consciousness.

This is especially true of China, as an ethnic group, a culture, a nation. The Chinese traditionally have upheld the ideal of ordering the world well in politics.[3] This ideal has been a central core of nostalgia in Chinese culture since the time of Confucius and before. Therefore, in China, politics is cultural and culture is often political in tone. This ideal has been tried, failed and tried again and the records of the vicissitudes of these cultural-political experiments are what make up the history of China.[4] No wonder China is a people, a culture, a land with such a strong historical consciousness. The Chinese are steeped in history as their background, source of norms of behavior and political management, and the final arbiter of their lives. History is that in and for which they live, move and hammer out their being.

Standing by a stream, Confucius (551–479 B.C.) sighed, "It passes on just like this, not ceasing day or night!"[5] Chen Zi-ang 陳子昂 (662–702) of the Tang dynasty (618–907) also lamented, "Beholding no ancients,/Beholding no one's coming,/Vainly thinking how vast the skies and broad the earth,/Being alone, I lament, shed tears." Bearing historical sentiments of this sort, the

---

[3] Cf. Robert P. Hymes & Conrad Schirokauer, eds., *Ordering the World: Approaches to State and Society in Sung Dynasty China* (Berkeley: University of California Press, 1993).

[4] It is lamentable that this interpenetration of culture and politics went more toward politicization of culture than toward an enculturation of politics. But, even here, we see the extent to which Chinese politics is close to culture and vice versa. For a recent treatment of this theme, see Frederick P. Brandauer & Chun-chieh Huang, eds., *Imperial Rulership and Cultural Change in Traditional China* (Seattle: University of Washington Press, 1994).

[5] The *Analects*, 9:16.

7. The Basis for Taiwan-Mainland Relations in the Twenty-First Century   195

Chinese, and especially their rulers, have been concerned with their legacy in history, whether in memories of their family and friends, or in the official annals of history. For instance, the emperors were all concerned with building their sepulchers, their "historic achievements" to be recorded by the imperial historians and their posthumous "temple names" (廟號, *miaohao*), such as "Wudi, 武帝" and "Wendi, 文帝" of the Han and so on.

In short, in China, the society, the people, the culture, the politics, all are history. To contact the Chinese and their culture is to contact their history. Their history constitutes their flavor, their atmosphere, in fact, the very existence of China. Chinese history is the very flesh and blood of China. Chinese people do not just live in history; they are their history. China (its people, its politics, its culture) is its history. China is the place where we see most clearly that the human being is *homo historiens* through and through.

Thus, both in a general sense and especially on the Chinese scene, historical consciousness and historical understanding are the *sine qua non* of important decisions in China and it would be unforgivable negligence on the part of those offering proposals for an amicable relationship between Taiwan and the Mainland, to fall short in mutual historical understanding of the two political groups across the Taiwan Strait.

Sadly, in Taiwan today we see two ahistorical quick-fix proposals for resolving the issue of cross strait relations: quick unification with the Mainland China and quick independence from the Mainland China. These two extremes meet, and share some regretable traits.

Adherents of both proposals press for quick solutions from mutually opposed angles, raising the stakes and making the problem increasingly incendiary. Adherents on both sides are impatient about tackling this complex problem.

Adherents on both sides insist on a quick fix. Their increasing insistence in their either/or, all-or-nothing approach is potentially counterproductive; they both would entail destruction of the very purpose for which they proposed their dilemma—sanctity of the state as itself a promotion of the integrity and welfare of the people. Still, both sides are becoming so impatient and ahistorical as to exacerbate and complicate current tensions between Taiwan and Mainland China.

Therefore, instead of siding with either one of these proposals, unification or independence, this essay seeks to undercut the very dilemma and bring out the basis, the common historical universe of their discourse, on and through which Taiwan and Mainland China can come together to hammer out a fresh approach, in the interests of both. This essay offers the proposal that mutual historical understanding can provide a common basis for both parties to meet and hold meaningful deliberatains.

Below, we first outline the relevant histories of Taiwan and Mainland China, then sketch out some risks of neglecting this mutual historical understanding, and finally offer a portrait of potential benefits of basing cross-strait talks and proposals on a historical understanding of both Taiwan and Mainland China.

7:3 Taiwan's Historicity: The Centripetal-Centrifugal Spirit

We are now in a position to look into what history is in China. Because Taiwanese are Chinese in appearance, yet differ in character and sentiment from Mainlanders, we must first consider the history of Taiwan. It is an exciting story, full of pathos and progress: a) outward tumultuous vicissitudes in every sense exhibit; b) an inner tension between yearning for the ideal China and political independence from Mainland which contributes to a youthful dynamism in Taiwan that is the gem, the pride, of modern China; c) the impatient proposal of Taiwan's unification with China, without profound appreciation of this historical, youthful, cosmopolitan virility of Taiwan, would prove a fatal blow to modern China.

a. First, we look at the history of Taiwan as it unfolded from an outward angle. We see that Taiwan has gone through much pathos in tension, frustration, confusion, bloodshed, on the one hand, while making impressive progress in terms of her industrial-economic miracle, international market, cosmopolitan outlook, rapid pragmatic change, on the other. We look at: (i) many political upheavals in Taiwan then; (ii) the attendant cultural ones; (iii) both of which forged the distinctively Taiwanese spirit, the Taiwan historical consciousness in radical inner tension.

i. It is common knowledge that Taiwan has undergone several violent changes in national sovereignty, from being occupied by the Dutch (1624–1662), to Koxinga of Ming times (1661–1683), followed by the Qing Manchus (1683–1895), then the Japanese (1895–1945) and the Nationalists (1945–present).

So many radical political ruptures in so short a period of time could not help but serve as political-cultural baptisms of radically diverse kinds, one after another, usually attended with bloodshed, thereby implanting centrifugal internationalism, progressivism and independence within Taiwanese hearts and minds. At the same time, the frequent political displacements provoked historical forlornness and centripetal yearnings to return home to the cultural roots of the "ideal China."

This oceanic-insular frame of mind, cultural and geographical, is anything b ut static; it is full of contrastive tensions. The basic tension that sets the stage for others—centripetal yearning after the ideal China, centrifugal flight from despotism, including that of Mainland, toward national independence—will be looked into in the next subsection (b).

ii. Another historical factor behind the centripetal-centrifugal tension typical of Taiwanese historical consciousness, the Taiwanese spirit, is the diverse cultural legacies in terms of the social, cultural and industrial "achievements" which the various political regimes bequeathed to Taiwan.

Two dramatic political changes helped to push Taiwan into international modernity. First, from 1895 the Japanese made impressive cultural contributions to Taiwan as they set about modernizing Taiwan. Japanese colonization provided the infrastructure of modernization, such as power companies, factories, railroads, an irrigation system and the Chianan Dam. At the same time, the Japanese helped to organize farm associations, institute household registration, and made primary school education compulsory.

The Nationalists arrived in 1945 and brought about four notable transformations: industrialization and urbanization, expansion of educational opportunity, social mobility and liberation of the female population. The latter three were accomplished in the urban society that resulted from rapid industrialization. The society became modern and people became more international-minded. The Land Reform Acts of the 1950s dramatically changed the economic outlook of the Taiwanese. Traditional soil sanctity and family-centeredness were replaced by mercantilism, individualism, industrialization and competition.[6]

iii. Political and cultural changes uprooted Taiwanese people from the traditional sanctity of their native soil, both agricultural and cultural. Again, this feeling of spiritual forlornness accompanied the mercantile spirit that envigorated and pushed Taiwan's

---

[6] For details of this dramatic modernization in postwar Taiwan, see my "Zhanhou Taiwan di shehui wenhua bianjian: Xianxiang yu jieshi," in *Kaohsiung lishi yu wenhua lunji*, ed. Huang Chun-chieh (Kaohsiung: Chen Chung-ho & Weng Tsu-shan jijinhui, 1994), pp. 1–60.

economy into international modernity.

All those cultural achievements instigated both centripetal longing for historical roots, the ideal China, on the one hand, and centrifugal spurring on forward in brave independence in every sense, on the other. Years of political oppression and cultural discrimination led by various political regimes instilled in Taiwan a historical consciousness that is both centrifugal and centripetal, forever Janus-faced, always in the interim, on the go, dynamic, unstable.

b. The above description of Taiwanese history is incomplete as it stands; if the above description shows how outward political and cultural turbulence provoked a distinctive Taiwan historical consciousness, we need now to reverse the direction and ask what it is that sets the unique Taiwanese tone, style and sentiment on all these breathtaking waves of external changes.

The answer lies in Taiwanese historical consciousness. It lies in the Taiwanese historical spirit,[7] which marks all the historical vicissitudes in Taiwan as typically and distinctively Taiwanese. And, having entertained this question, we now must consider what this Taiwanese historical consciousness means.

The Taiwanese historical consciousness is the spiritual[8] tension between profound nostalgia for the Chinese culture as an ideal amidst the rapid social, industrial and cultural modernization of Taiwan, on the one hand and a vigorous persistent dream for independence, political, social, economic, industrial, from all extra-Taiwanese ties, including those to the Mainland, on the other. This tension has kept Taiwanese people on their toes, always

---

[7] Cf. Note 11 below.
[8] Namely, cognitive, conscious, social, politica, and cultural—not just emotional and psychological.

thrusting toward a future full of possibilities.

Dramatic expressions of this Taiwanese spirit, of this historical consciousness, as tension-filled, appear in the writings of pivotal figures from Taiwan's history up to today. The six following examples will serve to instantiate the centrifugal-centripetal tension felt in Taiwanese historical consciousness. We will then conclude with a recent proclamation of Taiwanese intelligentsia, which cannot be understood apart from this sort of Taiwanese historical consciousness.

i. The first and most straightforward example is Koxinga (國姓爺 Cheng Cheng-kung), the embattled officer and military general of the defeated Ming dynasty. He was forced to flee to Taiwan, where he planned and prepared to launch a military and political-cultural recovery of the Mainland then under the barbarian rule of the Manchurians (1644–1912). To compound the problem, his father capitulated to the Manchurians, and urged him to do likewise.

Consequently, his nostalgic loyalty to the Ming clashed with his filial love and duty. He refused to capitulate and his pain was unspeakable. Trapped on an island, his heart yearned for his homeland and the Ming regime; meanwhile, his love of this island grew, as it provided him a base for gathering his military strength. He felt the ideal and the love and he felt the hatred and independence; these sentiments clashed in his heart, on the island of Taiwan. Thus, Taiwanese historical consciousness as centrifugal-centripetal tension first emerged and crystallized in him.

His ideal was to restore the Ming on the Mainland; his antipathy was to the current barbarian Qing regime, in protest against which he stayed in Taiwan. That tension-filled historical consciousness was the first example recorded in Taiwan's history.

Interestingly, the Ming royalty called Koxinga the Yenping junwang," 延平郡王 (the local ruler who prolongs peace) [presumably of the Ming rule], as a beacon of hope for the Ming. Thus, Koxinga was a crystallization of centripetal force toward an ideal. Yet, at the same time, Chinese immigrants in Taiwan called Koxinga the "Kaishan shengwang", 開山聖王 (the sagacious ruler who opened up the [virgin] mount [of Taiwan]); this name exhibits Koxinga as a crystallization of the centrifugal force of independence.[9]

ii. Our second example is Koxinga's contemporary Shen Kuang-wen 沈光文 who arrived at Kinmen in 1649 from Zhejiang province. He wrote a poem full of nostalgic scenes of Zhejiang, displaying his yearnings without shame.[10] Yet, his contemporary, Hsü Fu-yuan 徐孚遠 wrote a poem in praise of Taiwan as a precious abode, well-suited for evading the oppressive "Qin", an unmistakable allusion to the current despotic regime.[11] Again, this

---

[9] See Yang Ying, *Cong zhengshilu* (Taipei: Taiwan yinhang jingji yanjiushi, 1958), pp.39, 184–185; Chiang Jih-sheng, *Taiwan waiji* (Taipei: Shijie shu-ju, 1979), p. 191.
  The theme of our present concerns—the Taiwan spirit as centripetal yearning after the ideal China combined with a centrifugal going after authenticity—is echoed by the historians' continual debates over whether Cheng Cheng-kung "restored" the Chinese territory called Taiwan, or "opened up the new world of Taiwan" for immigrants from China. In my opinion, he did both. On these debates see, on the latter side, Yang Yun-ping, "Cheng Cheng-kung di lishi diwei kaichuang yu huifu," in Huang Fu-san & Ts'ao Yung-ho, eds., *Taiwanshi luncong* (Taipei: Zhongwen tushu gongsi, 1980), pp. 99–104; on the former side, see Huang Tien-chuan, "Cheng Yen-ping Taiwan shiye," *Op. Cit.*, pp. 105-24, and Sheng Ching-hsin, "Mingzheng di neizhi," *Op. Cit.*, pp. 125–162. In July 1987, an "International Conference on Cheng Ch'eng-kung" was held at The Institute for Taiwan Studies, Amoy University. Cf. Matsuda Yoshiro, "Tei Sei-ko Kenkyu Kokusai Gakujutsu Kaigi ni sanka shite," *Taiwanshih Kenkyu*, no. 7 (February 10, 1989), pp. 9–13.
[10] Lien Heng, *Taiwan shisheng* (Taipei: Taiwan yinhang jingji yanjiushi, 1960), pp. 7–8.
[11] *Taiwan shisheng*, pp. 13–14. For the centripetal-centrifugal sentiment expressed in Taiwan literature during the Ming of Cheng's period, see Chen Chao-ying, "Mingzheng shiqi Taiwan wenxue di minzu xing," *Zhongwai wenxue*, 22:4, 1994, pp. 18–47.

exhibits the centripetal-centrifugal tension experienced among the Taiwanese.

iii. Our third example is Li Chun-sheng 李春生 (1838–1924), a grassroots intellectual, wealthy self-made businessman, successful politician with the Japanese government, a Christian and a Confucian, all rolled into one person. He was sympathetic with both the foreign regime of Japan and popular welfare of Taiwan, with both the foreign Christian faith and the native Confucian ideals and thus, exhibited both centrifugal outreach and centripetal nativism, in politics, in culture, and in religion.[12]

iv. Our fourth example is Yeh Jung-chung 葉榮鐘, a follower of the eminent landlord, Lin Hsien-tang 林獻堂. In his "Memoir" he recorded the following reflection on himself:[13]

> Born in this occupied Taiwan, we have not been in our fatherland to touch its soil, to behold its rivers or its mountains. Without relatives or family there, we have no concretely experienced connection with the fatherland except in our minds, in our ideas, through written history, traditional culture. We feel a centripetal passion, perhaps to be called '*Volksgeist.*' Composed as it is out of written history we have read, this image of the fatherland, the object of our passion, is powerfully provoked by the acts and behaviors of the Japanese [in Taiwan] toward us. Whenever we oppose the Japanese oppression, they tell us, 'If you don't want to be Japanese nationals, return home to China.' Thus the bigger their oppression grows,

---

[12] Cf. Huang Chun-chieh and Ku Wei-ying, "Xinen yu jiuyi zhi jian: Li Chun-sheng di guojia centong zhi fenxi," in Li Ming-hui, ed., *Li Ch'un-sheng di sixiang yu shidai* (Taipei: Zhengzhong zhuju. 1995).

[13] Yeh Tsung-chung, *Dawu xiaoche ji* (Taichung: Zhongyang shuju, 1977), pp. 212–213.

the more fervent our Taiwanese yearnings for the fatherland become.

v. Our fifth example is that well-known writer, Wu Cho-liu 吳濁流 (1900–1978). Wu movingly depicted the fierce independence of the Taiwanese:[14]

> After all, the Taiwanese were produced in the physical and historical environment of Taiwan and so have traits distinctive of Taiwan. We are of course originally of the Han race, who migrated south after being defeated in battles with other races. We came down south to Fujian and Guangdong provinces because we would never capitulate to them. Similarly, political oppression brought us over to Taiwan (and elsewhere) to be overseas Chinese and develop the brave new world of our own freedom. We belong to the elements in the Han that always refused to capitulate to other ethnic groupd; they fought bravely for their independence in the Mainland, then continued their heroic struggles in Taiwan. Later, having been reduced to being nationals under the Qing, they continued their numerous rebellions. Thus the Qing Manchus characterized Taiwan as a terrible place of 'a small rebellion every three years, a great rebellion every five years.'

This passionate feeling for independence stems from an equally passionate love of the ideal China. Accordingly, he confessed poignantly:[15]

> The love of our fatherland, being invisible, is of course a mere idea. But, amazingly, this love forever draws my

---

[14] Wu Cho-liu, *Wuhuaguo* (Taipei: Qianwei chubanshe, 1988), p. 210.
[15] Wu, op. cit., p.40.

heart to it like a magnet. An orphan forever yearns for the parents he has never met, for what his parents are really like is not important to him at all. His heart just aches and pines after them, always thinking that as long as he is held safely in their bosoms he will live a life of warmth and comfort. Instinctively, we also long for our fatherland, pine after it. This is a feeling that only those who have it can understand. Except for those living under colonial foreign rule, there is perhaps no way to understand this feeling.

This "invisible fatherland" is the ideal China. He continued:[16]

Taiwanese have an ardent love of our homeland and our love of the fatherland is as intense. Everyone loves one's own country. But, the Taiwanese love of fatherland is not any love of the Qing Dynasty, which is ruled by the Manchus, not the Chinese. . . . Taiwan may be temporarily under the rule of Japanese but it will surely be brought back home to our fatherland. We Chinese people will surely rise again to build up our own country. Even old folks are dreaming that one day our Chinese army will come and save our Taiwan. At the bottom of Taiwanese hearts exists that beautiful and great fatherland, our 'China.'

Sadly, however, this image of a "beautiful great China" in Wu's Taiwanese heart was broken into pieces during his visit to the Mainland and encounter with the hard actuality there:[17]

After landing there, I understood not a word of what

---

[16] Wu, op. cit., p. 39.
[17] Wu, op. cit., pp. 120–123.

people said. Although it was my fatherland to which I had returned, it felt completely alien and foreign to me. The train to Nanking was packed with people to an appalling degree. Passengers queued up a long snake-like line for tedious inspections. Carrying a Japanese passport, I went to another line; on waving my passport, I was perfunctorily released, without having my luggage inspected. Since Shanghai recently had been bombed, we saw only temporary barracks. The rails were all wide guage, and the coach was wider on the inside than those in Taiwan. Passengers carried huge loads of luggage. All the train stations along the way were temporary ones, displaying recent damage from the bombardments. The scenes were all deserted, forlorn, quite a contrast to prosperous Shanghai, which is a veritable center of exploitation by foreign powers. Tall, luxurious buildings of banks and companies lined up to intimidate pedestrians. The foreigners there were so proud as to provoke indignation.

A visit of no more than three or four days to China convinced me of the miseries of being Chinese. Hoodlums boldly approached us like floods; beggars rushed in like rapid streams—these made wretched scenes of the struggle for survival. In contrast, foreigners were like despots, unspeakably haughty, behaving like they ruled over everything.

Wu was struck by the miserable actuality of China—the widespread devastation wrought by the Japanese invasion, the backwardness of Chinese society, the exploitation of foreign imperialism. This is the stark contrast of two Chinas, the ideal and the actual.

vi. Our final example is our contemporary, Peng Ming-min 彭

明敏. He holds a Ph.D. from France and taught at National Taiwan University until he was expelled from the post and exiled himself abroad. His vivid description of the impact his parents and he as a young boy received when they went together to Mainland China is well worth quoting:[18]

> When I was about five, I was brought to China. I still remember how cold Shanghai was, how long and many were the steps leading up to the Zhongshan Tomb in Nanjing were. This trip gave my parents an opportunity to compare the living conditions of Mainlanders with those of the Taiwanese after several decades of Japanese occupation. They were of course impressed by vastness of China, and felt nostalgia for the soil of our forefathers. In areas of social development, industrialization, education and public sanitation, however, they felt that, compared with conditions in Taiwan, China had much room for improvement.

The last two quotations vividly illustrate the shock felt at the sheer contrast between two Chinas—the actual versus the ideal. The shock was so great that it instigated a centrifugal thrust away from China toward the independent development of Taiwan.

This was what P'eng said on the Taiwanese spirit of independence:[19]

> During our fathers' generation, together with our own, thousands of educated Taiwanese have constantly sup-

---

[18] Peng Ming-min, *Zhiyou di zhiwei* (Taipei: Qianwei chubanshe, 1988), pp. 28–29. For Peng's China experience, see Lai Tse-han, Ramon H. Myers, and Wei Wou, *A Tragic Beginning: The Taiwan Uprising of February 28, 1947* (Stanford, Calif.: Stanford University Press, 1991), pp. 18–23.

[19] Ibid., p. 72.

ported the Taiwan self-government movement. At first, during the First World War they organized such a movement, encouraged as they were by the American President's call to the world to recognize the rights of the minority races in the world. In the 1920s Taiwanese leaders continuously demanded the Japanese government to let the Taiwanese participate in the government and legislature of Taiwan, until in 1935 Japan began to yield. From local elections to local town meetings, the right to vote gradually expanded. In the early part of 1945 the Japanese government finally announced that the Taiwanese were allowed to enjoy the same political rights as those enjoyed by the Japanese.

Peng was perhaps referring to the movement from 1921 to 1934 to petition the establishment of a Taiwan parliamentary system; this was in opposition to the Japanese policy of assimilation.[20] In the same vein, Hung Shih-chu 洪石柱, the founder of the Taiwan Culture Movement during the Japanese occupation, challenged the Nationalist government (in the early years of Retrocession) to set up a legal provincial system of government to replace the temporary and arbitrary military government at the time.[21]

c. (i) In light of above description of Taiwanese historical consciousness, we now understand the pathos and inner spiritual meaning of many struggles for political reforms in Taiwan, as crystallized in the recent epoch-making Declarations jointly issued by a group of young Taiwan intellectuals; ii) The unification proposal can ill afford to bypass this Taiwanese historical spirit to merely force its quick fix onto Taiwan. Doing so would destroy Mainland China as well as Taiwan.

---

[20] Cf. Chou Wan-yao, *Riju shidai yihui shezhi qingyuan yundong* (Taipei: Zhili baoxi wenhua chubanbu, 1988), p. 183.
[21] See Chung Yih-jen, *Xinsuan liushinian*, p.364.

In December 1993, on the eve of a visit to Taiwan by the delegation of the Association for Relations Across the Taiwan Strait in Mainland China, a Declaration of Taiwanese intent was issued jointly by no less than twenty-three organizations including the powerful Taiwanese Professors' Association. The Declaration concludes with:[22]

> The Taiwanese have the right to decide on the future of Taiwan and choose their own respective styles of living. Whatever regime desires to win the support of the Taiwanese must recognize their identity and organize with them a 'community for the Taiwan destiny.

This was a declaration of Taiwanese dignity, identity and subjectivity that occurred for the first time in the history of Taiwan, attended with all historical depths described in the preceding.

This Declaration was not a simple, naive protest out of frustrated individualism against a despotic Leviathan of statism. Such a simple individual-state antagonism, where each side neither can nor cannot do without the other, is a typical picture in the West. But, it is not Taiwanese. Taiwan's centripetal pole in the tension in its historical consciousness—the origin and spirit of the Declaration—bespeaks clearly its yearning after the ideal China to which Taiwanese pine to be reunited. What the individual is to society in Taiwan is more like what the child is to the parents than like what the enemy is to another.

Wu Cho-liu eloquently expressed this sentiment in his suffering-consciousness, "orphan"-mentality, presented in his justly celebrated novel, *The Orphan of Asia*, written during the Japanese occupation, yet suffering from the discrimination of "compatriots"

---

[22] *Zili Wanbao*, December 12, 1993, p. 14.

(同胞, *tongbao*) of Mainland China. Suffering from foreign oppression is understandable; but to suffer because of one's own compatriots is not so easily understood, and may be harder to take. Wu described the experience in this way:[23]

> I used to think that once I stepped out of Taiwan I would be free as a bird out of a cage. I found to my surprise that today's China has the same watchful eyes as the Japanese secret policemen sparkling at us from behind, just as they do in Taiwan. Our fellow Chinese, on their part, look suspiciously on us as Japanese spies dispatched from Taiwan. We dare not expose our identities under these circumstances; we merely say we are from Fujian or from Guangdong, and we use 'potatoes' as a secret password to identify ourselves with those from Taiwan.
>
> Today's Taiwanese people are like orphans deprived of parents. No matter whether in Zhongjing or in the territory of Chiang shadow regime, we are viewed as 'elements differing from us.' They not only refuse to recognize us as Taiwanese, they regard us as spies!

We are here struck by how apt, and how justly renowned, Wu's image of the orphan's mind was in crystallizing the complex historical consciousness of the Taiwanese. Exiled, alone on the lonely island of Taiwan, continually oppressed by aliens, the Taiwanese people came to yearn after their parents in the fatherland of the Mainland. This centripetal yearning for one's historical roots was, however, brutally stymied by the actual China, both backward and as brutal, as aliens. And so, the orphan's quest for parents turned to questing for the ideal China and the orphan took off in a new direction, centrifugally away from the actual China. All this

---

[23] Wu Cho-liu, *Taiwan lianjiao* (Taipei: Qianwei chubanshe, 1988), pp. 104, 223.

was graphically depicted both above and in section *II.b.v.* Thus, the mind of the orphan neatly synthesizes the centripetal-centrifugal tension in Taiwan's historical consciousness.

This orphan in the Taiwanese hearts does grow up and as he grows up, his yearning grows and changes, too. The orphan-sentiment, yearning after the ideal parent of ideal China, was true of the pre-1945 times under foreign rule; now it has undergone a contemporary metamorphosis, following the postwar economic miracles and educational, political reforms. The ideal parent of Chinese culture has changed into the ideal integrity of the self, grown out of orphanhood. One of the energetic young intellectuals puts it this way:[24]

> The Orphan of Asia now knows that his autonomy, his standing on one's own feet means his '*wofen*' consciousness, a resolute rising-up to struggle. The selfdignity of this Asia's Orphan consists not only in new developments in literature and philosophy, but in social, cultural, institutional achievements. And this Orphan's (*wofen*'s) growth and accomplishments imply the establishment of a new China. This Orphan's standing up from childish crawling shall result also in the standing up of all peoples in the world.

The sentiment now has become less forlornly nostalgic and more aggressively assertive, or rather, more nostalgic of the authentic Taiwanese subjectivity and integrity than of the ideal China. The image of the ideal China has been deconstructed, though far from lost, in the form of protest for Taiwanese sovereignty and individual integrity. Its focus is no longer the ideal old China but Taiwan's own ideal subjectivity and integrity, although it still lacks

---

[24] Chiang Nien-feng, *Taiwanren yu xin Zhongguo: gei minjindang di yige xingdong zhexue* (Taichung: author's own publication, 1988), p. 9.

7. The Basis for Taiwan-Mainland Relations in the Twenty-First Century 211

definition. This ignorance generates youthful Taiwan's eternal nostalgia, constituting a new centripetal force in Taiwan's transformed historical consciousness.

ii. The unification proposal, in light of above understanding of Taiwan *qua* Taiwan in its historical spirit, must be tempered with an appreciation of the modern, historical consciousness of its people, expressed elegantly in the recent Declaration for the silent majority. Otherwise, tragic destruction of Taiwan *qua* Taiwan would follow, and the destruction would bring irreparable damage to the Mainland.

Taiwan is anything but marginal to the Mainland, a negligible territory. Taiwan is a gem, the cutting edge of Chinese modernity, as international as Hong Kong and more historically Chinese than Hong Kong, a unique exhibition of Chinese strength to the contemporary world in democratic fervor, international marketing, industrial development, social dynamism and virile cosmopolitanism. In thousands of years of history, China has never been more progressive and prosperous, democratically and internationally self-aware, virile and forward-looking than Taiwan is today.[25]

---

[25] All observers from Mainland China were overwhelmingly impressed by the tremendous prosperity of Taiwan. For Liang Chi-chao's praise of Taiwan in 1911, see Liang Chi-chao, "Yu Taiwan shudu diyi xin," in his *Yinpingshi wenji* (Taipei: Shijie shuju, n. d., juan 4), p. 14. When Chen Yi, the governor of Fujian Province, visited Taiwan in 1935, he was so impressed, especially by the infrastructure in Taiwan constructed by the Japanese, that he invited the Japanese engineers responsible for constructing the Chianan Dam to visit Fujian. See Hurugawa Shozo, *Taiwan o Aishita Nihonjin—Kanan Taishin no Chichi Hatta Yoichi no Shogai* (Matsuyama Shi: Aoyama Tosho, 1989), pp. 260-61.

After World War II, technocrats of the Sino-American Joint Commission on Rural Reconstruction (JCRR) came to Taiwan and praised the socioeconomic situation in rural areas. See *Zhongguo nongcun fuxing lianhe weiyuanhui gongzo baogao* (Taipei: JCRR, 1950), p. 12. For a general discussion on postwar transformation in Taiwan, see chun-chieh Huang et. al. eds., *Postwar Taiwan Experience in Historical Perspective* (College Park: University Press of Maryland, 1998).

To crush this gem in blatant neglect of the Taiwanese spirit as the youthful vitality of China would be to crush the Chinese Treasure Island (*Baodao*), the envy of every Mainlander, the pride of China. If she were to crush the Taiwanese historical spirit, Mainland China would return to the impossible condition of pre-modern poverty in every respect—economically, politically, Industrially and internationally. The ease of destroying Taiwan—after all, it's just a small island-redounds to the lethal gravity of liability to the Mainland. The Mainland could never crush Taiwan's historical spirit without crushing its own forward-looking, modern, futuristic, international self.

7:4 Mainland's Historicity: Zealous Nationalism

This section can be as brief as its theme is simple: (a) the Mainland has nationalistic fervor, provoked by foreign invasions and domestic warfare among warlords, to protect "our own" territories, including Taiwan; (b) without understanding this historical sentiment felt on Mainland, any Taiwanese independence proposal simply will ruin Taiwan.

a. (i) Mainland China in recent years has been an embattled territory, torn apart by internecine and international warfare; (ii) one of the results provoked by these threats to national unity is a strong sentiment of nationalism and: (iii) nationalistic fervor entails zeal to control territories the government claims as theirs; the following provides historical evidence for these points.

i. Anyone familiar with the history of China knows she has been torn apart by continuous violence, from the demise of Qing dynasty until the Tiananmen Square Incident in 1989.

We recall the Boxer Rebellion, the eight Western Powers attacking Peking and the subsequent infamous Hinchou Treaty (1900–1901), followed the Xinhai Revolution of 1911 that finally ended Qing rule. But, from the moment of Sun Yat-sen's inauguration as president of the provisional government of the Republic of China, China was torn apart by endless violence, domestic and international. Yuan Shikai (1859–1916) proclaimed himself emperor and Japan proposed Twenty-One Demands with the intention of invading China (1915), followed by continual domestic warfare, especially from 1917 to 1924, until 1928 when China was officially unified.

But, on July 7, 1937 the Sino-Japanese War broke out, plunging China into misery for eight long years, intensified by additional domestic rivalries, ending in the retrocession of Taiwan from Japan to the Republic of China. The Communist takeover of the Mainland, however, failed to bring stability and concord to Mainland China. The Mainland suffered repeated waves of domestic violence, including the Anti-Right Movement of 1957–1958, the Great Leap Forward Movement of 1958–1960 and the long turmoil of Cultural Revolution of 1966–1976, all culminating in the tragic Tiananmen Square Incident of June 4, 1989. Such is a brief retelling of embattled miseries of Mainland China.

ii. Wartime miseries on the Mainland provoked nationalistic fervor. As early as January 1924, Sun Yat-sen (1886–1925) began his celebrated *Three Peoples' Principles* with a passionate nationalistic appeal:[26]

> The Three People's Principles are the Principles to save our nation. . . . These Principles promote the international prestige of our nation, so as to strengthen our economic and political position in the world, so that our nation can exist vigorously in the world. Therefore, I say,

---

[26] Guofu qüanji, ed., *Zhongguo Kuomintang zhongyangdangshi shiliao biancuan weiyuanhui* (Taipei: Zhonghuaminguo gejie jinian Guofu bainian danchen choubei weiyuanhui, 1965), Vol. 1, p. 2.

our Three People's Principles are the Principles that will save our nation.

At the Ceremony of the Founding of the Peoples' Republic of China, on October 1, 1949, Mao Zedong (1893–1976) opened his speech with, "From today on, the people of China stand up." Their political successes owed to this sort of manipulative incitement of seething nationalistic sentiment at the time.

Among Chinese intellectuals, Chang Chun-mai 張君勱 (Tung-sun, 1887–1969), the great architect of the Constitution of China, urged a Chinese translation of Fichte's (1762–1814) fervent *Speech to the German People—A Summary*. Chang often lectured on the spirit of nationalism, the reexamination of Chinese culture and its future, and related issues.[27] Thus, nationalism rose up out of the ashes of the war miseries felt on the Chinese mainland.

iii. Nationalism breeds protective zeal over territories the government regards as their own. As early as February 8, 1841, Qing Emperor Xüanzong 宣宗 (r. 1841–1850) issued an Edict of advice expressing worries over Taiwan:[28]

> [Many and varied violent incidents came up one after another in Taiwan.] I have dispatched officers with pay, both civil and military, to Taiwan to oversee, manage and pacify the region. It has been several months since then, and there are yet no reports on the outcome; we are much worried. Taiwan is our key strategic area in the Min Ocean region, traditionally much desired by many

---

[27] Cf. Hsueh Hua-yuan, *Minzhu xianzheng yu minzhuzhuyi di bianzheng fazhan* (Taipei: Daohe Publishers, 1993), p. 42.

[28] Yao Ying, "Cun zhi Fuzhou chuoyi Taiwan fuwuzhe," (February 16, 1843), in Hu Chiu-yuan, ed., *Zhongguo dui xifang zhi liehqiang zenshi ziliao huibian* (Taipei: Institute of Modern History, Academia Sinica, 1971), Vol. 1, Book I, p. 308.

barbarian nations. We do hope that our repulses of foreign vessels will ensure there won't be any more maritime invasions.

The governor of Fujian province in the latter half of the nineteenth century, Ting Jih-ch'ang 丁日昌 (?–1882), expressed the same sentiment over Taiwan in his official letter to the imperial court:[29]

[Various nations hold various places in Asia and our country as their respective exclusive ports and enclaves.] Germany alone has no port to harbor its vessels. And so, Germany would desire to take over Taiwan more than other nations.

On skimming through a travelogue to Taiwan written by a friend, an intellectual of the time, Mei Wen-ting 梅文鼎 (Ting-chiu 定九, 1633–1721) lamented in a poem, "[Many foreign nations] already tarry, stoop over and peep at the Southern part of our Ocean; the formation is set ominously."[30] All this shows that from the early days on, people in the Mainland, whether in the imperial court or among discerning commoners, have been concerned about the situation in Taiwan.

b. We must then understand Mainland's historicity—its nationalistic fervor and its protectionism. Protectionistic sensibility naturally breeds defensiveness over even slight indications of foreign influence, especially political or cultural, within their territories. And so those who propose Taiwan independence must be on

---

[29] Ting Jih-chang, "Minfu Ting Jih-chang chuo Xibanya kuishi Taiwan qingxing pien," in *Qing ji waijiao shiliao xuanji* (Taipei: Taiwan yinhang jingji yanjiushi, 1964), pp. 16–17.
[30] Mei Wen-ting, *Jixuetang wenchao*, Woodblock edition collected in the Naikaku Bunko, Japan, n. d., Chuan 4, pp. 5b–7a.

the alert. Their quick fix idea of clean-cut independence from Mainland China, as soon as possible, would prove fatal. This fatality would be two-edged—military and cultural.

i. On the eve of its fulfillment, Taiwan would be destroyed, first, by Mainland's mighty military, due to Mainland China's antipathy toward subversion of its sovereignty, whether domestic or foreign. Taiwan would be crushed in no time upon its declaration of independence. After all, "Taiwan the gem" is but a tiny irritant to the vast Mainland, easy to crush and discard.

ii. More radically, there would be no true Taiwanese remnants, and so not even a trace of hope for its future. Taiwan would be destroyed upon its declaration of independence because it would have thrown out the baby of the ideal China with dirty water of the actual one. Bereft of Chinese cultural legacies, Taiwan would be impoverished at its root.[31] Cut off from the base of its centripetal yearning, Taiwan would have no more subjectivity to treasure, fight for, enrich, develop and invigorate. It would simply drift away reactively, centrifugally, alone and rootless, destined to be lost in a centrifugal who-knows-what. Without deep appreciation of the historical roots of Mainland China, quick Taiwan declaration of independence would bring about the destruction of Taiwan without further ado.

7:5 Historical Understanding: The Hope of the Relationship

We have examined the necessity of mutual historical understanding of both parties in a relationship in order to achieve an amicable, interdependent and mutually thriving relationship.

---

[31] For an elaboration of this point, see Chun-chieh Huang and Kuang-ming Wu, "Taiwan and Confucian Aspiration: Toward the Twenty-First Century," in Stevan Harrell & Chun-chieh Huang, eds., *Cultural Change in Postwar Taiwan* (Boulder, Colo.: Westview Press, 1994), pp. 69–88.

We have shown that personal understanding in a true sense means historical understanding, by delving into what has made Taiwan what it is today and what has made Mainland what it is today—their respective historical experiences. And we have underscored the real risks of not going through this process of arriving at a historical understanding of both parties by both parties. Lack of mutual historical understanding would prove so disastrous as to endanger the existence of both sides.

And, the contrary is true, as well. Negotiators who are sensitive to each other's histories will reap complementarity, mutual satisfaction and thriving in an interdependent manner such that one party's prosperity will contribute to the prosperity of the other. But, how? To understand each other, both parties must communicate and that at a grassroots, people's level, not at an official, governmental level, to ensure a widespread, heart-to-heart understanding. Popular communication should include commercial dealings and negotiations, at both personal and institutional levels. Popular communication should also include cultural exchanges—scholarly, artistic, religious as well as popular. This is how one party can start to recognize the other in a deep personal manner. In short, understanding is needed in human relations and negotiations, history is involved in human understanding, and understanding in historical depth is facilitated by communication on a long-term personal basis. In the human world, patience in communication for historical understanding is the royal road, in fact, the only road, to a successful relationship. The Taiwan-Mainland relationship is no exception.

Epilogue

This book presents the great transformations in postwar Taiwan in production from farming to industry. It has also discussed the extent to which this change has affected changes in social and cultural outlook.

Part One analyzes how the rapid growth in Taiwan's economy after the World War II spurred the rapid change in the mode of production from agrarian hierarchical monism to industrial dynamic pluralism; and how, in turn, the change in production mode brought about changes in the mode of management to egalitarian coordination, with all its sociocultural-political implications.

The agrarian society, which characterized China from time immemorial, has emphasized quiet obedience. With everything regulated from the paternal top, the agraian economy has featured a monarchic centralism and a family submissiveness. However, in postwar Taiwan, industry started to pervade the society and changed everything. Quiet subordination to one central authority, be it a moral-familial center or an emperor, was replaced by mobile coordination among equal powers, be they productive, commercial, managerial or political. These radical changes paved the way for the outburst of "Taiwanese Consciousness," the rise of excessive self-assertiveness in the last decade. As discussed in Part Two, the egocentrism and selfish individualism in present-day Taiwan may lead to the self-destruction of Taiwan in the future.

Now, the question remains: what path will Taiwan take in the twenty-first century? I would like to start from a reflection upon the distinctiveness of the Chinese cultural tradition.

1. Distinctive Themes of Traditional Chinese Culture

Chinese civilization is noted for its age-old agrarian tradition.

Various archeological excavations attest that the cultivation of rice in North and South China started as early as 5000 B.C. Ever since the Neolithic Age, agriculture has permeated every aspect of life, making Chinese culture distinctly agrarian, lacking social mobility and featuring parochialism, extended family system, physiognomy, and the philosophy of harmony between heaven and man.

Because agriculture binds man to the soil, social mobility in China was limited. This, in turn, fostered local consciousness, even parochialism. Agriculture also required intensive labor, and so men placed high value upon the extended family. Since the beginning of the Christian era, this agrarian atmosphere led Chinese political systems toward physiocratic polities at the expense of commerce. The agrarian sentiment in socio-economy also produced the peculiar Chinese philosophy of harmony between heaven (natural or cosmic order) and man (or human order). The agrarian tradition created an agrarian mentality, which was earthbound, physiocratic and harmony-oriented.

Two features resulted from this agrarian mind that deeply affected the Chinese social fabric: (a) monarchic centralization, one-man imperial rule extending to all spheres of life and (b) people's overall attitude of submissiveness, a total embracing of the principle of subordination to authority.

Monarchic centralization, domination of one single force over all areas of culture, especially in the political sphere, was typical of Chinese civilization from as early as in the first millennium B.C.; the imperial order was a reality from the unification of China in 221 B.C. This domination can be seen in two spheres: political interpretation of the Confucian classics and politicization of all cultural areas.

Interpretations of the Confucian classics were permeated with political inputs and authorizations; many passages were read in political terms. A revealing case in point is the scholars' debates over Mencius' radical political thought, which revealed the fusion of political authority and intellectual pursuits. Politicization of intellectual pursuits is a clear indication of widespread permeation of political influence. All pursuits—economic, agricultural, religious and moral—were stripped of autonomy and free development. All spheres of life were subject to the interference of political power.

As a counterpart to the domination of a single authority, Chinese culture was pervaded, among the common folk, with the "principle of subordination" that refers to vertical, hierarchical webs of relationships. Such vertical hierarchy was typically manifested in the fundamental and "dominant kinship relationship" (DKR)—the father-son relationship. Submission to authority in traditional Chinese culture was intimately connected with this subordination principle.

In short, the agrarian tradition produced the imperial order of monarchic centralization and the principle of subordination and submissiveness. All these factors came to define what was traditional Chinese culture.

"Monism" may be the word that best describes this culture. The above two tendencies can be characterized as two features of agrarian monism—the monarchic order being its political monism, submission to authority being its social monism. Both sorts of monism paved the way to economic monism in the agrarian culture, where individuals count for little. This in turn explains how slow and difficult it was for this agrarian Chinese culture to enter the modern world of liberty, equality and individuality.

2. Restructuring of the Way of Life in Postwar Taiwan

After World War II, a great transformation took place in Taiwan; the agrarian mentality was replaced by the "industrial mentality." People bound to the earth in agriculture were "emancipated," or "uprooted," as others may call it, from the land. People were mobilized, and the society became pluralistic.

Many structural changes in Taiwanese society spurred by industrialization resulted in two major cultural shifts—monarchic centralization replaced by pluralistic community and subordination turned into coordination. Notably, such radical cultural, political and structural changes were caused by two factors: (a) change in the mode of production—industrial production replacing agricultural; (b) the spread of education by an increase in number both of schools and of returned students from abroad.

This said, I would like to look into a statistical substantiation of these two factors of change, and then consider the content of this cultural change.

Taiwan in the early 1950s was an agrarian society. The portion of people involved in agricultural population was 52.4 percent in 1952 and the net domestic product devoted to agriculture was 38.3 percent. The foreign exchange reserves Taiwan earned by exporting agricultural products paved the way for the industrial "take-off" from mid-1960s. From the implementation of the Four-Year Economic Plan in 1953, the portion of people involved in agriculture decreased steadily: from 49.8 percent as of 1960 to 45.4 percent as of 1987. Within thirty years, rural Taiwan was transformed into industrial Taiwan in terms of demographic changes. This demographic change was accelerated by the sharp contrast in the growth rates of the agricultural and industrial sectors. During this period, the annual growth rate recorded for agriculture was surpassed by that for industry. Their contrast in growth for the period of 1963–1972 is especially impressive: 18.5 percent for industry as opposed to 4 percent for agriculture.

Following this change in production structure were changes in the NDP, due to industrial production. The importance of agriculture in the NDP in early 1950s outweighed that of industry; since 1963, industrial output has steadily surpassed agricultural output. Accelerated industrialization from the implementation of the Third Four-Year Economic Plan in 1965 successfully turned Taiwan into a "newly industrialized country" (NIC).

During the socioeconomic restructuring in postwar Taiwan, the most noteworthy development has been the rapid growth of the private sector (43.4 percent) of industrial production, which had been lagging behind the public sector (56.6 percent). As Taiwan's economy developed, the private and the public sectors of industrial production became equal in 1958. The share of the private sector reached 79.5 percent in 1977 and 85.6 percent in 1987. The rapid growth of private sector in industry was responsible for the emergence of an unprecedented individual-oriented culture in Taiwan.

In addition to its impressive growth, the private sector in Taiwan exhibited the dynamism that made the "Taiwan Miracle" possible. This dynamism can be seen by a cursory look at the annual growth rates of private versus public industrial production. The annual growth rate of the private sector has been much higher than its public counterpart.

Many explanations may be offered for this. The major contributing factors to the dynamic growth of private industry include the incentives among the people, the greater autonomy in decision making, improved work ethics and so on. In terms of the rapid development of private industries, it may not be too farfetched to say that the major facets of postwar Taiwanese culture, especially dynamism and individualism have contributed immensely to the growth of people's confidence in themselves, as opposed to their previous reliance on the state.

Economic restructuring was not the only agent of cultural change in Taiwan, however. Of equal importance was the development of education. When we look at Taiwan's achievements in education over the past four decades, the most impressive statistic is the reduction in illiteracy from 42.1 percent of the population over the age of six in 1952 to percent in 1987. Moreover, the percentage of those who received secondary education increased from 8.8 in 1952 to 43.3 in 1987. This development has accelerated since the academic year 1968–1969, when the Nine-Year Compulsory Education Act was put into effect.

The increase in the number of schools in Taiwan meant easy access to and rapid spread of education. In 1950–1951 we had only 41.8 schools per 1000 square kilometers; by 1986–1987 we saw 179.51 schools per 1000 square kilometers.

Development in education created better availability of knowledge and wider circulation of information, which accelerated democratization. Further, developments in education in postwar Taiwan made people realize—only to be "disenchanted" with—all sorts of bonds (intellectual, political, legal and economic) in the traditional culture and society. Better educated, people became more eager to seek personal dignity and meaning in their life. Enlightenment has been the seed that yields liberalism, individualism and freedom in Taiwan. Moreover, the intellectual fruits of education in Taiwan were nourished by the return of students from abroad. The government statistics shows that since 1982 the returning Chinese students numbered 1,000 per year; by 1987, the number had increased to 1,920. Today, these students work for the government, industry, business and educational institutions. Not surprisingly, educated abroad, they have become disseminators of Western values, especially democracy, individualism and liberalism.

Having described factors responsible for socioeconomic and educational changes in postwar Taiwan, we can proceed to look into the content of these culture changes.

The radical cultural changes in postwar Taiwan with its rapid industrialization were twofold: a) vanishing of physiocratic mentality and b) flourishing of pluralism and coordination.

If the physiocratic mind goes with farming and if farming disappears when industry arrives on the scene, then we can expect that, as Taiwan industrializes, the vanishing of the physiocratic mentality will be a sure course of change. This change now can be witnessed in Taiwan farmers' attitudes to their own land and profession as we discussed in Chapter three.

With the vanishing of the physiocratic mentality came the flourishing of pluralism and coordination; the change amounted to no less than cultural transformation. Taiwanese culture has been changing from an attitude of introvert collective, past-oriented acceptance to that of extrovert, individualistic, future-oriented mastery.

We witness this cultural trend from monism to pluralism in the emerging social movements, such as the student rallies, political movements and worker demonstrations.

3. Conclusion

In a historical perspective, the prosperity of postwar Taiwan is a spectacle in its own right. In the foregoing pages, we have discussed how the economic "miracle" arose from changes in the modes of production from farming to industrial, and furthermore, how the "miracle" produced a far-reaching cultural change.

After experiencing the great transformation, individualism is currently on the rise in Taiwan. Therefore, it has become necessary to rethink the relationship between individualism and Chinese civilization. Because politics is crucial manifestation of social development, let us look at the future mode of politics in Taiwan.

Three factors affect political stability: production, cultural values and political system. Political stability can be maintained only in the milieu of cultural values supported by an appropriate production dynamism that, in turn, nourishes an appropriate political system. In the past, agriculture produced and supported an agrarian culture that nourished a monolithic and centralized political system for a long time; one central political authority was able to dominate the masses, because they submitted to moral hierarchic authority, thanks to agrarian culture. However, industrialization and education have changed the overall cultural milieu of postwar Taiwan: from subordination to coordination, from submission to an unquestioned authority to enlightened equality among various power units, from paternalistic centralization to capitalistic open society.

In sync with Taiwan's rapid democratization, the cultural-economic mode has shifted radically from monolithic subordination to pluralistic coordination, political stability in twenty-first-century Taiwan is guaranteed on the sole condition that the government changes its administrative style appropriately in accordance with the changing situation. If the government did contribute to economic growth in the past, it has proven itself to be an effective partner in the common project of shaping the future, no more and no less.

The twenty-first century is the time for the politics of partnership. Physiocratic paternalism should disappear with agrarian hierarchy, which has already given way to industrial coordination. The government is no longer the indispensable imperial father but one of the partners, working hand-in-hand with farmers, corporations and workers, serving the common cause of coordinated prosperity. In short, now is the crucial moment of political decision. It is up to both the powers that be and the people at large to come together and by mutual consultation, hammer out an appropriate governmental system that answers to the present cultural-economic milieu of coordinated partnership. This is democracy at work.

However, the rapid democratization in postwar Taiwan, especially in the time since the popular presidential elections in 1996, Taiwan has witnessed a volcanic eruption of self-assertiveness. We must see to it that its dangers be obviated and its healthy symbiotic growth be facilitated.

First, we are aware of some opportunities implied in the rise of self-assertiveness. To grow up in self-dignity and become truly oneself is a worthy project of individual life, whether personal or communal. Assertion of self-identity is a unique historical event in Taiwan, a precious opportunity to grow up as Taiwan for the sake of Taiwan. And this is Taiwan's unique opportunity, the very first time in its history, after its domination by oppressive regimes continually one after another of various cultural backgrounds—Dutch (1624–1662), Koxinga (1661–1683), Manchu (1683–1895), Japan (1895–1945), ROC (1945–today).

Yet at the same time we realize Taiwan is rife with perils brought about by this self-assertiveness. Given for the first time, self-identity excites people who are transfixed by their newly won freedom. This results in the preoccupation with oneself at the cost of others around oneself. And self-preoccupation all too easily leads to simple selfishness without considerateness, enjoyment of freedom without duties, responsibilities and obligations. Public decency and facilities are the first to disappear, then follow ugly rancid pollutions and confusions, predominantly the disregard of social convention, political hospitality and faithfulness and sociable thoughtfulness.

In other words, Taiwan is now in a state of budding teenage assertiveness against domination by outsiders, socially, economically, politically, culturally. Love of oneself is a stage in growth of personhood, saying *No* to everyone except to oneself. Unchecked, this potent self-awareness can become as brutal as slavery under authority and that all the worse for its unsuspected eruptions everyday everywhere. Self-assertion can grow out of hand in brutal callousness to others that results in mutual destruction; self-love destroys selves. This situation breeds Hobbes' world where life is solitary, poor, nasty, brutal and miserably short. Taiwan is now at the critical juncture in its history of growing into political and cultural autonomy. Dangers of self-destructive anarchy can be seen everywhere. Self-love must grow into "loving others as oneself" on pain of self-demise.

Let me cite Lin I-hsiung's 林義雄 remarks. Lin is a former provincial assemblyman and a conscientious intellectual whose family were assassinated (save his wife and daughter) because of his fervent love of Taiwan. He has an apt description of his people's value-orientation today: callous exploitation of natural environs, ruthless competition in total disregard of others, brutal racial prejudice and exclusive worship of money and power.

I concur that the first three dangers (exploitation of nature, competition, prejudice) are, as Lin pointed out, derived from the last, money-power-worship. But what is at stake is where these four vices come from; we see that they all arise out of self-assertiveness expressed as egocentrism, self-preoccupation manifested as self-confinement. This is sheer parochialism in the midst of internationalization of Taiwan economy.

This parochialism, as it were, is well expressed in an egocentric vision of Taiwan as the "center of the world"; Taiwan-centrism is simple ethnocentrism if not pure tribalism. It was graphically formulated as early as in August 10, 1941, toward the end of Japanese occupation of Taiwan, when Wu Hsin-jung 吳新榮, a well-known doctor in the historic city of Tainan (台南), mused to himself,

"Sitting alone in my study, I gazed long at the map on the south wall. My thoughts now being clear, the idea of 'Taiwan Centrism' took its shape in me:

1) Being at the center of Southeast Asia, Taiwan can be called geographical holy land;

2) To the east of Taiwan is the world greatest ocean, the Pacific, to the west is the world largest continent, Asia;

3) Taiwan is cut through at its center by the Tropic of Cancer, to the north of which is the temperate zone, and to the south, the torrid tropics."

And it went on like this for no less than ten reasons why Taiwan is the center of the world. Today, this Taiwan-centrism in the world is being enthusiastically embraced and developed by young "progressive" intellectuals and the new power holders fast becoming an essential part of the new culture of Taiwan for the twenty-first century. It is also taken as a new major dynamics that is impacting Mainland China.

This sort of self-assertive and egocentric mentality has become even more evident since 2000 as Taiwan marches boldly toward democracy. Therefore, the egocentrism in Taiwan today has rendered a "cunning of history," to use the term of Hegel. The "rationality" in the domestic and short-term context of Taiwan has soon turned over into the "irrationality" in the international and long-term context. It is in this way that Taiwan has been more and more self-marginalized in recent years. Standing at the crossroad of history, the future of Taiwan depends on whether or not it can enact a major shift from current self-assertiveness and egocentrism to an understanding of "others" in the age of globalization in the twenty-first century.

Works Cited

Ai Na 艾邢. "Hua-wei xiansheng yutaiji 華威先生遊台記," *Gonglun Bao,* September 23, 1948, p. 6.

Amano Motonosuke 天野元之助. *Chugoku Nogyou Keizailon* 中國農業經濟論. Revised edition. Tokyo: Ryukei Shusha, 1978.

Baker, John Earl. *JCRR Memoirs, Part II: Formosa, Chinese-American Economic Cooperation,* February 1952 (Mimeograph).

Barrington, Moore Jr. *Social Origins of Dictatorship and Democracy: Lord and Peasant in the Making of the Modern World.* New York: Beacon Press, 1966.

Bell, Daniel. *The Cultural Contradictions of Capitalism.* New York: Basic Books, Inc. 1976.

Benedict, Ruth. *Patterns of Culture.* New York: New American Library, 1934.

Berger, Peter L. "Secularity: West and East," paper presented to the Kokugakuin University Centennial Symposium on Cultural Identity and Modernization in Asia Countries, 1983.

Brandauer, Frederick P. and Huang Chun-chieh, eds. *Imperial Rulership and Cultural Change in Traditional China.* Seattle: University of Washington Press, 1994.

Brown, James R., and Sein Lin, eds. *Land Reform in Developing Countries.* Hartford: University of Hartford Press, 1968.

Chan Wing-tsit, ed., trans. with notes, *Instructions for Practical Living and Other Neo-Confucian Writings by Wang Yang-ming.* New York: Columbia University Press, 1963.

Chang Hsun-shun. "Jiashu nongcun jieshe zhongyao zoshi duidong qingxing 加速農村建設重要措施推動情形," *Taiwan nongye* 9, no. 2 (1973).

Chang Jaw-Ling Joanne. "The Taiwan-Strait Crisis of 1995–1996: Causes and Lessons," in Chun-chieh Huang et. al. eds., *Post-war Taiwan in Historical Perspective.* College Park: University Press of Maryland, 1998.

Chang Liang-tse. *Sishiwu zishu* 四十五自述. Taipei: Qianwei chubanshe, 1988.

———, ed. *Wu Hsin-jung Riji [Zhanqian]* (吳新榮日記〔戰前〕). Taipei: Yuanjing chubanshe, 1981.

———. *Wu Hsin-jung Riji [Zhanhou]* (吳新榮日記〔戰後〕). Taipei: Yuanjing chubenshe, 1981.

Chang Wang. "Women duoshi Zhongguoren 我們都是中國人," X*insheng Bao,* June 26, 1946.

Chen Chao-ying 陳昭瑛. "Mingzheng shiqi Taiwan wenxüe di minzuxing 明鄭時期台灣文字的民族性," *Zhongwai wenxue*, 22, no. 4, (1994).

———. *Taiwan shi xuanzhu* 台灣詩選註. Taipei: Zhengzhong shuju, 1996.

———. *Taiwan wenxue yu bentuhua yundong* 台灣文學與本土化運動. Taipei: Zhengzhong shuju, 1998.

———. *Taiwan yu chuantong wenhua* 台灣與傳統文化. Taipei: Zhonghua minguo zhongshan xueshu wenhua jijinhui, 1999.

Chen Cheng 陳誠. *Ruhe shihxian gengzhe you qitian* 如何實現耕者有其田. Taipei: Zhengzhong shuju, 1954.

Chen Chi-nan 陳其南. *Chuantongzhidu yu shehuiyishi di jiegou—Lishi yu renleixue di tanso* 傳統制度與社會意識的結構:歷史與人類學的探索. Taipei: Unchen wenhua shiye gongsi, 1998.

———. *Taiwan di Chuantong Zhongguo shehui* 台灣的傳統中國社會. Taipei: Yunchen wenhua shiye gongsi, 1987.

Chen Han-kuang 陳漢光. "Riju shidai Taiwan hanrenzu ji diaocha 日據時代臺灣漢人祖籍調查," *Taiwan Wenxian*, Vol. 23, no. 1 (1972).

Chen Hsu-ching 陳序經. "Zhongguo wenhua di chulu 中國文化的出路," in Lo Zongqu 羅榮渠, ed., *Cong xihua dao xiandai hua* 從西化到現代化. Beijing: Beijing daxue chubanshe, 1990.

Chen Kuo-chang 陳國章. "Cong diming keyi bianbie Quan-Zhang yuqun di fenbu—yi Taiwan diming weili 從地名可以辨別泉、漳語群的分布－以台灣地名爲例," *Dili jiaoyu*.Vol. 24., Taipei: National Normal University, 1998.

Chen Li-fu 陳立夫. "Zhonghua wenhuafuxingyundong weiyuanhui gongzo shulue 中華文化復興運動委員會工作述略," *Zhongyang Monthly*, July 1991.

Cheng Chih 鄭梓. *Taiwan shengyihui zhi yanjiu* 台灣省議會之研究 Taipei: Huashi chubanshe, 1985.

Chiang Mon-lin 蔣夢麟. *Nongfuhui gongzo yanjin yuanze zhi jiantao* 農復會工作演進原則之檢討. Taipei: Council of Agriculture, Executive Yuan, 1990.

Chiang Nien-feng 蔣年豐. "Taiwanren yu xin Zhongguo—gei Minjinindang di yige xingdong zhexue 台灣人與新中國：給民進黨的一個行動哲學." Taichung, printed and distributed by the author, 1988.

Chien Mu 錢穆. *Zhuzi xin-xuean* 朱子新學案. Taipei: Sanmin shuju, 1971.

———. *Zhongguolishi yanjiufa* 中國歷史研究法. Taipei: Sanmin shuju, 1969.

———. *Zhongguo jinsanbainian xueshu shi* 中國近三百年學術史. Taipei: Taiwan Commercial Press, 1972.

———. *Zhongguo sixiangshi* 中國思想史. Taipei: Taiwan xuesheng shuju, 1983.

———. *Wenhuaxue dayi* 文化學大義. Taipei: Zhengzhong shuju, 1952.

———. *Guoshi dagang* 國史大綱. Revised 7th ed. Taipei: Taiwan Commercial Press, 1980.

———. *Shjie jushi yu Zhongguo wenhua* 世界局勢與中國文化. Taipei: Dongda tushu gongsi, 1985.

Chou Hsien-wen 周憲文. "Riju shidai Taiwan zhi nongye jingji 日據時代台灣之農業經濟." *Taiwan yinhan qikan*, 8, no. 4 (1956).

Chou Wan-yao 周婉窈. *Riju shidai yihui shezhi fayuan yundong* 日據時代議會設置法願運動. Taipei: Zhili baoxi wenhua chubanbu, 1988.

Chu Chao-yang 朱昭陽. *Chu Chao-yang huiyilu* 朱昭陽回憶錄. Taipei: Qianwei chubanshe, 1995.

Chu Chien 朱謙 et. al. *Taiwan nongcun shehui bianqian* 台灣農村社會變遷. Taipei: Taiwan Commercial Press, 1984.

Chu Hsi (Zhu Xi). *Zhu Wengong wenji* 朱文公文集. Sibu congkan cupian soben edition.

Chu Hung-lin. "Dui nongmin yinyou xindi renshi 對農民應有新的認識," *Chongguo shibao*, Dec., 6, 1979, p. 3.

Chung I-jen 鍾逸人. *Xinsuan Liushinian—Ererbashijian erqi budui zhang Chung I-jen huiyilu* 辛酸六十年：二二八事件二七部隊長鍾逸人回憶錄. Taipei: Ziyoushidai chubanshe, 1986.

Clough, Ralph N. "Taiwan-PRC Relations," in Robert G. Sutter and William R. Johnson, eds., *Taiwan in World Affairs*. Boulder, Colo: Westview Press, 1994,.

Creel, Herrlee G. *The Origins of Statecraft in China*, Vol. 1, *The Western Chou Empire*. Chicago: University of Chicago Press,

1970.

Fairbank, John K., Edwin O. Reischaure, and Albert M. Craig. *East Asia: The Modern Transformation.* Boston: Houghton Mifflin Company, 1965.

Fang Thome H. *Chinese Philosophy: Its Spirit and Its Development.* Taipei: Linking Publishing Co. Ltd., 1981.

Fei Hsiao-tung. *Peasant Life in China: A Field Study of Country Life in the Yangtze Valley.* London: G. Routledge and Sons, 1939.

Galenson, Walter, ed. *Economic Growth and Structural Change in Taiwan: The Postwar Experience of the Republic of China.* Ithaca and London: Cornell University Press, 1979.

Gallin, Bernard. "Rural Development in Taiwan: The Role of the Government," *Rural Sociology*, XXIX, no. 3 (1964).

———. "Land Reform in Taiwan: Its Effect on Rural Social Organization and Leadership," *Human Organization*, XXX, no 2 (1963).

———. *Hsin Hsing, Taiwan: A Chinese Village.* Berkeley and Los Angeles: University of California Press, 1966.

Gold, Thomas B. "Colonial Origins of Taiwanese Capitialism," in Edwin A. Winckler, et. al., eds., *Contending Approaches to the Political Economy of Taiwan.* New York: M. E. Sharp, Inc., 1988.

Han Shih-chuan 韓石泉. *Liushi huiyi* 六十回憶. Taiwan: Han Shih-chuan xiansheng sishi sanzhounian juanji weiyuanhui, 1996.

Herbert H. P. Ma. "The Role of Law in the Land Reform of Taiwan," *Soochow Law Review*, no. 1 (Nov., 1976).

Ho Ping-ti 何炳棣. *Huangtu yu Zhongguo nongye di qiyuan* 黃土與中國農業的起源. Hong Kong: Chinese University of Hong

Kong Press, 1969.

———. *The Cradle of the East: An Inquiry into the Indigenous Origins of Techniques and Ideas of Neolithic and Early Historic China, 5000–1000 B.C.* Chicago: The University of Chicago Press, 1975.

Ho, Samuel. P. S. *Economic Development of Taiwan, 1860-1970.* New Haven: Yale University Press, 1978.

Hsia Nai 夏鼐. *Zhongguo wenmin di qiyuan* 中國文明的起源. Taipei: Changlang Publishing Company, 1986.

Hsiao Chien 蕭乾. *Rensheng zaifang* 人生探訪. Taipei: Lianjing chuban gongsi, 1990; the first edition published in Shanghai, 1948.

Hsiao, Kung-chuan 蕭公權. *Compromise in Imperial China.* Seattle: School of International Studies, University of Washington Press, 1979.

———. *Xianzheng yu minzhu* 憲政與民主. Taipei: Lianjing Publishing Company, 1982.

———. *Rural China: Imperial Control in the Nineteenth Century.* Seattle: University of Washington Press, 1960.

Hsiao, Michael H. H. *Government Agricultural Strategies in Taiwan and South Korea: A Macrosociological Assessment.* Taipei: Institute of Ethnology, Academia Sinica, 1981.

Hsu Chia-ming 許嘉明. "Cai Jisi quan zhiyü jütai hanrendi shehuidi dutexing 祭祀圈之於居台漢人社會的獨特性," *Zhonghua wenhuafuxing yuekan* 中華文化復興月刊, 11, no. 6, June 1978.

Hsu, Francis L. K. "Dominant Kin Relationships and Company Ideas," *American Anthropologist*, 68 (1968).

Hsu Fu-kuan 徐復觀. *Zhongguo renxinglun shi: Hsian-Qin pian* 中國人性論史—先秦篇. Taipei: Taiwan Commercial Press, 1969.

———. *Rujia zhengzhi sixiang yu minzhu ziyou renquan* 儒家政治思想與民主自由人權. Taipei: Bashi niandai chu-she, 1979.

———. *Liang-Han sixiang shi* 兩漢思想史. Taipei: Taiwan xue-sheng shuju, 1979.

Hsu Hsueh-chi visited, Tseng Chin-lan recorded. *Lan Min xiansheng fangwen jilu* 藍敏先生訪問紀錄. Taipei: Zhongyang yanjiuyuan jindaishi yanjiusuo, 1995, p. 93.

Hsueh Hua-yuan 薛化元. *Minzhu xianzheng yu minzhu zhuyidi bianzheng fazhan* 民主憲政與民族主義的辯證發展. Taipei: Daohe Publishers, 1993.

Hu Chang-chih 胡昌智. *Lishi zhishi yu shehui bianqian* 歷史知識與社會變遷. Taipei: Lianjing Publishing Company, 1988.

Hu Shih 胡適. "Fan lixüe di sixiang jia—Dai Dongyuan," in Yu Ying-shih, et al., *Zhongguo zhexüesixiang Lunji* 中國哲學思想論集, *Qingdai pian* 清代篇. Taipei: Mutong chupanshe, 1976, pp. 229–240.

Huang Cheng-tsung 黃呈聰. "Yinggai zho chuangshe Taiwan tese di wenhua, 應該著創設台灣特色的文化" *Taiwan Min-bao*, Vol.3, no.1 (Jan. 1,1925).

Huang Chun-chieh 黃俊傑. "Hsiao Kung-chuan yu Zhongguo jindai renwen xueshu 蕭公權與中國近代人文學術," in his *Juxue chuantong yu wenhua chuangxin* 儒學傳統與文化創新. Taipei: Dongda tushu gongsi, 1983.

———. "Zhongguo nongye chuantong jiqi jingsheng neihan: wenti yu jieshi 中國農業傳統及其精神內涵：問題與解釋," in *Chungguo wenmingdi jingshen* 中國文明的精神. *(I)* Taipei: Guangbo tianxin wenhua jihui, 1990.

———. *Zhongguo nongcun fuxing lianhe weiyuanhui shiliao huibian* 中國農村復興聯合委員會史料彙編. Taipei: Sanmin shuju, 1991.

———. "Chen Jung-chieh (Chan Wing-tsit) xiansheng di xuewen yu zhiye 陳榮捷先生的學問與志業," *Newsletter of Institute of Chinese Literature and Philosophy, Acadmia Sinica*, Vol. I, no. 1 (March, 1991).

———. *Chungguo Nongcun fuxing lianhe weiyuanhui guoshu lishi fanwen jilu* 中國農村復興聯合委員會口述歷史訪問紀錄. Taipei: Institute of Modern History, Academia Sinica, 1992.

Huang Chun-chieh 黃俊傑 and Cheng-hung Liao. *Zhanhou Taiwan nongmin jiazhi quxiang di zhuanpian* 戰後台灣農民價置取向的轉變. Taipei: Lianjing Publishing Company, 1992.

———. *Nongfuhui yu Taiwan jingyan* 農復會與台灣經驗. Taipei: Sanmin shuju, 1994.

———. "Industry, Culture, Politics: The Taiwan Transformation" in Richard Hardey Brown, ed., *Culture, Politics and Economic Growth: Experience in East Asia*. Studies in Third World Societies, Vol. 44. Williamsburg, Va.: College of William and Mary, 1994.

———. and Wu Kuang-ming. "Taiwan and Confucian Aspiration: Toward the Twenty-First Century," in Stevan Harrell and Chun-chieh Huang, eds., *Cultural Change in Postwar Taiwan*. Boulder, Colo.: Westview Press, 1994.

———. "Transformation of Farmer Social Consciousness in Postwar Taiwan," in Stevan Harrell and Chun-chieh Huang, eds., *Cultural Change in Postwar Taiwan*. Boulder Colo: Westview Press, 1994.

———. "Zhanhou Taiwan di shehui wenhua bianqian: xianxiang yu jieshi 戰後台灣的社會文化變遷：現象與解釋," in *Kaohsiung lishi yu wenhua lunji* 高雄歷史與文化論集. Huang Chun-chieh, ed. Kaohsiung: Chen Chung-ho and Weng Tsu-shan jijinhui, 1994.

---. *Zhanhou Taiwan di zhuanxing jiqi zhanwang* 戰後台灣的轉型及其展望. Taipei: Zhengzhong shuju, 1995.

---.and Ku Wei-ying. "Xin-en yu jiuyi jijian: Li Chun-sheng di guojia rentong zhi fenxi," in Li Ming-hui 李明輝, ed., *Li Chun-sheng di sixiang yu shidai* 李春生的思想與時代. Taipei: Zhengzhong shuju. 1995.

---. *Daxue tongshi jiaoyu ti linian yu shijian* 大學通識教育的理念與實踐. Taipei: Chinese Association for General Education, 1999.

---. *Mencian Hermeneutics: A History of Interpretations in China.* New Brunswick, N.J. and London: Transaction Publishers, 2001.

Huang Kuang-kuo 黃光國. *Rujia sixiang yu dongya xiandaihua* 儒家思想與東亞現代化. Taipei: Zhulin chubanshe, 1988, p. 20.

Huang Li-ching 黃麗卿. "Women duoshi Taiwanren 我們都是台灣人," *Chongyang zhonghe yuekan* 中央綜合月刊, Vol.32, no. 1 (Jan., 1999), pp.8–9.

Huang, Philip C. C. *The Peasant Economy and Social Change in North China.* Stanford, Calif: Stanford University Press, 1985.

Hung Chin Chu 洪金珠. "Tingting nongmin zenmo shuo 聽農民怎麼說," *Shibao Zazhi* 時報雜誌, no. 92 (September 1981).

Hung Li-wan 洪麗完. "Qingdai Taiwan difang fuke guanxi chutan— jianyi Ching-shui pingyüan Sanshan Guowang Miao zhi xingshuai weili 清代台中地方福客關係初探－兼以清水平原三山國王廟之興衰為例," *Taiwan Wenxian* 台灣文學, 42:2 (June 1990).

Hymes, Robert P., and Conrad Schirokauer eds. *Ordering the World: Approaches to State and Society in Sung Dynasty China.* Berkeley: University of California Press, 1993.

Kahn, H. *World Economie Development: 1979 and Beyond.* London: Croom Helm, 1979.

Kan Wen-fang 甘文芳. "Xin Taiwan jianshe shangdi wenti he Taiwan qingnian di juewu 新台灣建設上的問題和台灣青年的覺悟," *Taiwan Minbao* 台灣民報, no. 67, August 26, 1925.

Kao Hsi-chun 高希均. "'Xin Taiwanren: Gaixie Taiwan shengmingli di xin juben 「新」台灣人：改寫台灣生命力的新劇本," *Zhongyang zonghe yuekan* 中央綜合月刊, Vol.32, no.1.

Kawano Shigetani. *Riju shidai Taiwan migu jingjilun* 日據時代台灣米穀經濟. trans. by Lin Yin-yen .Taipei: Bank of Taiwan, 1960.

Kirby, E. Stuart. *Rural Progress in Taiwan.* Taipei: JCRR, 1960.

Ko Piao 柯飄. "Taiwan chufang 台灣初訪," *Lianhe Bao*, October 25, 1951.

Kogawa Katsumi. *Taiwan o ai shida Nihojin* 台灣を愛する日本人. Matsuyama: Aoyama Tosho, 1989.

Kublin, Hyman. "Taiwan's Japanese Interlude, 1895–1945", in Paul K. T. Sih ed., *Taiwan in Modern Time.* New York: St. John's University, 1973.

Kuo Min-hsueh 郭敏學. *Hezuohua nonghui tizhi* 合作化農會體制. Taipei: Taiwan Commercial Press, 1982.

———. *Taiwan nongye fazhan guiyi* 台灣農業發展軌跡. Taipei: Taiwan Commercial Press, 1984.

———. *Duo mubiao gongneng di Taiwan nonghui* 多目標功能的台灣農會. Taipei: Taiwan Commercial Press, 1977.

Kuo Shui-tan 郭水潭. "Heren jütai shijidi Zhongguo yimin 荷人據台時期的中國移民," *Taiwan wenxian* 台灣文獻, Vol. 10, no. 4, 1959.

Lai, Tse-han, Ramon H. Myers, and Wei Wou. *A Tragic Beginning: The Taiwan Uprising of February 28, 1947.* Stanford, Calif: Stanford University Press, 1991.

Lao Sze-kuang 勞思光. *Xinbian Zhongguo zhexueshi* 新編中國哲學史. Taipei: Sanmin shuju, 1981.

Lau, D. C. *Mencius.* Hong Kong: The Chinese University Press, 1979, 1984.

Lee Teng-hui. *Intersectoral Capital Flows in the Economic Development of Taiwan, 1895–1960.* Ithaca, N.Y.: Cornell University Press, 1972.

———. *Taiwan di zhuzhang* 台灣的主張 Taipei: Yuanliu chubanshe, 1999, p. 264.

Leh Po-erh (Raper). *Taiwan muqian zhi nongcun wenti yuqi jianglai zhi zhanwang* 台灣目前之農村問題與其將來之展望. Taipei: JCRR, 1952.

Li Chun-sheng 李春生. *Zhujin xinji* 主津新集. Fuzhou: Meihua shuju, 1984.

Li Li-ching 李麗卿. *Guozhong guowen jiaokeshu zhi zhengzhi shehuihua neirong fenxi* 國中國文教科書之政治社會化內容分析. unpublished Master's Thesis Taipei: Institute of Education, National Taiwan Normal University, 1989.

Li Yih-yuan 李亦園. "Wenhua jianshe gongzo di rogan jiantao 文化建設工作的若干檢討," in Zhongguo luntan bianzhi weiyuanhui ed., *Taiwan diqushehui pianqian yu wenhua fazhan* 臺灣地區社會變遷與文化發展. Taipei: Lianjing Publishing Co., 1985.

———. and Yang Kuo-shu 楊國樞 eds. *Zhongguoren di xingge: Ke ji zhenghe xing di taolun* 中國人的性格:科際整合性的討論. Taipei: Institute of Ethnology, Academia Sinica, 1972.

Liang Chi-chao 梁啓超. *Yinbingshi wenji* 飲冰室文集. Taipei: Xinxing shuju, 1966.

Liang Sou-ming 梁漱溟. *Zhaohua* 朝話 Taipei: Longtian chuban-she, 1979.

———. *Chungguo minzhu zijiu yundong zhi zuihou juewu* 中國民族自救運動之最後覺悟. Taipei, n. d.

———. *Dongxi wenhua jiqi zhexue* 東西文化及其哲學. Taipei: Photo reproduction, n. d.

Liao Cheng-hung 廖正宏 et. al. *Guangfuhou Taiwan nongye zhengche di yanbianlishi zhi shehui di fenxi* 光復後台灣農業政策的演變－歷史及社會的分析. Taipei: Institute of Ethnology, Academia Sinica, 1986.

Lien Heng 連橫. *Taiwan Shisheng* 台灣詩乘. Taipei: Taiwan Commerical Press, 1960.

Lien Wen-hsi 連文希. "Kejia zhi nanqiandongyi jiqi zai Tai di liubu—jianlun qi kaido fendou jingshen 客家之南遷東移及其在台的流佈－兼論其開拓奮鬥精神, *Taiwan Wenxuan* 台灣文學, 23:4 (1972).

Lilley, James R. and Chunk Downs eds. *Crisis in the Taiwan Strait.* Washington D.C.: National Defense University Press, 1998.

Lin I-hsiung 林義雄. "Taiwanren jiazhiguandi zhongjian 台灣人價值觀的重建," *Tianxia* 天下, December 1, 1994.

Lu Jiuyuan 陸九淵. *Lu Jiuyuan ji* 陸九淵集. Beijing: Zhonghua shuju, 1980.

Liu Kuang-ching 劉廣京 ed. *Jinshi Zhongguo jingshi sixing yantaohui lunwenji* 近世中國經世思想研討會論文集. Taipei: Institute of Modern History, Academia Sinica, 1984.

Mei Wen-ting 梅文鼎. *Jixuetang wenchao* 績學堂文鈔. Woodblock edition collected in the Naikaku Bunko, Japan, n. d.

Mintz, Sidney W. "A Note on the Definition of Peasantries," *Journal of Peasant Studies*, no. 1, 1973.

Mou Tsung-san 牟宗三. *Zhongguo wenhua di shengcha* 中國文化的省察. Taipei: Lianjing Publishing Company, 1983.

———. *Zhongguo zhexue shijiu jiang* 中國哲學十九講. Taipei: Xuesheng shuju, 1983.

———. *Zhongguo zhexue di tezhi* 中國哲學的特質. Taipei: Xuesheng shuju, 1963, 1976).

———. *Xinti yu xingti* 心體與性體. Taipei: Zhengzhong shuju, 1968), 3 Vols.

———. *Cong Lu Xiangshan dao Liu Jisha* 從陸象山到劉蕺山. Taipei: Xuesheng shuju, 1979.

———. *Wushi zishu* 五十自述. Taipei: E-hu chubanshe, 1989.

———. *Yuanshan lun* 原善論. Taipei: Xuesheng shuju, 1985.

Myers, Ramon H. and Mark R. Peattie, eds. *The Japanese Colonial Empire, 1895–1945.* Princeton, N.J.: Princeton University Press, 1984.

Okada, Takehiko. *Jukyo Seisin to Gendai* 儒教精神と現代. Tokyo: Meitoku Shuppansha, 1994.

———. *Oyomei to Min-matsu no Jugaku* 王陽明と明末の儒學. Tokyo: Meitoku Shuppansha, 1970.

Peng Ming-min 彭明敏. *Ziyou di zhiwei* 自由的滋味. Taipei: Qianwei chubanshe, 1988.

Popkin, Samuel L. *The Rational Peasant: The Political Economy of Rural Society in Vietnam.* Berkeley and Los Angeles: University of California Press, 1979.

Popper, Karl R. *The Open Society and Its Enemies.* Princeton, N.J.: Princeton University Press, 1933.

Scott, James C. *The Moral Economy of the Peasant: Revolution and Subsistence in Southeast Asia.* New Haven, Conn., and London: Yale University Press, 1976.

Shen, T. H. *The Sino-American Joint Commission on Rural Reconstruction: Twenty Years of Cooperation for Agricultural Development.* Ithaca, N.Y. and London: Cornell University Press, 1970.

Shih Tien-fu 施添福. "Qingdai zai Taiwan hanrendi zu jifenbu yu yuanxiang shenghuo fangshi 清代在臺漢人的祖籍分布與原鄉生活方式," Taipei: National Taiwan Normal University, Geography Department, 1987.

Shiomi Shunji 塩見俊二. "Jingcha yu jingji 警察與經濟," tr. by Chou Hsien-wen 周憲文, in Chou Hsien-wen, *Taiwan jingji shi* 台灣經濟史. Taipei: Taiwan kaiming shujü, 1980.

Sung Kuang-yu 宋光宇. "Cong zuijin jishinian lai nuanzo yujishi shanshu tan Zhongguo minjian xinyang li di jiazhiguan 從最近幾十年來鸞作遊記式善書談中國民間信仰裏的價值觀," paper presented to the International Conference on Values in Chinese Societies: Retrospect and Prospect, May 23–26, 1991, Taipei.

Tang Chun-i 唐君毅. *Zhongguo zhexue yuanlun:daolun pian* 中國哲學原論：導論篇. Hong Kong: Dongfang renwen xuehui, 1966.

―――. *Zhongguo zhexue yuanlun: yuanxing pian* 中國哲學原論：原性篇. Hong Kong: New Asia College, 1968.

―――. *Zhongguo zhexue yuanlun: yuanjiao pian* 中國哲學原論：原教篇. Hong Kong. New Asia Colloge, 1975.

―――. *Zhongguo zhexue yuanlun: yuandao pian* 中國哲學原論：原道篇. Hong Kong: New Asia College, 1974.

Teng Hsueh-ping 鄧雪冰. *Taiwan nongcun fanwenji.* 台灣農村訪問

記. (n. p., 1954) p. 135.

Ting Zih-chang 丁日昌. "Minfu Ting Zih-chang zhuo Xibanya kuishi Taiwan qingxing pian," in *Qingmo waijiao shiliao xuanji* 清末外交史料選集. Taipei: Taiwan yinhang jingji yanjiushi, 1964.

Treagold, Donald W. *The West in Russia and China: Religious and Secular Thought in Modern Times, Vol. 1, Russia, 1472–1917.* Cambridge, U.K.: Cambridge University Press, 1973.

Tuma, Elias H. *Twenty-six Centuries of Agrarian Reform.* Berkeley and Los Angeles: University of California Press, 1965.

Wang Yang-ming. *Chuan Hsi Lu*, tr. by Wing-tsit Chan, *Instructions for Practical Living and Other Neo-Confucian Writings by Wang Yang-min.* New York: Columbia University Press, 1963.

Winckler, Edwin A. and Susan A., et al., eds. *Contending Approaches to the Political Economy of Taiwan.* New York: M. E. Sharpe, Inc., 1988.

Wolf, Eric R. *Peasant Wars of the Twentieth Century.* New York: Harper & Row, 1969.

Wu Cho-liu 吳濁流. *Wuhuaguo* 無花果. Taipei: Qianwei chubanshe, 1988.

———. *Taiwan lianqiao* 台灣連翹.Taipei: Qianwei chubanshe, 1989.

Wu Feng-shan 吳豐山. "Jintian di Taiwan nongcun xilie baodao 今天的台灣農村系列報導," *Rili wanbao*, Jan. 19, 1971.

———. and dictated by Wu San-lien, *Wu San-lien huiyilu* 吳三連回憶錄. Taipei: Zili baoxi, 1991.

Wu Hsin-jung 吳新榮. *Wu Hsin-jung riji (zhanqian)* 吳新榮日記(戰前). Taipei: Yuanjing chubanshe, 1981.

———. *Wu Hsin-jung shujian* 吳新榮書簡. Taipei: Yuanjing chubanshe, 1981.

Wu Kuang-ming. *History, Thinking, and Literature in Chinese Philosoph.* Taipei: Academia Sinica, 1991.

Wu Wen-hsing 吳文星. *Riju shiqi Taiwan shehui lingdao jieceng zhi yanjiu* 日據時代台灣社會領導階層之研究. Taipei: Zhengzhong shuju, 1992.

Yager, Joseph A. *Transforming Agriculture in Taiwan: The Experience of the Joint Commission on Rural Reconstruction.* Ithaca, N.Y. and London: Cornell University Press, 1988

Yager, Martin M.C. *Socio-Economic Results of Land Reform in Taiwan.* Honolulu: East-West Center Press, 1970

Yamanabe Kentaro 山邊健太郎. "Riben diguozhuyi yu zhimindi 日本帝國主義與殖民地," tr. by Cheng Chin-jen 鄭欽仁, Shihuo 食貨 Monthly, n. s. 2:1 (1972), p. 48.

———.*Riben diguozhuyi xiadi Taiwan* 日本帝國主義下的台灣. tr. by Chou Hsien-wen 周憲文. Taipei: Bamier shudian, 1985.

Yang Chao-chia. *Yang Chao-chia huiyilu* 楊肇嘉回憶錄. Taipei: Sanmin shuju, 1977.

Yang Chi-chuan 楊基銓. *Yang Chi-chuan huiyilu* 楊基銓回憶錄. Taipei: Qianwei chubanshe, 1996.

Yang Ju-pin 楊儒賓. "Renxing, lishi qieji yu shehui shijian—cong youxiandi renxinglun kan Mou Tsung-san di shehui zhexue" 人性、歷史契機與社會實踐－從有限的人性論看牟宗三的社會哲學," *Taiwan shehui yanjiu jikan* 台灣社會研究季刊, Vol. I, no. 4 (Winter, 1988).

Yang Kuo-shu et. al. "Chuantong jiazhiguan, geren yu xiandaihua jiqi zuzhixingwei: hourujia jiashedi yixiang weiguan yanzheng 傳統價值觀、個人與現代化及其組織行為：後儒家假設的

一項微觀驗證," *Bulletin of the Institue of Ethnology, Academia Sinica,* no. 64 (1989).

———. "Xiaodao di shehui taidu yu xingwei: lilun yu celiang 孝道的社會態度與行為：理論與測量," *Bulletin of the Institute of Ethnology, Academia Sinica,* no. 65 (1989).

Yang, Martin M.C. *Socio-Economic Result of Land Reform in Taiwan* Honolulu: East-West Center Press, 1970.

Yang Yih-jong 羊憶蓉. "*Xiandaihua yu Zhongguoren di jiazhi bianqian: jiaoyu jiaodu di jieshi* 現代化與中國人價值變遷：教育角度的解釋," paper presented to the International Conference on Values in Chinese Societies: Retrospect and Prospect, May 23–26, 1991, Taipei, p. 18.

Yang Ying 楊英. *Cong zheng shilu* 從征實錄 Taipei: Taiwan yinhang jingji yanjiushi, 1958.

Yao Chun 姚隼. "Renyuren zhijian jiqi ta 人與人之間及其他," *Taiwan yekan* 臺灣月刊, no. 2 (November, 1946).

Yao Ying 姚瑩. "Cun zhi fu zhuo chuoyi Taiwan fuwu zhe," (February 16, 1843), in Hu Chiu-yuan 胡秋原, ed., *Zhongguo dui xifang zhi lieqiang renshi ziliao huibian* 中國對西方之列強認識資料彙編 Taipei: Institute of Modern History, Academia Sinica, 1971.

Yeh Jung-chung, *Xiaowu dache ji* 小屋大車集 Taichung: Zhongyang shuju, 1977.

———. ed. *Lin Hsien-tang xiansheng jinianji* 林獻堂先生紀念集. Taipei: Privately published, 1960.

Yeh Kuang-hui 葉光輝 and Yang Kuo-shu 楊國樞. "Xiaodao di renzhi jiegou yu fazhan: gainian yu jianheng 孝道的認知結構與發展：概念與鑑衡," *Bulletin of the Institue of Ethnology, Academia Sinica,* no. 65 (1989).

Yin Chang-yi 尹章義. "Minyue yimin di xiehe yu duili—yi keshu Chaozhouren kaifa Taipei yiji Hsin-chuang Sanshan Guowang Miao di xingshuai shiwei zhongxin sozo di yanjiu 閩粵移民協和與對立：以客屬潮洲人開發台北以及新莊三山國王廟的興衰史爲中心所做的研究," *Taipei Wenxian* 台北文獻, Vol. 74 (December 1985).

Yu Ying-shih 余英時. *Chungguo jinshi zongjiao lunli yu shangren jingshen* 中國近世宗教倫理與商人精神 Taipei: Lianjing Publishing Co., 1987.

Index of Names

Aisin Chuelo, 7

Amano Motonosuke, 44

Anderson, W. A., 36, 73

Baker, John Earl, 46, 167

Bentham, Jeremy, 25

Berger, Peter, 111

Buck, John L., 44

Buck, Pearl S., 7

Buddha, 105

Carlyle, Thomas, 25

Chang Chun-mai, 213

Chang Hai-peng, 113

Chang Hsun-shun, 34, 49

Chang Liang-tse, 11, 172

Chen Chao-ying, 132, 161

Chen Cheng-tien, 18

Chen Hsin, 162

Chen Yi, 25, 42, 173

Chen Zi-ang, 194

Cheng Mingdao, 107, 109

Cheng Yi, 108

Chen-ying. *See* Wu Hsin-jung

Chiang Kai-shek, 7

Chiang Meng-lin, 46, 47, 48, 49

Chien Mu, 91, 92, 95, 140, 145

Chiu Fu-li, 71

Chuang Chui-sheng, 161

Chung Yi-ren, 8, 13, 19, 165

Coleridge, Samuel Taylor, 25

Confucius, 26, 27, 90, 93, 100, 104, 106, 108, 137, 140, 194

Deng Xiaoping, 144

Duke of Zhou, 27, 120

Fang Tung-mei, 102, 104, 105, 110

Fei Hsiao-tung, 86

Feng Youlan, 93, 94

Gallin, Bernard, 63

Guo Moro, 93, 131

Hada Yoichi, 42

Ho Yen, 71

Ho Ying-chin, 23

Hsiao Chien, 169, 172

Hsiao Kung-chuan, 64, 91, 95, 128, 129

Hsu Fu-kuan, 90, 91, 92, 95, 97, 125, 127, 129, 131, 133, 136, 137, 142, 143, 145, 147, 149

Hsu Fu-yuan, 201

Hsu Hsien-yao, 20

Hu Shih, 142, 187

Hu Wufeng, 109

Huang C. C. (Philip), 68

Huang Cheng-tsung, 179

Huang Kuang-kuo, 112, 113
Huang Shun-chien, 22
Huang Tsu-hsiang, 71
Hua-wei, 172
Hung Shih-chu, 207
Ito Takio, 167
Jen-kung. *See* Liang Chi-chao
Jiang Qing, 93
Kaishan shengwang. *See also* Zheng Chenggong
Kan Wen-fang, 179
Kanda Masao, 167
Kao Hsi-chun, 182
Kaozi, 109
King De, 6
King, Martin Luther, 27
Kirby, E. Stuart, 62
Koxinga, 7, 197, 200, 201, 227
Kublai, 7
Kung-chia. *See* Chen Yi
Kuo Min-hsueh, 36, 37, 74, 75
Ladjinski, Wolf, 50
Lan Min, 23
Lan Ting-yuan, 23
Lao Sze-kwang, 102
Laozi, 26, 105
Li Chung-tao, 48

Li Chun-sheng, 11, 201, 202
Li Fu-hsu, 22
Li Yih-yuan, 114, 119
Liang Chi-chao, 42, 161
Liang Sou-ming, 66, 137, 146
Lianheng, 161
Lim Hian-tong, 12
Lin Chin-lin, 71
Lin Chin-sheng, 76
Lin Hsien-tang, 4, 40, 161, 202
Lin I-hsiung, 228
Lin Yu-chun, 161
Liu Jishan, 107, 108, 109
Liu Shu-hsien, 102
Lu Ah-chih, 71
Mei Wen-ting, 215
Mencius, 26, 90, 97, 100, 104, 106, 107, 108, 109, 110, 118, 130, 131, 137, 139, 141, 220
Milton, John, 25
Mizoguchi Yuzo, 102
Mou Tsung-san, 90, 102, 106, 110, 141
Moyer, Raymond T., 46
Ou Hsiu-hsiung, 180
Peng Ming-min, 16, 180, 205
Popper, Karl, 47
Qing Emperor Xuanzong, 214

Raper, Arthur F., 59
Shakespeare, William, 25, 26
Shen Kuang-wen, 201
Shen Tsung-han, 46
Shih-chih. *See* Hu-shih
Shih-min. *See* Wu Hsin-jung
Si Shao-wen, 11
Sima Qian, 143
Sun Yat-sen, 19, 168, 212, 213
Sung Chu-yu (James), 176, 177
Sung Fei-ju, 173
Sung Kuang-yu, 120
Tang Chun-i, 90, 102, 105, 110, 139
Thome H. Fang. *See* Fang Tung-mei
Ting Zhi-chang, 214
Ting-chiu. *See* Mei Wen-ting
Tsai Huang-chin, 81
Tsai Hui-ju, 161
Tung-sun. *See* Chang Chun-mai
Waley, Arthur, 27
Wang Chin-ping, 180
Wang Kemin, 6
Wang Min-ning, 11
Wang Yangming, 109
Weber, Max, 66, 113
Wing-tsit Chan, 95
Wolf, Eric R., 54

Wu Chin-chuan, 16
Wu Cho-liu, 4, 5, 9, 14, 19, 20, 21, 24, 77, 165, 202, 208
Wu Hsin-jung, 4, 6, 11, 162, 179, 228
Wu San-lien, 4, 12, 18, 22
Wu Yung-fu, 162
Yamanoi Yu, 102
Yanaihara Sadao, 43
Yanaihara Tadao, 44, 57, 166
Yang Chao-chia, 7, 10, 163
Yang Chi-chuan, 164, 172
Yang Kuo-shu, 112, 113, 114
Yang Lien-sheng, 91
Yang Tai-shun, 181
Yatang. *See* Lianheng
Yeh Jung-chung, 3, 4, 11, 15, 25, 161, 182, 202
Yen Yang-chu, 46
Yenping junwang. *See also* Zheng Chenggong
Yichuan. *See* Cheng Yi
Yu Kuo-hua, 48
Yu Ying-shih, 100, 110, 112, 113, 140
Yue Fei, 7
Zhang Hengju, 107
Zheng Chenggong, 7, 161, 200

Zheng Xiaoxu, 6
Zhou Lianxi, 107, 109

Zhu Xi, 65, 96, 97, 99, 108, 109, 234
Zhuangzi, 26, 99